Reading Recovery and Every Child a Reader

Reading Recovery and Every Child a Reader

History, policy, and practice

Edited by Sue Burroughs-Lange and Amanda Ince

IOEPress

First published in 2013 by the Institute of Education Press,
20 Bedford Way, London, WC1H 0AL
www.ioe.ac.uk/ioepress

© Penny Amott, Sue Bodman, Sue Burroughs-Lange, Julia Douëtil, Janet Ferris, Glen Franklin, Val Hindmarsh, Angela Hobsbaum, Amanda Ince, Phyl Maidment, Helen Morris, John Smith, Susan Taylor 2013

British Library Cataloguing in Publication Data:
A catalogue record for this publication is available from the British Library

ISBNs
978-0-85473-996-7 (paperback)
978-1-78277-034-3 (PDF eBook)
978-1-78277-035-0 (ePub eBook)
978-1-78277-036-7 (Kindle eBook)

Every effort has been made to trace copyright holders and to obtain their permission for the use of copyright material. The publisher apologizes for any errors or omissions and would be grateful if notified of any corrections that should be incorporated in future reprints or editions of this book.

The opinions expressed in this publication are those of the authors and do not necessarily reflect the views of the Institute of Education, University of London.

Typeset by Quadrant Infotech (India) Pvt Ltd
Printed by CPI Group (UK) Ltd, Croydon, CR0 4YY

Contents

List of figures and tables

Abbreviations

BRP	Better Reading Partnership
DCSF	Department for Children, Schools, and Families
DfE	Department for Education
ELS	Early Literacy Support
ECaR	Every Child a Reader
ECRR	European Centre for Reading Recovery
FFT	Fischer Family Trust
GEST	Grants for Education, Support, and Training
HMI	Her Majesty's Inspectorate of Schools
IOE	Institute of Education, University of London
IRRTO	International Reading Recovery Trainer Organization
LSP	Link Support Person
LT	Link teachers
LIFT	Literacy Initiative from Teachers
LTF	Literacy Task Force
LA	Local authority
NC	National Curriculum
NLP	National Literacy Project
NLS	National Literacy Strategy
OECD	Organisation for Economic Co-operation and Development
PNS	Primary National Strategy
QFT	Quality First Teaching
RRiPLLe	Reading Recovery in Primary Literacy Leadership
RRT	Reading Recovery teacher

SATs	Standard Assessment Tests
SEN	Special educational needs
TL	Teacher leader
TA	Teaching assistant

Acknowledgements

We the editors would like to acknowledge the insights and knowledge of our co-writers, freely shared. We wish to thank all those who responded to our call for recollections, reflections and critique, insider perceptions, and analysis of events – among them teachers and managers from schools, local authority advisers and managers, university researchers and teachers, education departments in government, and charitable trust and educational association leaders. Some are named in the text (with permission) and some not. We have valued their willingness to be involved and their frankness in the telling and evaluating of this story. We also appreciate those who helped in constructing, editing, and preparing the text.

About the authors

Penny Amott is a lecturer in Initial Teacher Education at the Institute of Education, University of London (IOE). She teaches Primary English and works across the PGCE and Teach First programmes. Prior to that she was a Reading Recovery trainer and coordinator and part of the team managing the Every Child a Reader programme based at the European Centre for Reading Recovery (ECRR). She has a particular interest in the teaching of early reading and supporting children with literacy difficulties. She has taught for many years across the Early Years and Primary age range and has also worked with teachers in Jamaica, Sierra Leone, and Liberia. She is currently studying for a doctorate in education.

Sue Bodman joined the Institute of Education in 2002, after starting her career in schools and advisory roles in Wales. She now works with teachers and teacher educators in many international contexts, including in England, Wales, Ireland, Denmark, the USA, and New Zealand. She contributes to master's degree programmes in literacy development and literacy difficulties, and to the Doctor in Education programme. She is a member of the European Centre for Reading Recovery at the Institute of Education, which over a six-year period, worked in partnership with the KPMG Foundation and the English government education department to develop and deliver the Every Child a Reader project. Dr Bodman's research and teaching interests include teacher education, continuing professional development, early literacy acquisition, and literacy interventions. Her research, publications, and conference work to date have focused on designing professional development for literacy educators. She considers herself fortunate to have a job that allows her to work with children, teachers, teacher educators, education managers, national government departments, and academics – an invigorating mix that maintains her enthusiasm and creativity.

Sue Burroughs-Lange came to the Institute of Education in 1999 from Australia, where she led the establishment of professional programmes and the implementation of Reading Recovery across Queensland. She had previously spent a year of preparatory work with Professor Marie Clay and her team at the University of Auckland, New Zealand. She began her career in education in 1965 as a primary class teacher and moved into consultancy roles with schools, management, and teachers of children with special needs while completing research for her master's degree. Her later career focused on teaching, research, and publication in the area of literacy difficulties for initial and postgraduate courses in the UK and USA and in Queensland, Australia. As a member of the leadership team at the European Centre for Reading Recovery, and alongside external collaborators, Dr Burroughs-Lange led the development and early years of what became Every Child a Reader. As an essential part in enabling and quality-assuring its rapid expansion, she developed and led the doctoral specialism course at the Institute of Education that won international agreement for the establishment of the European centre for qualifying Reading Recovery national leaders. The challenge of effecting sustained change in experienced educators through professional development and action research is a common thread throughout her work.

Julia Douëtil is head of the leadership team at the Institute of Education, of the European Centre for Reading Recovery and Every Child a Reader. After ten years of teaching and leadership in primary schools, Julia Douëtil joined the Institute of Education and for more than 20 years has led the professional learning of adults, teaching on both master's and doctoral programmes. She has been at the centre of Reading Recovery in the UK and Ireland from its beginnings and was instrumental in the development of Every Child a Reader. She represented the European enterprise on the first Reading Recovery International Leadership Team, and subsequently on the executive board of the International Reading Recovery Trainers Organization. In her current role she leads on the successful implementation, evaluation, and further development of interventions for low-attaining children. She has overseen systemic change in response to changing contexts and imperatives, including the development of web-based systems for quality assurance and evaluation, for communication, and for the development and dissemination of resources. She writes extensively for teachers, has an international profile as a writer and speaker on early literacy intervention, and is a national authority on the strategic management of literacy intervention.

Janet Ferris has worked in education for 33 years. In 2009 she joined the Institute of Education to become a Reading Recovery national leader. Prior to this she worked as a teacher leader in Devon, completing the research for her master's degree at the Institute of Education in 2008. Janet

Ferris was in the second cohort of teacher leaders who joined the Institute of Education's doctoral programme for Reading Recovery national leaders supported through the rollout of Every Child a Reader. As a national leader, Janet is particularly interested in enabling Reading Recovery teachers (RRTs) to use their expertise to support literacy interventions both in their own school and in their Local Learning Communities, and she has published and developed resources for this role. Her previous professional career included 4 years' working as a literacy consultant for the Primary National Strategy and 17 years' experience as a deputy headteacher in a primary school. Janet Ferris has presented papers at national and international conferences. The focus of her current doctoral research is on the professional development of experienced adults, with a particular interest in transformative learning and the relationship between emotion and learning.

Glen Franklin is a Reading Recovery national leader at the European Centre for Reading Recovery (ECRR) at the Institute of Education. A particular responsibility is to lead the management of the centre's extensive data collection and analysis processes of the Reading Recovery and Every Child a Reader annual monitoring. She has worked in education for over thirty years, initially as a primary teacher, then as a deputy headteacher and Reading Recovery teacher. In 1995, she joined the National Literacy Association as teacher/coordinator for the Docklands Learning Acceleration Project, which supported the use of ICT (information communication technology) in schools as a tool for learning. Prior to joining the ECRR, she worked as a Reading Recovery teacher leader and consultant for the Primary National Strategy in an Inner London local education authority. Glen Franklin completed her master's degree in 2007 at the Institute of Education. She is currently working on her doctorate, in which she explores the unique practice of Reading Recovery teacher educators in maintaining an ongoing commitment to teaching children as integral to their personal professional learning and their work with adults.

Val Hindmarsh is the programme leader of the Institute of Education's master's degree in Reading Recovery and Literacy Leadership, having previously led this course in a regional hub. Dr Hindmarsh taught first in Scottish primary schools. On moving to England she worked for many years as a special educational needs (SEN) teacher and as a local authority reading advisory teacher and manager, gaining qualifications in the teaching of pupils with Specific Learning Difficulties and in education management. She became a Reading Recovery teacher leader in 2004 and was awarded her MA in 2006. She has been a Reading Recovery national leader since 2006, including in that role successfully running extensive national professional development conferences for Every Child a Reader and Reading Recovery regional leaders. She is especially interested in professional development as a means of bringing about transformative change in teachers, and in 'affect' as a compounding but productive factor in that process, the topic of her doctorate, which she was awarded in 2012.

Angela Hobsbaum worked at the Institute of Education until her retirement in 2004. She was active in establishing Reading Recovery in England and worked as a national coordinator since its introduction in 1991. She was the co-developer and first programme leader for the course that trained teacher leaders at the Institute of Education. As part of her involvement with Reading Recovery, she worked on the early editions of Book Bands for Guided Reading, and co-authored *Guiding Reading*, a handbook for teachers in Key Stage 2. She has also taught and supervised research on a number of master's and doctoral courses. She maintains her work in research and consultancy roles in the field. Her passion and curiosity lead her to continue to work informally with young children, trying to apply what she learnt through Reading Recovery.

Amanda Ince is currently a member of the Primary Initial Teacher Education teaching team at the Institute of Education. She joined the Institute of Education in 2007 as a member of the national leadership team at the European Centre for Reading Recovery and taught on the master's degree programme for Literacy Learning and Literacy Difficulties. Previously, Dr Ince worked in local education authorities as an Early Years/literacy consultant, children's centre advisor, and Reading Recovery teacher leader. She gained her MA in 2004 and has presented papers at conferences in the UK and internationally on early literacy and professional learning. Her prior roles include head of school in further education, training manager for a childcare company, and primary school teacher. Her research interests focus on professional learning and the subject of her doctoral thesis concerned the role of cognitive dissonance in transforming practice.

Phyl Maidment has wide experience in education. This has included teaching in a variety of schools in England and overseas, and across the age range from 4-year-olds to 16-year-olds. She has worked as a language and curriculum development officer for a local authority language support service and as a literacy consultant. For several years she combined the role of Reading Recovery teacher leader with that of adviser, later becoming a school improvement officer. In her current role as a national leader at the ECRR at the Institute of Education, she works with postgraduate and MA students and provides professional development and support for teacher leaders in the field. Her particular research and publication interests are working with children for whom English is an additional language and the teaching and learning of children with literacy learning difficulties, the topic of her current doctoral research.

Helen Morris is a Reading Recovery national leader at the Institute of Education, offering support for Reading Recovery professionals in the field. She also works with postgraduate and MA students and leads a module in Literacy Development. She has extensive experience of primary teaching and school leadership, both in Australia and the UK. She worked for eight years in school improvement in England, specializing in literacy and literacy difficulties and developing action research with class teachers. During the development of Every Child a Reader, Helen Morris's role in a local authority included that of link manager for a Reading Recovery teacher leader, and supporting the rollout and evaluation of the programme. Her MA research explored multi-modal texts as a scaffold for writing, with a particular focus on potential impact on boys' attainment. In her doctoral research she is investigating the ways in which close observation and socially constructed learning contribute to the development of critical reflection in professional change.

John Smith is a Reading Recovery national leader at the Institute of Education. His extensive experience includes a wide range of roles in primary education in New Zealand and England, teaching all primary-school age ranges, and leading senior management teams. While teaching in New Zealand he trained as a Reading Recovery teacher and Reading Recovery teacher leader. Dr Smith's research and publication interests include neuroconstructivism, the theory and practice of Reading Recovery, and models of reading that can influence effective professional development for teachers.

Susan Taylor has over thirty years' experience of teaching, initially as a head of department in a secondary school and later within the Early Years and Primary age phases. She completed her master's degree while working as a manager for learning and teaching in further and higher education. She began working at the Institute of Education in 2001 as a national leader at the ECRR, providing initial and on-going professional development for teachers and teacher educators including internationally. She is programme leader of the MA in Literacy Learning and Literacy Difficulties and contributes significantly to the work of the doctoral school as programme leader for the Master of Research as well as a course leader within the Doctor in Education programme. Dr Taylor's research interests include initial and continuing professional development, curriculum design for developing generative learning, and early literacy acquisition and literacy interventions. Her publications and conference work to date have focused on designing professional development in generative learning in the education sector and also in relation to flight safety.

Foreword

Many years ago, as an educational psychologist, I witnessed at first hand, over and over again, the stark consequences of illiteracy. I would be asked to 'see' children when they were seven because they had not learnt to read, I would see them again at ten because of general learning difficulties and low self-esteem, and yet again in secondary school because they still could not read well and were, unsurprisingly, behaving badly or attending poorly.

Later, I was managing services in Bristol when an unexpected windfall (proceeds from the sale of the city's council-owned airport) led to local education authority initiatives to improve citizens' future through education. Using this money, we were able to bring Reading Recovery to the city, and open the door of learning to the lowest-achieving children on its deprived council estates. Some of these children are now at university.

But it was slow going. There were so many children, then and now, who needed help. Headteachers found it hard to contemplate an intervention that would benefit a small number of children when others had to be turned away.

Now, however, Reading Recovery is thriving in a large proportion of schools in Bristol. What made the difference, there as elsewhere in the country, was the Every Child a Reader initiative. Every Child a Reader added value to the core Reading Recovery one-to-one lessons for children with the greatest difficulties. This was achieved by using the skills of its highly trained specialist teachers to support a range of broader literacy work in their schools, from lighter-touch interventions provided by teaching assistants and volunteers through to improving the match between children's reading levels and the books available to them, and the more effective teaching of phonics.

This book elegantly charts the story of how the national Every Child a Reader initiative was tested, refined, and embedded over the period 2005–11. My role in its early days was to work with the KPMG Foundation and the Institute of Education to develop and trial the model, funded to the tune of £4.5 million by a range of businesses and charitable trusts. It was then time to make the business case to the British Government that matching this funding and expanding the initiative across the country was a sound proposition.

The business case had to demonstrate that the need was there. That was not difficult, since national data told us that every year some 35,000 children (6 per cent of the cohort) were leaving primary school having failed to acquire even the most basic literacy skills, and attaining below National Curriculum Level 3 in English. The data also showed that this figure had changed little in the previous eight years – at a time when standards for higher attainers were rising rapidly.

The business case also had to offer a solution: that an intervention proven to work for this bottom 6 per cent, and was 'system ready' for the UK context, could be scaled up without loss of fidelity and quality and could also raise standards for a broader group of children. We never claimed that Reading Recovery was the only answer – but the Institute of Education's controlled research did provide solid evidence of its effectiveness in 'real-world' circumstances. This made for a convincing proposition, when put together with Reading Recovery's unique infrastructure of professional support and quality assurance at national, local, and school level, which secures year-on-year results with no loss of quality as the number of schools involved grows.

Finally, the business case had to demonstrate to government that investing in Every Child a Reader would be economically worthwhile. We did this through the *Long Term Costs of Literacy Difficulties*, a report published in 2006, showing that every £1 invested in the initiative would save government in the order of £17 annually over the lifetime of the children involved, as a result of increased tax and national insurance receipts and decreased government spending on welfare benefits, adult literacy classes, health services, and the costs of crime.

Essentially, the government's decision in 2006 to earmark funding for Every Child a Reader was made on economic rather than on ideological grounds. The current policy climate of non-earmarking, of leaving schools free to make their own choices about how to spend their money, sometimes forgets this. Ultimately, if government neither earmarks money nor re-frames the accountability system so as to give schools the incentive to support their hardest-to-teach children through their most skilled adults, rather than their least, it is central government that will bear the financial consequences.

But governments are not all that matters. Involvement in Every Child a Reader has a transformational effect on the belief systems of headteachers and class teachers, which of itself engenders sustainability. A teacher I know once said: 'If you can teach John to read, I'll eat my hat.' Reading Recovery proved her wrong. Whether the hat was eaten I never found out, but I do know that something has changed in that school. The lid has been taken off aspirations, and teachers know that it is truly possible for every child they teach to become a reader.

Big ideas like this stay in the system through thick and thin. Big ideas like this also bear deep analysis to identify what works, and why. This book provides that analysis. It offers a reflective, academic exploration of how a big idea can be enacted in practice, and shows us how every child can achieve, if we only apply the right science. I commend it to you.

Jean Gross, CBE

Introduction
Amanda Ince

This book describes the origins of Every Child a Reader,[1] an approach to early literacy designed to ensure that every child leaves primary school able to read. It was launched in England in 2005 and by 2011 it had expanded to reach over 28,000 children who needed literacy support. Every Child a Reader was developed from the established early literacy intervention, Reading Recovery. This book describes the main features of Reading Recovery – how it operates for each child, how teachers are trained to teach them, and the infrastructure necessary for Reading Recovery to make an effective impact on the poorest literacy learners in primary school. The introduction of Reading Recovery into the rest of the UK and the Republic of Ireland, and its implementations there, are traced and contrasted, and the influence of systemic and societal influences on the transfer of innovation recorded. The story of Every Child a Reader is one that shows how such interventions need to be supported to ensure that their effectiveness is not jeopardized as they expand in scale and scope.

This book will therefore be relevant to those interested in early literacy and in the prevention of literacy failure through effective intervention. It will also be of interest to those who have heard about Reading Recovery but are not familiar with its operation in the UK, and to those involved in managing large-scale interventions in schools and systems.

Every Child a Reader offers primary schools a comprehensive approach to ensuring that all struggling readers are given the most appropriate support, tailored to their needs. It does this by training a specialist teacher who will manage and monitor a variety of forms of assistance for children who are struggling to learn to read and write. Children having the greatest difficulty will receive Reading Recovery, an individual approach designed to help them to learn effectively; those who require less intensive support will receive additional help in small groups. In all situations where Every Child a Reader operates in the UK and Republic of Ireland, a specially trained Reading Recovery teacher is responsible for individual teaching, for providing in-school professional development, guidance, and advice, and for monitoring the outcomes for all the school's low-achieving children. Through Every Child a Reader in England these layers of support-teaching and activity are expanded and systematized to ensure that each child benefits from the most appropriate teaching.

Every Child a Reader grew out of Reading Recovery, an early literacy intervention developed in New Zealand in the 1980s by Professor Marie Clay. Reading Recovery was adopted by the New Zealand Ministry of Education in 1985 and was gradually disseminated to primary schools across the country. Interest in this approach spread to other English-speaking countries and in 1984 a training site was established in Ohio, USA. During the next decade, Reading Recovery became established in a number of American states. In England, meanwhile, Surrey's local education authority started to train the country's first Reading Recovery teachers in 1990 (Wright, 1992). In 1991 Professor Clay was invited by the Institute of Education, University of London, to lead a team from New Zealand to introduce Reading Recovery to England. Over the next 15 years, Reading Recovery was introduced to primary schools in a number of local education authorities in England, and later spread to Wales, Scotland, Northern Ireland, and the Republic of Ireland. This book describes how Reading Recovery, an individualized literacy intervention, became incorporated into the more comprehensive approach to literacy provision called Every Child a Reader, which had governmental support to expand in order to tackle low literacy achievement in schools across England.

The chapters in this book build the story of why and how Every Child a Reader developed from working with relatively few children in Reading Recovery to a wide-scale systematic approach to managing early literacy interventions. Evidence, insights, and cautions are recounted here in many voices, and critique of research and theory, policy and practice, political history and government action are used to draw out implications for those involved not only in early literacy but also in any drive to expand the scale of an effective educational response.

The book begins by exploring the history and origins of Reading Recovery, describing its introduction to England in the political context of the 1990s, and subsequently across the UK and the Republic of Ireland. The argument for early intervention, the features that contribute to the effectiveness of Reading Recovery, and the significance of the case for cost-effectiveness are juxtaposed against a context of policy change.

Chapter 2 argues the evidence of the political and educational necessity for Every Child a Reader as a logical development from Reading Recovery's early progress in reshaping the learning trajectory of those failing to read.

The theoretical and research base of Every Child a Reader and Reading Recovery, set out in Chapter 3, marks out these initiatives from other, largely resource-based, responses promoted as quick fixes for underachievement in early literacy.

One of the strengths, and a surprise to many, was the consistency of results achieved by Reading Recovery and Every Child a Reader despite the numbers of newly trained teachers and newly trained teacher leaders doubling each year – the results did not dip despite the majority of people involved being inexperienced. This was entirely due to the effectiveness of the initial and ongoing professional development that underpins the implementation of Reading Recovery and Every Child a Reader. Chapter 4 uses a series of interwoven case studies to draw out the key features of this professional development so as to explain the theory and practice that enables experienced class teachers to gain and maintain this expertise in addressing literacy difficulties.

The challenges, changes, and adaptations in rolling out a system-wide approach to early literacy intervention are discussed in Chapter 5. Drawing on interviews with and data from those most involved in implementing Every Child a Reader, the authors offer a critique of what was achieved in addressing these challenges.

The whole story of Every Child a Reader and its key messages provide the focus for Chapter 6. Lessons learnt from the initiative are examined alongside evidence and theory on embedding change. The author considers the threat from current economic constraints. For the sake of expediency, and without an appropriate evidence base, such constraints are imposed without recognition of the consequences of a lost opportunity for successful early literacy intervention – which offers the potential to contribute to economic recovery further into the future.

The authors are uniquely placed to write this book since they have been closely involved in both Reading Recovery and Every Child a Reader from the beginning, and from a variety of perspectives and roles. Some academic texts are criticized for their reliance on theory that is too far removed from the reality of practice. It appears easy for academics and researchers to critique literacy interventions when they have no, or only limited, experience of working with struggling learners. By contrast, in this text the authors combine theory and practice with the understanding and personal experience of teaching children day by day how to read and write, with all its frustrations and delights, and of enabling teachers to gain the expertise necessary to challenge their assumptions of what all children can achieve. The authors' insights are supported by their extensive experience as class teachers, school managers, Reading Recovery teachers, teacher leaders, local education authority managers, consultants, advisers, university teachers and researchers, and as members of the national leadership team at the ECRR at the Institute of Education, University of London.

Notes

[1] 'Reading Recovery' and 'Every Child a Reader' are names trademarked by the Institute of Education, University of London. 'Reading Recovery' implementations in Scotland, Wales, Northern Ireland and Republic of Ireland also have agreements with the Institute of Education, University of London. Internationally, 'Reading Recovery' also takes place in New Zealand, Australia, the USA and Canada. There are institutional trademark holders for 'Reading Recovery' in those countries.

Chapter 1

Reading Recovery, an early literacy intervention

Julia Douëtil, Angela Hobsbaum, and Phyl Maidment

Introduction

This chapter considers the case for early intervention for children with literacy difficulties. It describes Reading Recovery and the background to its development, and introduces evidence concerning its effectiveness. The chapter then gives a historical overview of Reading Recovery in the UK. It is suggested that, despite central government initiatives and the injection of major funding aimed at addressing literacy failure, there remains a need for effective early intervention.

The case for early intervention in literacy

Early intervention programmes aim to close the gap between pupils at risk of literacy difficulties and their classroom peers. Effective early intervention has two potential benefits:

(i)   Literacy failure is avoided for those pupils whose difficulties are preventable.

(ii)   Pupils with more intractable learning needs are identified early in their school career (Clay, 1998).

Before investing time, effort, and resources into early intervention, it is vital that there is a strong evidence base for its efficacy (Brooks, 2007, 2013). Evidence of achievement gains and long-term sustainability has implications for the timing of intervention and the allocation of resources to schools and within schools (Shanahan and Barr, 1995).

For 20 years, there has been a growing consensus that early detection and intervention are vital to a student's literacy success (e.g. Wasik and Slavin, 1993; Al Otaiba and Fuchs, 2002). Research has shown that effective early intervention can ensure that the majority of those falling behind catch up with and maintain their progress alongside their classmates (Vellutino *et al.*, 1996, 2004). Once an achievement gap has developed, however, it is very resistant to change (Alakeson, 2005; Bynner and Parsons, 1997) and signs of wider difficulties begin to emerge early in the primary years (Wanzek *et al.*, 2006).

Views on 'how early is early?' have changed over the years. For example, Piagetian stage theory might be interpreted as meaning that children would not be 'ready' to read until later in their educational career, perhaps as late as seven or eight years old. Even by the early 1990s, children in England were not usually offered additional help with reading problems until they were at least seven or eight years old.

> I argued with headteachers about early identification. At that time (1995) intervention was left until Key Stage Two, even though you could see kids at Key Stage One who needed help ... There was a lot of resistance.
>
> (Anwyll, a former LA English Inspector, 2011)

Those experiencing difficulty were often regarded as late developers who would 'grow out of their problems' (Hurry, 2000). However, a 'wait and fail' approach to identification and remediation condemns children to protracted failure (Gersten and Dimino, 2006: 100).

Research into effective instruction should also include evidence of the optimum point of intervention for achieving the most effective outcomes that are sustainable. A year of good-quality tuition, known as 'quality-first' instruction, prior to preventative action, allows some children to catch up with their peers. Screening earlier than the first year cannot reliably distinguish between those who lack appropriate early environmental opportunities but can catch up without special help and those who have other cognitive difficulties. Children who have not managed to keep up with their peers' progress after a year in a good classroom will benefit from further support. This is preferable to allowing unhelpful literacy behaviours to become further ingrained. Figure 1.1 illustrates how children in an intervention have to learn at a quicker pace than their average classroom peers in order to regain a normal learning pathway. Monitoring of children's progress in Reading Recovery intervention in Year 1 suggests that the rate of learning must be four times that of their average peers to close the gap (European Centre for Reading Recovery, 2011).

Mapping reading ability

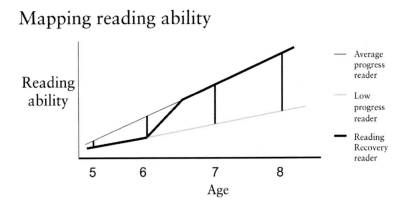

Figure 1.1: Mapping reading ability: The learning trajectory

The downward spiral caused by an older poor reader's 'view of self' as failing can dominate the learning process (Meek, 1982: 114), leading to reading less and to lower levels of motivation (Strickland *et al.*, 2002). The task of breaking these attitudes later in school life becomes increasingly difficult (Clay, 1979). This is why decisive preventative action is required at an optimum point in a child's educational career. A cost-effective 'surgical strike' (Stanovich, 1986) is necessary to alter the poor outcomes predicted for young children already falling behind after a year in school (Juel, 1988; Francis *et al.*, 1996; Shaywitz *et al.*, 1999), 'before accumulating failure disorders their natural learning' (Holdaway, 1979: 167).

While this line of argument is concerned with preventing educational failure at school, a second strand relates to the long-term costs to society of literacy failure, considering its impact on the individual's well-being and on opportunities for his or her employment in adult life.

Counting the cost of failure to learn to read

Calculating the cost benefits of an intervention in education is extremely difficult. It is hampered by many considerations: what counts as evidence; how the effect can be measured in isolation from the context in which it occurs; how much of what is measured can be attributed to the impact of the intervention; how long it should be monitored so as to establish that the effects do not 'wash out'; and more (Ashdown and Hummel-Rossi, 2002; Hummel-Rossi and Ashdown, 2010). However, a study in 2006 calculated the short-term costs and benefits to schools and the longer-term savings to society of teaching all children to read and write (figure 1.2). Professional analysts subjected a range of relevant, large-scale, longitudinal data to detailed fiscal analysis and concluded that these benefits were substantial and could be determined sufficiently accurately to strengthen the argument that effective early literacy intervention can contribute to savings in the longer term (KPMG Foundation, 2006).

Figure 1.2: Human and societal costs of persistent poor literacy (KPMG Foundation, 2006)

The 2009 revision of these calculations estimated that, year-on-year, for every £1 spent on effective early intervention (specifically Reading Recovery) annually about £13 was saved per individual up to the age 37, with a lifetime saving to society of almost twenty-fold.

When these figures are multiplied by 30,000 (the number of children in English schools *each year* who are known to be starting their secondary education with the reading ability of, at best, a 7-year-old) the sociopolitical and economic benefit of effective early intervention is undeniable.

Reading Recovery early literacy intervention

Background to the development of Reading Recovery

Marie Clay's theory of early reading acquisition was developed from her research in New Zealand. She undertook a large-scale, longitudinal observation of children learning to read over their first year in school. Her analysis showed that their learning had to range wider than simply letter-learning and word-reading. It began by involving children in an understanding of the written word and its functions in reading and writing. Familiarity with letters and with the sounds that they represent was found to be central to this understanding, and this could be developed more quickly when pupils had experience both of printed text and of their own attempts at writing letters, words, and 'stories'. A growing familiarity with books introduced children to the differences between spoken and written language, necessary for early reading success. Throughout her academic life Clay continued to research and develop ways of communicating to teachers, researchers, and families the appreciation that many skills have to be orchestrated to achieve text reading. Clay's premise was always that the goal of reading was the ability to understand written texts (see Chapter 3).

Early identification of slow entry into literacy

Clay's research demonstrated that children acquire effective control of early reading and writing behaviours at different rates (Clay, 1966). By the end of their first year in school it was possible to reliably identify those who had succeeded and those who needed extra support to learn to read.

The first practical outcome of Clay's research was her response to New Zealand teachers' requests for help with ways of assessing what might be getting in the way of some children's literacy. The 'Concepts about Print' observation task was the first tool that she published, followed soon after by 'Taking a Running Record of Reading Continuous Texts'.

The fully developed profile assessment, *An Observation Survey of Early Literacy Achievement* (first published 1993, revised 2002, in process of 2nd revision 2013), comprises:

- A **Letter Identification** task to observe which letters are known and whether the most automatic response for each letter is alphabetic, phonemic, or linked to a word
- A **Word Reading** task to analyse progress towards building a corpus of known high-frequency words
- A **Concepts about Print** task to observe what is known about how spoken language is represented in print
- A **Writing Vocabulary** task to capture words that the child can write in every detail
- A **Hearing and Recording Sounds in Words** assessment of phoneme–grapheme correspondence and how spoken language is recorded
- A **Text Reading** task using a running record to observe text reading behaviour and to find an appropriate level of text difficulty for instruction

In addition, in the UK and the Republic of Ireland a standardized test for word reading is used: this is from the British Ability Scales II (Elliott *et al.*, 1996, re-standardized 2012).

This collection of assessment tasks provides valid and reliable measures of the skills necessary for early literacy (Clay, 2002; Denton *et al.*, 2006; Rodgers, 2012). National norms are used to assist in interpreting scores and to ensure that literacy levels at the end of Reading Recovery intervention fall within the average band of attainment for the child's age. Text levels[1] are also used to ensure that children whose series of Reading Recovery lessons has been completed (or 'discontinued' (Clay, 2005: 52)) are able to operate at the literacy attainment norms for a particular classroom.

Reading Recovery lessons

Clay recognized that individual differences make group programmes less efficient; individual tuition is the most effective in adapting to each child's unique profile.

She developed Reading Recovery as a short-term intervention for those who, after about one year of formal schooling, were identified as the lowest achieving in their cohort. The intervention was designed to run for 12 to 20 weeks. Within this time, learners who start with the lowest level of literacy need to progress at a faster rate in order to catch up with the 'average' literacy of their peers. This accelerated rate is achieved through daily, half-hour, one-to-one lessons with a specially trained teacher.

The design of components within Reading Recovery lessons allows for changes from child to child, day by day, as their learning develops. In each half-hour they typically read four or five books and write a sentence or two of text that they have composed, with specific and embedded work on letters and words. Opportunities to develop perceptual and cognitive processes are paramount as the child:

(i) READS FAMILIAR BOOKS

Lessons begin with reading familiar texts that the child has read once to three times before. This gives the child contexts to which he/she can rapidly apply his/her decoding and comprehension skills, read with fluency, and sound like a successful reader (Stanovich, 1986).

(ii) READS THE PREVIOUS DAY'S NEW BOOK ON WHICH THE TEACHER WILL TAKE A RUNNING RECORD

The teacher takes a running record of the child's reading behaviours as he/she reads a new book, which will have been introduced and read through once in the previous lesson. This assessment practice demands that the teacher consider progress from quantitative and qualitative perspectives: a measure of accuracy in reading texts of increasing difficulty and use of visual print information by recording the accuracy of words read (an additive view of progress) and how the child perceives information, links information, and makes decisions about that information (a transformative view of progress).

Assessment of this nature inevitably involves inspection of letters attended to, words read accurately, and processes of decoding from left to right. However, the complexity of taking a running record is often overlooked. During the observation, the teacher is also alert to signs of fluency – how the reading sounds. Stress, pace, pitch, and juncture are important signals regarding how information is picked up and worked on. From this record of the child's independent reading strategies, the teacher can adopt contingent teaching immediately and also use the record to monitor progress over time and to shape the overall direction of the child's lesson.

(iii)   WORKS WITH LETTERS AND/OR WORDS USING MAGNETIC LETTERS
Word-level work can appear anywhere in the lesson and also in a discrete component of the lesson, including explicit teaching of sound and letter/letter cluster relationships.

(iv)   COMPOSES AND WRITES A STORY OR MESSAGE
Teacher and child engage in a real conversation, providing an opportunity for the development of spoken language. This is also focused on capturing the child's use of language as the base for composing a piece of text, such as a story or message. The child's experience of writing also involves receiving explicit tuition on such aspects as letter formation, phonics, punctuation, grammar, syntax, and comprehension, all tailored to individual need and level of complexity.

(v)   ASSEMBLES THE CUT-UP STORY
With the story written on a strip of card, which the teacher has cut up, the child then works on the reciprocity between reading and writing by putting the text into sequence and re-reading it.

The lesson builds towards the new book, 'tempting the child to lift his or her processing to another level' (Clay, 2001: 230). The placement of the new text at the end of the lesson allows the most recent literacy behaviours of the child to be uppermost in the teacher's mind during the interaction to introduce the new book and to respond to the child's first reading. It also allows the child to apply his/her most recent learning immediately in a new problem-solving context.

(vi) Reads a new book

The new book is introduced to the child. The new text will stretch the child's emerging reading skills as he/she reads it. It is also carefully chosen to interest the child and to bring together many aspects of the child's current processing. A new book acts as a 'testing ground for emerging strategies, consolidating some and [providing] an opportunity for learning others' (Clay, 2001: 227). This new book will provide the text for the next lesson's running record.

All this takes place within one daily, 30-minute session. The skills of the teacher are the main resource in gaining rapid progress in literacy. The professional development programme undertaken to qualify as a Reading Recovery teacher is both extended and rigorous.

Professional training in Reading Recovery

Unique to Reading Recovery is a 'three-tiered system' (Schmitt *et al.*, 2005) of professional development designed to ensure consistent, positive results. University-based national leaders provide an initial one-year, full-time course for Reading Recovery teacher leaders, followed by ongoing professional development. In turn, these teacher leaders work with local education authorities to provide a one-year, part-time professional development programme for school-based teachers. Professionals in each of these three tiers continue to teach children in Reading Recovery so that their understanding is continually enriched by recent experience. The importance of this infrastructure is not only its ability to provide professional development but also to support quality practice in existing and new implementations, to monitor recruitment and outcomes, to collect data periodically, and to report it annually.

Chapter 4 provides insights into this professional development model and explains how Reading Recovery professionals gain expertise, why generative learning is necessary, and how it is developed. Supported and structured critical reflections from a blend of learning environments are used to link theory and practice in the courses of professional development for Reading Recovery professionals. Communities of learners (Moore, 1997) are established during both the initial and ongoing professional development as sources of self-generating quality assurance. Professional learning around literacy is fostered in other colleagues who provide wider benefits to whole school teams.

Reading Recovery in England: The early years (1990–95)

In 1987 Marie Clay was invited by Peter Bryant and Lynette Bradley to visit the Department of Experimental Psychology at the University of Oxford.

During her stay she made a number of conference presentations about her developments in the assessment of very early literacy, and the intervention that had grown from it, Reading Recovery. As a result, in April 1989, Surrey's education authority sent a local adviser, Jean Prance, formerly the headteacher at an infant school, to New Zealand to train as a Reading Recovery teacher leader. On her return in January 1990, she established the first teacher-training group in Surrey, supported by an experienced New Zealand tutor. A second group began training in September 1990.

In 1991, the Institute of Education, University of London, invited Clay back, this time to set up a training programme for teacher leaders. It was initially disseminated to seven Inner London boroughs, each of which had areas of considerable social disadvantage. During the intensive one-year course Clay's team of teacher leaders trained literacy coordinators. In the following year the Department for Education granted funding for Reading Recovery through Grants for Education, Support, and Training (GEST) as part of the Raising Standards in Inner City Schools programme. A second centre also began a training programme in Sheffield. This grant provided sufficient funds for a three-year project to expand to include a further 20 education authorities outside London, spread across the North of England and the Midlands. Thus Reading Recovery cut its teeth in England in some of the most socially deprived areas, in schools where reading standards were very low.

Between 1991 and 1993, 169 teachers were trained and over 900 children benefited from Reading Recovery teaching. Clay was keen to evaluate how well its implementation had adapted to the English education system. Her report noted that, when children in England were selected for Reading Recovery, they had lower literacy scores than did a comparable group in New Zealand (not surprisingly, perhaps, given that they were the weakest readers in very deprived areas). However, they made good progress during Reading Recovery and by the end of their lessons they were performing as well as children in New Zealand. Her report went further than an analysis of the children's literacy scores; it also investigated other factors that influenced the effectiveness of Reading Recovery in England. Clay noted that Reading Recovery teachers in England experienced many interruptions; for example, they were asked to cover for other staff, obliged to accompany classes on trips, or sent on training courses. This prevented them from teaching their Reading Recovery pupils every day, which meant that the intervention did not provide the intensive daily support that it was intended to deliver. Clay was concerned that these schools did not safeguard teachers' time for daily Reading Recovery lessons, but used them as an extra pair of hands to be redeployed when necessary. The link between daily lessons and accelerated learning for Reading Recovery to operate effectively was not yet understood. A further concern was that teachers frequently underestimated what these children could achieve and had low expectations about their potential for progress. Clay urged that 'Teachers should not allow their sympathies for children to erode their expectations of achievement' (Hobsbaum and Clay, 1993: 21). Clay also reported that reading books available in schools were often inadequate for supporting poor readers in the early stages of the intervention. It was at this point that Reading Recovery's contribution to improving resources for early reading began, eventually culminating in the first publication of *Book Bands for Guided Reading* (Bickler *et al.*, 1998).

These observations of how teachers and children in English schools responded to Reading Recovery were useful in ensuring that in future clear messages were conveyed to schools and local authorities about how to implement the intervention in order for it to work most effectively. The Department for Education's own report on the projects funded by GEST was extremely favourable and recognized that 'projects have been most effective in pupils' early years before failure has had time to take hold' (Hollingsworth, 1995: 4). Despite this positive conclusion, earmarked funding for Reading Recovery ceased after 1995, leaving local authorities to seek funds from a variety of other sources.

Reading Recovery in England 1995–2005

During the 1990s in England, there were growing concerns about standards of literacy. England did not perform well in international comparisons:

> International comparisons of children's achievements in reading suggest Britain is not performing well, with a slightly below average position in international literacy 'league tables'. Most studies show also a long 'tail' of underachievement in Britain and a relatively poor performance from lower ability students.
>
> (Literacy Task Force, 1997: paragraph 21)

While children in England and Wales in the middle and upper ranges were performing well, Britain's international ranking suffered because of this long 'tail of underachievement'.

The predominant view described in two Ofsted reports (1993, 1996) was that the teaching of literacy was poor, and that standards of literacy in the UK were falling. Beard (2011: 68) describes literacy teaching in England at that time as largely individualized and in need of 'radical change'. Schools had failed to respond to research into effective literacy teaching: this highlighted the importance of a structured approach and effective learning time, together with motivating pupils through challenge and praise, and maintaining high expectations.

Ofsted's report (1996) on the teaching of reading in 45 London primary schools highlighted the scale of the problem. It found only 25 per cent of teaching to be satisfactory and revealed that about one third of children in Year 6 (aged 10–11) had reading ages two or more years below their actual age. The report diagnosed a number of reasons: poor and uneven teaching of reading; limited understanding of National Curriculum requirements and a failure to incorporate these into clear, detailed policies; inadequate initial teacher training and continuing professional development; and poor resources.

This report received considerable publicity and, despite some questioning of parts of the evidence for these damning claims (Mortimore and Goldstein, 1996), the British Government felt compelled to act swiftly. It promptly established the National Literacy Project, directed by John Stannard, a former inspector of schools, whose goal was to raise the standards of literacy teaching in primary schools. Working initially with 15 local authorities, the project drew heavily on the Literacy Initiative from Teachers (LIFT) project, which had been set up in the London borough of Westminster by Shirley Bickler in 1993. Bickler had been one of the first teacher leaders to be trained in Reading Recovery in London in 1991. This, together with her encounters with teachers from New Zealand who were critical of the teaching practices they found in London classrooms, had led her to establish the LIFT project, designed to improve literacy teaching in all Key Stage 1 classes. Although initially established in only six primary schools, this project generated considerable interest and became an influential model for the National Literacy Project. In LIFT classrooms, literacy was taught in daily one-hour sessions; these included shared reading using big books, group work including guided reading led by a teacher, and different kinds of independent work appropriate for each group's abilities. In these classrooms, the individual hearing of reading by the teacher – which had previously been the predominant teaching approach, much criticized by Ofsted – was replaced by more direct input from the teacher and by a new approach – guided reading, with small groups of children of similar ability.

Evaluation of the project (Hurry *et al.*, 1999) emphasized the extent to which Reading Recovery had influenced the LIFT model. The use of Clay's Observation Survey of Early Literacy Achievement in assessing children and raising teachers' awareness; the focus on the teacher's role in shared and guided reading; the grading of early reading books used in classrooms to ensure a gradual increase in difficulty level; attention to fluent, accurate text reading through giving children opportunities to re-read familiar texts; all these were recognizable as features of a Reading Recovery lesson and of New Zealand classroom literacy practice. After six months, the children in the LIFT classrooms were significantly better at word reading than a comparison group, and a year later they were better at both word and text reading (Hurry *et al.*, 1999). The project's evaluation also indicated that less attention was paid to phonological skills (the children were correspondingly less advanced in this area), and recommended that this aspect be given more attention. This aspect was addressed in Reading Recovery lessons, and in the National Literacy Project's development from LIFT's model.

The LIFT project attracted considerable attention and hosted visits from at least 20 local education authorities, assisting them to start their own versions of LIFT. In May 1996, the director of the National Literacy Project visited the LIFT project and was sufficiently impressed to use it as a model. The National Literacy Project adopted similar methods of in-service training, approaches to classroom organization, and lesson structures but applied these across the primary age-range, not just in Key Stage 1. The National Literacy Project also incorporated writing as well as reading in the directed literacy tasks.

When the Labour Government came to power in 1997, its plans for the National Literacy Strategy extended the National Literacy Project nationwide. The National Literacy Strategy aimed to change the teaching practice of 190,000 primary schoolteachers so that, within five years, 80 per cent of 11-year-olds would reach the standard for English (Level 4) set by the National Curriculum, an increase of over 20 per cent. The National Literacy Strategy was evaluated by an international team, whose three reports provide a thorough examination of this ambitious reform programme (Earl *et al.*, 2000; 2001; 2003). The achievements of the National Literacy Strategy have been amply reported elsewhere (e.g. Stannard and Huxford, 2007).

In his review of the teaching of early reading, commissioned by the government, Rose (2006: 11) concluded:

> The National Literacy Strategy, which is now part of the Primary National Strategy, has been in place for seven years. When it was introduced in 1998 only 65% of 11-year-olds reached the target level in English, i.e. Level 4, at the end of Key Stage 2. By 2005, after seven years of the NLS, nearly 80% of them reached that level. These Year 6 pupils were the first cohort to have been part of the NLS from the beginning, i.e. when they were in the Reception year.

However, the problem of those children who were still struggling to read and write, the large number who constituted the 'long tail' of underachievement, seemed intractable. The Literacy Hour, with its emphasis on whole-class and small-group teaching, described as a 'one-size-fits-all approach to teaching' (Earl *et al.*, 2003: 7), could not meet the needs of children who did not follow the expected developmental route. Concerns about these children's needs had been raised as early as 2000 (Lingard, 2000; Stainthorp, 2000). The support that these pupils had received prior to the creation of the National Literacy Strategy, when children were 'heard to read' individually, was in some cases replaced by poor and often irregular guided reading sessions. Added to this, in thrall to the high status of publicly reported achievement levels, many schools probably focused on children projected to narrowly miss the desired targets in national tests. Time and money were therefore directed towards boosting the performance of older children who were just below average, and were diverted from early intervention and from the lowest achievers.

Nevertheless, supplementary programmes aimed at children in the bottom 20 per cent of literacy achievement were developed. From 2003, the National Literacy Strategy introduced the model of 'waves' of support for particular target groups, possibly derived from Clay and Tuck (1993). Wave 1 offered quality-first teaching (QFT) for all children in a class, while Wave 2 provided additional small-group interventions for children who were just below average, typically offered by teaching assistants for whom the NLS provided training and materials. Wave 3 was designed for children with more complex literacy difficulties. Although it recognized that these children needed more intensive support, the NLS did not recommend or devise specific programmes for this group. However, Reading Recovery was cited as an example of an effective Wave 3 approach.

With workplace reform, many more teaching assistants were employed in classrooms. They became increasingly responsible for working with the slower children at a lower cost to schools than a Reading Recovery teacher. Subsequent research provided some evidence that well-trained teaching assistants can be effective (Savage and Carless, 2005; Bowyer-Crane *et al.*, 2008). However, Blatchford *et al.* (2009) found a negative relationship between the amount of support that children received from teaching assistants and their academic progress. Teaching-assistant support was generally not additional to teacher support but a substitute for it; teaching assistants spent one third of their time working outside the classroom, resulting in 'varying degrees of pupil separation (being cut off from their teachers, the curriculum and their peers) and dependency' (ibid.: 60). The authors also found differences between teaching-assistant talk and teacher talk, with teaching assistants spending less time explaining concepts to children and their explanations being 'sometimes inaccurate or confusing'.

Schools seldom monitored the effectiveness of interventions, and of any such teacher-assistant support, so as to ensure that children were making sufficient progress to catch up. Gross (2003: 18) stated: 'If you are not achieving at least twice the "normal" rate of progress through your existing Wave 3 literacy provision, you may need to re-evaluate what you are offering.' In Reading Recovery, such monitoring of progress was integral to teaching, and continued to ensure that children's progress was maintained in the classroom. Every year data were collected and published on the whole national cohort of children who received Reading Recovery, allowing outcomes from individual schools within an education authority and results for each authority to be evaluated against the national benchmark.

Despite the lack of earmarked governmental support after 1995, some local authorities managed to continue to implement Reading Recovery through a patchwork of bids and grants. By the time the National Literacy Strategy was introduced in 1997, Reading Recovery was still operating in 36 local authorities in England, over 1,300 teachers had been trained, and 12,000 children had received tuition. By 2003, when planning for Every Child a Reader began, 320 teachers were teaching in Reading Recovery in 19 local authorities, their data showing effective early literacy intervention in action, but it was still not widely available throughout England.

The spread of Reading Recovery across the UK and the Republic of Ireland

The pressures that gave impetus to the introduction of Reading Recovery were not confined to England. Concerns about underachievement in literacy, especially for socially disadvantaged children, were prevalent across the UK and the Republic of Ireland. Impressive early results from Reading Recovery in England led schools in each country to adopt the programme. Each implementation was distinctive, shaped by the particular features of the education system within which it had to operate, and bringing unique challenges and insights. Each country of the UK controls its own education system whose organization, funding, curriculum, and examination systems differ from England's.

Northern Ireland

Initial interest in Reading Recovery in Northern Ireland was strongly associated with the peace process of 1994–8 because of concerns about boys' poor attainment at school and the likelihood of their later being drawn into sectarian violence. The first reported results of Reading Recovery in Surrey (see page 13) attracted the attention of the Northern Ireland Office, and in the autumn of 1993 two of the province's Education and Library boards began the process of establishing an implementation by each appointing a teacher leader to train at the Institute of Education in London.

This was the period of ethno-political conflict in Northern Ireland known as 'The Troubles' (late 1960s–1998), and the sensitive social and political context created unique issues to be resolved before work could begin in schools. It was agreed that the Reading Recovery programme should serve both Catholic and Protestant schools without distinction, and that teachers would be drawn from schools in both communities. Twenty years on this may not appear unusual, but the accomplishment of officials in the Department of Education of Northern Ireland (DENI) in achieving this should not be underestimated. The role of teacher leader in Northern Ireland also carried unique challenges. Inevitably drawn from one side or the other of what at the time was a very real social divide, teacher leaders had to commit to working with both communities, which meant visiting schools in areas that they might otherwise have avoided. As the programme expanded and the number of teacher leaders increased, it seemed fortuitous that, with no apparent manipulation, colleagues from Northern Ireland in each training year were evenly balanced between Catholic and Protestant communities. During the second year of operation in Northern Ireland, a teacher leader commented that her Reading Recovery teacher-training group represented the first time she had worked with, or mixed socially with, members from across the religious divide. This story was heard time and again from Reading Recovery teachers: that, working together to unpick the literacy problems of a small and vulnerable child, was the first time that they came to know and respect members of 'the other' community as colleagues and friends.

The location of Reading Recovery centres for the professional development of teachers was critical, not just for teachers to feel safe and secure while attending sessions, but also to be acceptable to the families of children who would be brought there for live teaching sessions. This was not a matter of ideology but a very real concern for the personal safety for all involved, as young children were not spared the impact of hostility between the two communities. Visiting a teacher in a primary school in Omagh, the London-based trainer was shocked at the end of the day to see fully armed, battle-ready soldiers working their way through the infant playground. The local teacher leader did not bat an eyelid; on that housing estate it was routine.

The Reading Recovery centre in Belfast was opened in 1994 by Lady Jean Mayhew, wife of Sir Patrick Mayhew, then Secretary of State for

Northern Ireland. The local press photographer posed Lady Mayhew for a photograph but, as soon as his back was turned, she switched the book she had been given for one she had spotted in the display, Jill Murphy's classic picture book of Mr Bear's attempts to get a good night's sleep. Several times the photographer replaced the book with something more serious but each time, as soon as he turned away, Lady Mayhew changed it back. She got her way, and the photograph in the press the next day clearly displayed the title of the book: *Peace at Last*.

The implementation of Reading Recovery in Northern Ireland proved to be highly successful, and it quickly spread to all five of the province's Education and Library Boards. As a fragile peace process began to grow in the province, talk of a peace dividend brought hope of economic and social regeneration, with financial support given through the European Union Peace Fund and the International Fund for Ireland. In 1998, DENI published a Literacy Strategy for Northern Ireland. This included the target for all schools to have, or have access to, a Reading Recovery teacher by 2007. The strategy was backed by funding to enable schools to train a teacher, and in 2001 the Executive Programme Fund added further support, enabling schools to continue to provide Reading Recovery after their teacher was trained. In 2002 an evaluation of the Northern Ireland Literacy Strategy listed Reading Recovery as an example of best practice, an effective intervention strategy for lower-achieving children (NILSG, 2002: 9, 51).

In May 2001 Martin McGuinness, as Minister for Education in Northern Ireland, addressed a conference for Reading Recovery teacher leaders in Belfast. A controversial figure, he spoke frankly and movingly about his own early struggle with literacy and its impact on his teenage years. He left school at 15 with no formal qualifications, and acknowledged that his failure in education was a factor in his being drawn into the sectarian violence of the time. He echoed the thoughts of many in expressing his determination that future generations in Northern Ireland should be spared his experiences; he saw Reading Recovery as a significant part of the strategy for achieving that goal. The implementation peaked in 2003–04, when 2,775 children were served across the province.

However, in 2002 the peace process faltered and between 2002 and 2007 decision-making in the province became bogged down between Stormont and Westminster, so that, when the funding programme for Reading Recovery came up for renewal, a local administrator described the decision as 'falling into a black hole'. The much-vaunted peace dividend failed to deliver and in 2005, as Northern Ireland faced significant budget cuts, funding for Reading Recovery was significantly reduced. By 2007, in spite of protests from schools, no funding for Reading Recovery remained. A small number of schools tried to provide the programme from their own resources but the infrastructure of teacher leaders was no longer sustainable. By 2009, 15 years after Reading Recovery first started in Northern Ireland, only a handful of children had received the programme and it closed that year.

Important lessons were learnt in Northern Ireland. Independent evaluations (Gardner *et al.*, 1998; Munn and Ellis, 2005) showed the programme to have been highly effective for those children whom it had helped. But they also suggested the need for closer integration with classroom programmes and better use of professional resources and expertise to ensure that all children with literacy needs, including those not weak enough to receive Reading Recovery, should receive appropriate help. This influenced the development of Every Child a Reader in England, and in particular led to a growing emphasis on the strategic management of intervention to ensure that all children received a level of support that would be effective for them.

At the time of writing, Reading Recovery was not available in any school in Northern Ireland, although poor literacy standards among children across the province, especially those in poverty, continue to be a major cause of concern. In January 2012 the Literacy and Numeracy Taskforce reported to the Northern Ireland Assembly Education Committee. One member of the taskforce, Mrs Maureen Smyth, formerly a trained Reading Recovery teacher, reported:

> We have a lot of very short-lived initiatives; it is one initiative after another. [Some of] those have been proven to have good effect. One of them was Reading Recovery, which was phased out in 2005 or 2006 ... If we look to the Finnish model, we will see that they have had sustained programmes ... I think we should have some continuity and sustained programmes of improvement rather than have short-lived initiatives that make an impact but then end again.
>
> (Hansard, 2012)

The Republic of Ireland

In the Republic of Ireland there had been interest in Reading Recovery from late 1994. At a conference in Limerick that year an Education Inspector for the Department of Education and Science (DES) declared that there were only three obstacles to implementing Reading Recovery in Ireland, and held up a piece of paper on which was written:

Cost

Cost

Cost

However, St Mary Immaculate College, University of Limerick, had a close association with the Congregation of the Sisters of Mercy, a religious order with a particular commitment to education for children in poverty. Leaders of the order were closely following the implementation of Reading Recovery in Northern Ireland, and in 1999 they arranged to have one of the Sisters of Mercy trained as a teacher leader, to test the programme in the counties of Monaghan and Louth, bordering the province. As in Northern Ireland, the order made a generous commitment that, although they would fund the teacher leader, her work would not be confined to Catholic schools but would be available to all schools in the district.

There were practical issues to be resolved; Reading Recovery operates through a network of teacher leaders at district, board, or local authority level. In the Republic of Ireland there was no such local infrastructure through which teacher leaders could be employed or where training centres could be based.

In collaboration with Ireland's Department of Education and Science, agreement was reached to incorporate a training facility for Reading Recovery in a new teacher centre planned for Monaghan. The flagship Monaghan Education Centre was finally opened by Mary McAleese, President of Ireland, in 2004.

In 2001, a second Sister of Mercy, from Galway, in the west of Ireland, began training as a teacher leader. Galway is a region in which Irish is the first language for many children and, because of its distance from London, she relocated there for her year of training. During that year the DES made a commitment to expand Reading Recovery across Ireland so that, instead of returning to Galway, the newly trained teacher leader returned to Dublin, to establish the first of two centres there.

From 1995 the Republic of Ireland experienced an astonishing rate of economic growth. Investment in education was identified as one of the key catalysts in this rapid transformation from 'the poorest of the rich' to 'Europe's shining light' (Murphy, 2000). As Ireland grew into a modern knowledge-based economy, addressing the low educational attainment of large numbers of children in poverty became a significant government priority. In 2002, the DES set up the Educational Disadvantage Committee 'to advise the Minister on policies and strategies to be adopted to identify and correct educational disadvantage'. In 2003, the committee recommended a more integrated and effective delivery of school-based educational inclusion measures. In 2004 the Minister for Education and Science, Noel Dempsey, announced the allocation of an additional 350 teaching posts for special educational needs and a more reliable system for allocating resources for SEN in primary schools. The DES identified the most disadvantaged schools and offered Reading Recovery to those in the greatest need, 'starting at the bottom and gradually working up' (DES, personal communication, 2004).

With excellent results in Dublin and Monaghan, interest in the programme grew as schools wished to train their allocated resource teachers in Reading Recovery. In 2005, three more education centres began to offer professional development in Reading Recovery. In the same year, the DES published a detailed plan for social inclusion, Delivering Equality of Opportunity in Schools (DEIS), which included a new integrated School Support Programme. This would bring together and build upon existing interventions, including Reading Recovery, for schools and communities with a concentrated level of educational disadvantage (DES, 2005).

In spite of the economic downturn that began in 2008, and that hit Ireland far harder than it did the UK, that pledge to overturn disadvantage has been honoured. The implementation of Reading Recovery in Ireland grew from just over 500 children in 2005 to more than 3,000 in 2012. It has produced outstanding results, with a consistently 90 to 94 per cent of children completing programmes and achieving standards for discontinuing, the rate rising to 100 per cent in some districts.

The implementation of Reading Recovery in the Republic of Ireland has a number of distinctive features from which lessons may perhaps be drawn: Reading Recovery in Ireland is clearly embedded in a strategic national endeavour to overcome the divisive effects of poor educational outcomes for disadvantaged children. In outlining the strategy, one oft-repeated sentiment is that overturning longstanding and deeply embedded effects of disadvantage is a responsibility shared by all, including government, schools, families, and wider society:

> Education cannot be seen as an isolated process whereby the outcomes are the sole responsibility of schools ... the wider view has to be taken beyond that which applies in any one school. The impact of difficulties faced by an individual school and the outcomes for individual children are felt by other higher-level schools, by alternative education & training providers and by the wider community at an economic, social and behavioural level. The stakeholders in education have to be prepared to come

together to pro-actively plan for better outcomes taking the view that children and young people need to be helped throughout all their educational phases. Their success at the end is not 'owned' by any one stakeholder but is a shared achievement and one which everyone involved can take pride in.

(Ryan, 2004: 42)

The implication of this view is that government must have a dynamic leadership role in managing resources, enabling intervention, and monitoring outcomes.

In the absence of a local authority infrastructure within which Reading Recovery is organized elsewhere, the Reading Recovery network in the Republic of Ireland has developed interlinking and cooperative clusters of teacher leaders, based around regional teacher centres but coordinated and sustained centrally. This has proved to be an exceptionally robust model for quality assurance, as programme outcomes testify. Teacher leaders are enabled to focus closely on their unique role, they are able to refine and grow their expertise through consistent practice, and the clusters provide a strong basis supporting further professional learning.

Throughout the implementation of Reading Recovery in both Northern Ireland and the Republic of Ireland, teacher-leader training was provided through the Institute of Education in London. There are sound reasons why it may be appropriate for a centre for teacher-leader training, and for much of the national-level leadership and quality-assurance activity currently undertaken by the IOE, to be transferred to accredited national leaders based in Ireland.

Wales

Implementation

Reading Recovery in Wales, unlike in England or the Republic of Ireland, has never been a nationally implemented programme and it has never had support at government level. Instead Reading Recovery in Wales has been driven by demand from schools in two local authorities, almost entirely focused in the industrial/urban south of the principality, around Newport and Cardiff.

In 1992 the then Welsh Minister, Sir Wyn Roberts, announced three-year GESTs for projects to improve reading standards both in English and in Welsh. This paralleled the first trials of Reading Recovery in England. Six Welsh local authorities successfully bid for a variety of projects to address the problem of poor attainment in literacy and, though Reading Recovery was not among them, it is indicative that the active search for solutions to low attainment in literacy has been ongoing in Wales for at least 20 years.

At a conference in South Wales in September 1993, trainers from London shared information about the fledgling Reading Recovery implementation in England. In 1994 Gwent local education authority used some of its GEST funds to trial Reading Recovery. From 1994 teachers from Cardiff, Torfaen, Monmouth, and Blaenau Gwent participated in training in Newport, and in 1998 and 1999 Cardiff and Newport trained their own teacher leaders.

When the National Literacy Strategy was rolled out across England in 1998, the Welsh Assembly opted out of a national plan, instead leaving local authorities to develop their own programmes. Following the reorganization of many local authorities in Wales into several small unitary authorities, many struggled with very limited resources with which to provide expertise. This made the employment of a Reading Recovery teacher leader and the creation of an observation facility for training more difficult. Collaboration between neighbouring authorities was hard to achieve so, in spite of interest from schools across South Wales, the infrastructure was never able to expand beyond Newport and Cardiff. Nevertheless, over the period 1995 to 2000 the implementation grew steadily, and between 2001 and 2008 it served 250 to 300 Welsh children each year, with eight out of ten achieving the challenging goals of the intervention.

In spite of support from schools that valued the programme's successful outcomes, as in any small implementation it remained fragile. Reading Recovery in Wales was badly affected by key supportive personnel retiring or moving on and not being replaced, and by a lack of funding for the teacher-leader role. By 2012, only a few schools were able to support an implementation using teacher leaders in Bristol and serving only a handful of children.

The PISA (Programme for International Student Assessment) report of 2009 showed Wales slipping behind its UK counterparts and again in the Organisation for Economic Co-operation and Development (OECD) report of 2010. This was supported by a report by HM Inspectorate of Education and Training in Wales (ESTYN) in its finding that around 40 per cent of pupils entered secondary school in Year 7 with reading ages significantly (at least six months) below their actual age. Around 20 per cent of these pupils were functionally illiterate, with reading ages of below nine and a half years (ESTYN, 2012: 2).

In May 2012 the Welsh Assembly, in a reversal of the decision of 1998, launched a statutory National Literacy Programme (NLP) for Wales. In a comment echoing statements made in the Republic of Ireland, the NLP states:

> The Welsh Government cannot raise standards of literacy alone. Literacy standards will only improve if there is commitment from regional school improvement consortia, local authorities, governing bodies, head-teachers, teachers and support staff.
>
> (DES, 2012: 3)

The NLP identified among key issues the need for 'more and earlier' targeted support for pupils who struggle, and enhanced professional development for teachers (DES, 2012: 5). Both of these are readily available in Reading Recovery.

Welsh language developments

The first attempts to apply Reading Recovery to the Welsh language proved illuminating and helped to establish the clear understanding that considerably more was involved than a straight translation from English. As the Welsh academic Anne Jones had found, the assessment tools and teaching programme needed to be redeveloped, or reconstructed, to take account of subtle differences, and the specific demands, of Welsh.

Gwelais aderyn ar y gangen

a cherrig

ar y llawr.

Figure 1.3: A sample of the draft redevelopment of Concepts about Print text, Cerrig (Stones, 1997). Reproduced by kind permission of the Marie Clay Literacy Trust.

One particular assessment item made the point very clearly: in the Concepts about Print assessment, one task requires the child to use masking cards to show just one letter, two letters, just one word, and finally two words. Its purpose is to reveal the child's understanding of the hierarchy of letters and words. In the original English version both sentences that form the alternative versions for the context of this task begin with 'The'. Translated directly into Welsh both sentences begin with 'Y', a one-letter word. The meaning is the same but the potential for confusion between 'one letter' and 'one word' immediately invalidates the task. This valuable experience led to the subsequent establishment of clear protocols and guidance for any future redevelopments of the Observation Survey and of the transference of Reading Recovery into new languages (International Reading Recovery Trainers Organization, 2010). In these the starting point is not the translation of existing texts, but an exploration of the nature of the new language and its impact on the way literacy operates and can be assessed, learnt, and taught.

A redevelopment of the full Observation Survey in Welsh was completed in 1997, but to date has not been published.

Scotland

The implementation of Reading Recovery in Scotland has been perhaps the most perplexing and frustrating of all European literacy ventures. The requirement for teacher leaders in Scotland to travel to London for a year of training not only added to the costs and logistical problems for a Scottish local authority wishing to engage with the programme, but also deterred potential teacher leaders from coming forward. It was also unfortunate in that, in contrast with their counterparts elsewhere in the UK, and for a variety of personal reasons not associated with the role, three of the four teacher leaders trained for work in Scotland stayed in post for only one or two years after training. An attempt in 1998 to establish a centre for teacher-leader training at Jordanhill College (now part of the University of Strathclyde, Glasgow) failed to bear fruit. Had that been achieved, it is possible that the programme could have become more widely embedded. Without Scottish 'ownership', the cost and other cultural issues associated with a London-based initiative gave rise instead to alternative 'Reading Recovery lite' programmes (Leslie and McMillan, 1999). While they had some positive effect, they did not have a satisfactory impact on the lowest-attaining children.

It was acknowledged that there was a great need for effective literacy intervention. Some schools experienced such high levels of underachievement that, at a conference in Scotland in 1996, a local headteacher commented to the Reading Recovery trainer: 'You described Reading Recovery as a precision tool, but what we need is a sledgehammer.'

In June 1997 the Scottish Office launched the Early Intervention Programme (EIP) to raise standards of literacy in primary Years 1 and 2. With the Excellence Fund announced in 1998 this became a five-year project, with £60 million in funding to support 'the right start' in literacy and maths for all children (SOEID, 1998).

North Lanarkshire arranged for two members of staff to join the teacher-leader course in London. When they returned at the end of their training course to set up training for teachers in Scotland in 1998–9, the response was overwhelming, and in the first year of implementation more than 200 children were served.

Schools in this first cohort received funding to release teachers full-time, rather than 0.5 of the working week as was usual elsewhere. This meant that teachers taught six or seven children in Reading Recovery each day, rather than the usual four. The outcomes were remarkable, with 85 per cent of children reaching the criteria for programmes to be discontinued, compared with the national average at the time of 78 per cent. This was in spite of a greater proportion of the cohort being eligible for free school meals, high levels of non-attendance, and the fact that all the teachers were in training under novice teacher leaders.

In that first year lessons were learnt from the generous funding that had been made available. The impact of schools' being able to reach eight to ten children in the first year demonstrated what was possible and helped to overturn low expectations for children with multiple disadvantages. An analysis at the time found an association between the number of children taught each day and higher outcomes (Figure 1.4). The drop associated with eight programme places appeared on closer investigation to be linked to larger schools with two teachers each teaching four children daily. This supported anecdotal evidence that teachers working full-time in Reading Recovery were able to focus on the job in hand and developed their skills very rapidly as they dealt with a wide range of children each having distinct problems and requiring different approaches.

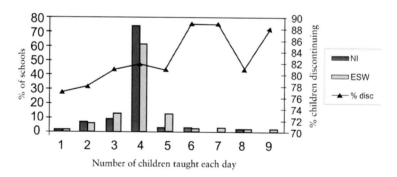

Figure 1.4: Percentage of children reaching levels for discontinuing, by number of Reading Recovery programme places (children taught each day) in the school. Data from 1999–2000 cohort, internal analyses. Data for Northern Ireland and for England/Scotland/Wales.

However, there were warnings too. Teachers reported that one-to-one teaching throughout the day required a level of intensity, concentration, and focus that was extremely draining. Many reduced their commitment to four places after the first year and, of those who continued to teach full-time, many left the role after the second year, saying that they felt 'burnt out'.

Fully funding schools at government level was unsustainable in the long term so that, having made no contribution to costs initially, schools subsequently struggled to arrange their budgets to provide daily teaching. Schools that had been fully funded were less likely to accept responsibility for self-funding the programme than those who had already accommodated some of the costs. Indeed some headteachers made it a matter of principle, insisting that, if their local authority wanted them to engage in the programme, the local authority should pay for it.

In 2001, a formal evaluation of the EIP reported that in the 67 per cent of Scottish primary schools that had taken part, most serving areas with multiple disadvantages, the increase in reading attainment was greater in those schools where Reading Recovery approaches had been implemented (Fraser *et al.*, 2001: 4).

Local authorities had been given freedom to distribute funds equally among all schools, or to direct it to those in greatest need. The impact of EIP was greater where funds were channelled to fewer schools with the greatest needs (Fraser et al., 2001: 10).

Between 2000 and 2006, the centre in North Lanarkshire provided training for individual schools in Highland, Inverness, Aberdeen, Falkirk, Stirling, and Inverclyde.

Sadly, with the retirement of the teacher leader in 2006, and a fourth teacher leader unable to take over the role because of illness, the centre closed. Although a number of schools continued to use their Reading Recovery teachers to support low-attaining children, without professional development or further funding the programme ceased in 2007.

Jersey

Jersey was one of the earliest parts of the British Isles besides England to introduce Reading Recovery, in 1993–94. The initial connection was made through a self-employed tutor/teacher leader who was already delivering Reading Recovery in the south of England and was bought in by Jersey's Department for Education on a part-time basis for two years to provide training for Jersey schools. In 1995, this teacher leader retired but Jersey was able to take advantage of the end of the GEST-funded project in England (see p. 14) to employ another trained teacher leader full-time, granting residency status to her and her family so that she could fully support the schools on the island community.

By 1999, Jersey had Reading Recovery teachers in 23 of its 24 primary schools. Some schools had taken advantage of the professional development opportunity to have two or even three of their teachers trained, though not all delivered the programme. The impact in schools over the next few years was considerable, anticipating many of the wider school approaches that would later be developed as part of Every Child a Reader. Between 2005 and 2010 (when Jersey stopped providing data to bodies outside their system) more than 80 per cent of children who received Reading Recovery attained Level 2 or above each year.

Jersey provides a model of what can be achieved with full implementation. Jersey has a system to determine the proportion of children who experience financial disadvantage and it is clear that, even in an otherwise wealthy context with highly effective schools, there are some children who need intensive literacy support.

An important lesson was learnt in the first year of implementation in Jersey when, in order to recruit sufficient schools for a viable training group, the teacher leader made an exception to accommodate a teacher attending training sessions without teaching the minimum number of children (four). This, a significant deviation from existing guidelines, was intended to address a specific problem in one school but, in an island community news spreads quickly and within months the teacher leader found herself struggling to maintain the requirement for teachers to teach the minimum number of children in any school. The impact on outcomes was catastrophic and almost undermined the fledgling implementation. The situation was remedied, and the implementation went on to become one of the most successful in the UK, but the experience led to the development and articulation of clear standards and guidelines for the implementation of Reading Recovery. These became the foundation for quality assurance, which has considerably strengthened the programme while enabling innovation and adjustment through controlled and monitored trials.

A European perspective

As Reading Recovery spread across the UK and beyond, what was learnt?

We learnt that the need for such a programme is universal. From the toughest estate in Belfast to the sandy coves of Jersey there are children who, for whatever reason, need intensive help if they are to learn to read and write within the same time frame as their peers and with the same relish and positive attitude as children who have never struggled. Showing what is possible for children facing multiple disadvantages raises expectations for others, whatever the context.

We learnt that Reading Recovery can be transferred with equal success across a wide range of settings. In each country, implementations acquire a unique local character, shaped by culture, context, and conditions. Those engaged with Reading Recovery across the whole of the UK and the Republic of Ireland, and probably internationally, have been enriched by the different perspectives, challenges, and achievements of each country. Sensitivity to and respect for one another's national systems, priorities, and customs has broadened horizons and encouraged a reflective critique of one's own assumptions.

Those involved in solving children's individual problems, though they may work in very diverse contexts, are supported by being part of a wider infrastructure. In the European Reading Recovery network, all implementations are of equal worth, whether large and thriving or small and struggling, because they serve the needs of low-attaining children. Each teacher and teacher leader contributes to a better understanding of how to overcome a child's idiosyncratic difficulties; each manager offers ways of enhancing implementations, and through the community of learners the overall network is strengthened.

A number of factors are essential for the programme to be effective across different settings: core principles must be clearly articulated and well understood by all; leaders must be sensitive to and respectful of the subtleties of each new context; communication should be efficient, consistent, and coherent both within and between nations; and the infrastructure needs a capacity for controlled adaptation that can be tested and refined or rejected, as changes in one site impact on all others.

Each national implementation is affected as political support waxes and wanes. Where implementation is piecemeal and schools are left to struggle, the risk of a fragile infrastructure breaking apart is significantly increased. Leadership needs to be neither complacent nor defeatist but to focus on children who need support. In Clay's early articulation of Reading Recovery she described three concentric circles representing the child, the teacher, and the education system within which they are located (figure 1.5).

Experience across the whole of the UK and the Republic of Ireland highlights the importance of the third ring, the system whose role is to enable both the teacher and the child to benefit. Reading Recovery thrives, and children thrive, where overall leadership drives a will to change the status quo and to break the link between disadvantage and poor literacy.

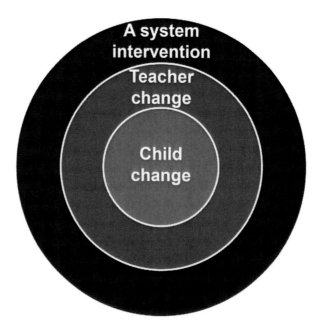

Figure 1.5: The spheres of change (developed from Clay, 2009)

Summary

This chapter has presented the case, on both individual and societal grounds, for effective early literacy intervention. It has shown how Reading Recovery, an example of such an intervention, came to be introduced first to England in 1991, and subsequently to Northern Ireland, Scotland, and the Republic of Ireland. During the 1990s in England, a number of reports, highly critical of England's standards of literacy, were published and, in reaction to these, the ambitious National Literacy Strategy was introduced, which aimed to radically change the classroom teaching of reading and writing in primary schools in England. Similarly, in other parts of UK and the Republic of Ireland where interest resulted in implementation of Reading Recovery, various reports were made and monitoring undertaken with the same strong results for children. Under political and economic stresses, these implementations waxed and waned, but were most consistently sustained in the Republic of Ireland. In England, despite the considerable improvements that the National Literacy Strategy produced, there was still a substantial minority of children who failed to achieve sufficient literacy to leave primary school able to cope with the demands of the secondary school curriculum. Although a number of supplementary programmes were devised for this group, they did not achieve the gains needed to enable slow learners to catch up with their peers. After six years of the National Literacy Strategy, attention turned to the needs of this group and Reading Recovery was poised to provide an effective model of support.

Notes

[1] Texts used in Reading Recovery are graded numerically from 1 to 20+, with Level 1 being most supportive of emergent readers and Level 20 representing more sophisticated texts for 6- to 7-year-olds. Readily available books from a range of reading schemes, types, and genres are levelled into a fine gradient of difficulty through evaluation criteria and field trialling.

References

Alakeson, V. (2005) *Too Much, Too Late: Life chances and spending on education and training*. London: Social Market Foundation.

Al Otaiba, S. and Fuchs, D. (2002) 'Characteristics of children who are unresponsive to early literacy intervention: A review of the literature'. *Remedial and Special Education*, 23 (5), 300–17.

Ashdown, J. and Hummel-Rossi, B. (2002) 'What is cost effectiveness analysis?' *Journal of Reading Recovery*, 2 (1), 44–6.

Beard, R. (2011) 'The origins, evaluations and implications of the National Literacy Strategy in England'. In A. Goodwyn and C. Fuller (eds), *The Great Literacy Debate*. London: Routledge.

Bickler, S., Baker, S., and Hobsbaum, A. (1998) *Book Bands for Guided Reading: A handbook to support Foundation and Key Stage 1 teachers*. London: Institute of Education, University of London.

Blatchford, P., Bassett, P., Brown, P., and Webster, R. (2009) 'The effect of support staff on pupil engagement and individual attention'. *British Educational Research Journal*, 35 (5), 661–86.

Bowyer-Crane, C., Snowling, M.J., Duff, F.J., Fieldsend, E., Carroll, J.M., Miles, J., Götz, K., and Hulme, C. (2008) 'Improving early language and literacy skills: Differential effects of an oral language versus a phonology with reading intervention'. *Journal of Child Psychology and Psychiatry*, 49 (4), 422–32.

Brooks, G. (2007, 3rd ed.) *What Works for Pupils with Literacy Difficulties? The effectiveness of intervention schemes*. London: Department for Children, Schools, and Families.

– (2013, 4th ed.) *What Works for Children and Young People with Literacy Difficulties? The effectiveness of intervention schemes*. Bracknell: Dyslexia-SpLD Trust.

Bynner J., and Parsons, P. (1997) *It Doesn't Get Any Better*. London: Basic Skills Agency.

CBI Northern Ireland (1994) *Peace – A Challenging New Era*. Belfast: Northern Ireland Confederation of British Industry.

Clay, M.M. (1966) 'Emergent Reading Behaviour'. Unpublished PhD thesis. University of Auckland.

– (1979) *The Early Detection of Reading Difficulties*. Portsmouth, NH: Heinemann.

– (1998) *By Different Paths to Common Outcomes*. Portsmouth, NH: Heinemann.

–. (2001) *Change Over Time in Children's Literacy Development*. Portsmouth, NH: Heinemann.

– (1993, revised 2002, in process of 2nd revision 2013) *An Observation Survey of Early Literacy Achievement*. Auckland, New Zealand: Heinemann.

– (2005) *Literacy Lessons Designed for Individuals: Part One: Why? When? How?* Auckland, New Zealand: Heinemann.

Clay, M.M. and Tuck, B. (1993) 'The Reading Recovery sub-groups study, 1991'. In M.M. Clay: *Reading Recovery: A guidebook for teachers in training*. 86–95. Auckland: Heinemann.

Denton, C.A., Ciancio, D.J., and Fletcher, J.M. (2006) 'Validity, reliability and utility of the Observation Survey of early literacy achievement'. *Reading Research Quarterly,* 41 (1), 8–34.

Department for Education and Skills (DES Wales) (2012) *National Literacy Programme*. Cardiff.

Department of Education and Science (2003) *School Development Planning Initiative: National Progress Report 2002*. Dublin.

Department of Education and Science (2005) DEIS (Delivering Equality Of Opportunity In Schools) *An Action Plan for Educational Inclusion*. Dublin.

Earl, L., Fullan, M., Leithwood, K., Watson, N., with Jantzi, D., Levin, B., and Torrance, N. (2000) *Watching and Learning 1: First annual report*. London: Department for Education and Employment.

Earl, L., Levin, B., Leithwood, K., Fullan, M, Watson, N., with Torrance, N., Jantzi, D., and Mascall, B. (2001) *Watching and Learning 2. Second annual report*. London: Department for Education and Employment.

Earl, L., Watson, N., Levin, B., Leithwood, K., Fullan, M., Torrance, N. with Jantzi, D., Mascall, B., and Volante, L. (2003) *Watching and Learning 3. Final report of the external evaluation of England's National Literacy and Numeracy Strategies*. London: Department for Education and Employment.

Elliott, C.D., McCulloch, K., and Smith, P. (1996) *British Ability Scales (BAS II) (2nd edition) Early Years*. GL Assessment.

Educational Disadvantage Committee (2003) *A More Integrated and Effective Delivery of School-based Educational Inclusion Measures*. Dublin: Department of Education and Science.

Educational Disadvantage Committee (2005) *Moving Beyond Educational Disadvantage: Report of the Educational Disadvantage Committee*. Dublin: Department of Education and Science.

ESTYN (2012) *Literacy in Key Stage 3*. Cardiff.

European Centre for Reading Recovery (2011) *Every Child a Reader Annual Report 2010–11*. Online. http://readingrecovery.ioe.ac.uk/reports/documents/ECaR_annual_report_2010-11.pdf (accessed 30 April 2013)

Francis, D.J., Shaywitz, S.E., Stuebing, K.K., Shaywitz, B.A., and Fletcher, J.M. (1996) 'Developmental lag versus deficit models of reading disability: A longitudinal individual growth curves analysis'. *Journal of Educational Psychology*, 88, 3–17.

Fraser, H., MacDougall, A., Pirrie, A., and Croxford, L. (2001) *Early Intervention in Literacy and Numeracy: Key issues from the national evaluation of the programme*. Edinburgh: Scottish Executive Education Department.

Gardner, J., Sutherland A., and Meenan-Strain, C. (1998) *Reading Recovery in Northern Ireland: The first two years.* Belfast: Blackstaff Press.

Gersten, R. and Dimino, J.A. (2006) 'RTI (Response to Intervention): Rethinking special education for students with reading difficulties (yet again)'. *Reading Research Quarterly,* 41 (1), 99–107.

Gross, J. (2003) 'Waves of intervention'. *Special Children,* Feb–March, 16–20.

Hansard, January 2012 (2012). Online. www.niassembly.gov.uk/Assembly-Business/Official-Report/Committee-Minutes-of-Evidence/Session-2011-2012/January-2012/Committee-for-Education---Literacy-and-Numeracy-Taskforce/ (accessed 30 April 2013).

Hobsbaum, A. and Clay, M.M. (1993) 'A training scheme for the Reading Recovery programme: The pilot years, 1991–1993'. Unpublished paper. Institute of Education, University of London.

Holdaway, D. (1979) *The Foundations of Literacy.* Gossford, Australia: Ashton-Scholastic.

Hollingsworth, M. (1995) Effective Raising Standards projects. *Grants for Education Support and Training: Raising standards in inner city schools 1992 – 1995.* London: DfEE.

Hummel-Rossi, B. and Ashdown, J. (2010) *Cost-effectiveness Analysis as a Decision Tool in Selecting and Implementing Instructional Interventions in Literacy.* Columbus, OH: Reading Recovery Council of North America.

Hurry, J., Sylva, K., and Riley, J. (1999) 'Evaluation of a focused literacy teaching programme in reception and Year 1 classes: Child outcomes'. *British Educational Research Journal,* 25, 637–49.

Hurry, J. (2000) *Review of Intervention Strategies to Support Pupils with Difficulties in Literacy during Key Stage 1.* London: QCA.

International Reading Recovery Trainers' Organization (IRRTO) (2009) 'Establishing Reading Recovery in a New Nation where the Language of Instruction is not English'. Procedural document. Online. www.irrto.com (behind paywall).

Juel, C. (1988) 'Learning to read and write: A longitudinal study of fifty-four children from first through fourth grades'. *Journal of Educational Psychology,* 80 (4), 437–47.

KPMG Foundation (2006) *The Long Term Costs of Literacy Difficulties.* London: Every Child a Chance Trust.

Leslie, M. and McMillan, G. (1999) 'Early intervention in the teaching of reading: The Edinburgh projects'. *Educational and Child Psychology,* 16 (1), 14–21.

Lingard, T. (2000) 'Is the National Literacy Strategy raising the achievement of lower attainers?'. *British Journal of Special Education,* 27 (3), 117–23.

Literacy Task Force (1997) 'A Reading Revolution: How we can teach every child to read well: The preliminary report of the Literacy Task Force. Online. www.leeds.ac.uk/educol/documents/000000153.htm (accessed 23 December 2011).

Matic, M., Byrne, S., and Fissuh, E. (2007) 'Awareness and Process: The Role of the European Union Peace II Fund and the International Fund for Ireland in Building the Peace Dividend in Northern Ireland'. *Journal of Conflict Studies.* Online. http://journals.hil.unb.ca/index.php/JCS/article/view/8290 (accessed 23 September 2012).

Meek, M. (1982) *Learning to Read.* London: The Bodley Head.

Moore, P. (1997) 'Models of Teacher Education: Where Reading Recovery teacher training fits'. Online. www.readingrecovery.org/development/archives/moore.asp (accessed 18 February 2010).

Mortimore, P. and Goldstein, H. (1996) *The Teaching of Reading in 45 Inner London Primary Schools: A critical examination of OFSTED research*. London: Institute of Education, University of London.

Munn, P., and Ellis, S. (2005) 'Interactions between school systems and Reading Recovery programmes – evidence from Northern Ireland'. *The Curriculum Journal*, 16 (3), 341–62.

Murphy, A.E. (2000) 'The "Celtic Tiger": An Analysis of Ireland's Economic Growth Performance'. Robert Schuman Centre for Advanced Studies, RSC no. 2000/16, Badia Faisolana, Italy, European University Institute.

Northern Ireland Literacy Steering Group (NILSG)(2002) *An Evaluation of the Northern Ireland Literacy Strategy 1998–2002*. Belfast: Belfast Education and Library Board.

OECD (2010) *PISA 2009 Results: Executive Summary*. London: OECD.

Ofsted (1993) *Reading Recovery in New Zealand*. London: HMSO.

Ofsted (1996) *The Teaching of Reading in 45 Inner London Primary Schools*. London: Office for Standards in Education.

Ofsted (2000) *The National Literacy Strategy: The second year*. London: Office for Standards in Education.

O'Hearn, D. (2000) 'Peace dividend, foreign investment, and economic regeneration: The Northern Irish case'. *Social Problems*, 47 (2), 180–200.

Rodgers, E. (2012), 'Using Systematic Observation to Assess Early Literacy Development and Plan Instruction'. In E. Ortlieb and E.H. Cheek (eds), *Using Informative Assessments towards Effective Literacy Instruction*. Bingley, W. Yorkshire: Emerald. Online. www.emeraldinsight.com/books. htm?chapterid=17021001

Rose, J. (2006) *Independent Review of the Teaching of Early Reading: Final report*. London: DfES.

Ryan, G. (2004) *Get it Right First Time – An education strategy for Ballymun*. Dublin: Department of Education and Science.

Savage R. and Carless S. (2005) 'Learning support assistants can deliver effective reading interventions for "at-risk" children'. *Educational Research*, 47, 45–61.

Schmitt, M.C., Askew, B.J., Fountas, I.C., Lyons, C.A., and Pinnell, G.S. (2005) *Changing Futures: The influence of Reading Recovery in the United States*. Worthington, OH: Reading Recovery Council of North America.

Scottish Office Education and Industry Department (1998) *The Early Intervention Programme: Raising standards in literacy and numeracy*. Edinburgh: The Stationery Office.

Shanahan, T. and Barr, R. (1995) 'Reading Recovery: An independent evaluation of the effects of an early instructional intervention for at-risk learners'. *Reading Research Quarterly*, 30 (4), 958–96.

Shaywitz, S.E., Fletcher, J.M., Holahan, J.M., Shneider, A.E., Marchione, K.E., Stuebing, K.K., Francis, D.J., Pugh, K.R., and Shaywitz, B.A. (1999) 'The persistence of dyslexia: The Connecticut longitudinal study at adolescence'. *Pediatrics*, 104, 1351–9.

Stainthorp, R. (2000) 'The National Literacy Strategy and individual differences'. *Journal of Research in Reading,* 23 (3), 299–307.

Stannard, J. and Huxford, L. (2007) *The Literacy Game: The story of the National Literacy Strategy.* Abingdon: Routledge.

Stanovich, K. (1986) 'Matthew effects in reading: Some consequences of individual differences in the acquisition of literacy'. *Reading Research Quarterly,* 21, 360–407.

Strickland, D.S., Ganske, K., and Monroe, J.K. (2002) *Supporting Struggling Readers and Writers: Strategies for classroom intervention 3–6.* New York: Stenhouse.

Vellutino, F.R., Fletcher, J.M., Snowling, M., and Scanlon, D.M. (2004) 'Specific reading disability (dyslexia): What have we learned in the past four decades? A comprehensive review of intervention studies'. *Journal of Child Psychology and Psychiatry,* 45, 2–40.

Vellutino, F.R., Scanlon, D.M., Sipay, E.R., Small, S.G., Pratt, A., Chen, R.S., and Denckla, M.B. (1996) 'Cognitive profiles of difficult to remediate and readily remediated poor readers: Early intervention as a vehicle for distinguishing between cognitive and experiential deficits as basic causes of specific reading disability'. *Journal of Educational Psychology,* 88, 601–38.

Wanzek, J., Vaughn, S., Kim, A.H., and Cavanaugh, C.L. (2006) 'The effects of reading interventions on social outcomes for elementary students with reading difficulties: A synthesis'. *Reading and Writing Quarterly,* 22, 121–38.

Wasik, B.A. and Slavin, R.E. (1993) 'Preventing early reading failure with one-to-one tutoring: A review of five programs'. *Reading Research Quarterly,* 28 (2), 179–200.

Chapter 2

How Every Child a Reader grew from Reading Recovery

Sue Burroughs-Lange, Julia Douëtil, and Angela Hobsbaum

Introduction

This chapter describes the factors that provided the momentum for the emergence of Every Child a Reader from the nucleus of Reading Recovery. It shows that Every Child a Reader, with its strong theoretical and practical base, is an example of an educational initiative that can demonstrate high achievement levels even during rapid expansion.

The scale of the problem of low literacy achievement

By 2003, it was generally acknowledged that, while the National Literacy Strategy had improved literacy for the majority of primary school pupils, there remained a sizable minority who had failed to benefit sufficiently from this ambitious initiative. By then, an entire cohort of children had experienced the National Literacy Strategy during their whole primary school career, and so might have been expected to show the benefit of changes in teaching, through the Literacy Hour, and in the more detailed curriculum with its greater specification of, for example, genres, text features, and progression in phonic knowledge.

In 2003 national testing showed that more than 30,000 children were entering secondary school with a reading ability at or below the level of a 7-year-old. This meant that around 7 per cent of 11-year-olds were still not reaching the level needed to make a smooth transition to secondary school. The issue of this persistent 'tail of underachievement' in literacy rose up the political agenda as it threatened the Government's claims for success in the educational arena, an issue that would also be reflected in the UK's international ranking.

Research now began to show a link between poor attainment in literacy and long-term personal and social problems, and so quantified its impact on the public purse. Feinstein's analysis of the social benefits of learning in relation to crime (1999) and, perhaps more surprisingly, to health (2002) extrapolated the true costs of low educational attainment. Reports from national cohort studies for the Basic Skills Agency highlighted the links between literacy and employment, in-work training, benefit dependency, social engagement, stability of personal relationships, and mental health (Bynner and Parsons, 1997; Flood-Page *et al.*, 2000; Parsons, 2002; Rack, 2005; Godfrey *et al.*, 2002; Green *et al.*, 2003). The Social Exclusion Unit showed the impact on social cohesion of disparities in educational attainment (Parsons and Bynner, 2002; Scott *et al.*, 2001). So, far from being confined to the educational arena, the impact of achievement in literacy was shown to have far-reaching social and economic implications.

How could Reading Recovery help?

Given this growing recognition of the potential cost of failing to address the problem of poor literacy, and the evidence that whole-class approaches were not capable of solving the problems of a substantial proportion of underachieving pupils, might Reading Recovery be a possible solution?

Although Reading Recovery was acknowledged as an effective early literacy intervention, a number of factors limited its take-up and restricted its spread. The principal barriers to schools adopting Reading Recovery were the costs of the infrastructure required to start a new implementation in an area, including the costs to a local authority of setting up a centre and training a teacher leader; the costs to a school of releasing a teacher for training and for one-to-one teaching; and the relatively few children served directly through the intensive individual Reading Recovery intervention. These costs were a disincentive for local authorities and, unless their local authority was committed to investing in Reading Recovery, schools could not access it. In some cases, schools that had used Reading Recovery found that, where there were large numbers of children needing support, this demand exceeded the available Reading Recovery resource. Despite Reading Recovery's success as an individual teaching response, criticisms were levelled at it for the cost of its provision, and for it not reaching enough children given the level of need that many schools experienced. Critics argued that, since one Reading Recovery teacher could support only eight to ten children in a year, this would be a drop in the ocean given the levels of need in many primary schools, especially those in deprived inner-city areas (referred to in ECaR annual report, 2009–10).

Even where the needs of the poorest readers were served by Reading Recovery, there was still a lack of effective provision for children who were not the lowest-attaining but still needed some help. The support offered to those children was often poorly designed and inadequately monitored. In a number of places, skilled Reading Recovery practitioners had begun to develop a range of 'lighter touch' support programmes for children with less complex needs, alongside Reading Recovery for children with the greatest difficulties. These developments capitalized on the professional skills of the Reading Recovery teacher to organize, support, and monitor a range of interventions suited to children with varying levels of need. They included children who simply needed additional opportunities to practise their reading in a supportive setting, those who needed help to improve their speaking and listening skills, and those who needed more assistance with writing and spelling. Through these innovations, Reading Recovery began to have an enhanced impact in schools that was recognized by professionals working within the National Literacy Strategy. However, it was still regarded as too costly for national implementation.

The need for well-designed research evidence

Another criticism frequently levelled at Reading Recovery was that it lacked a well-designed evaluation. In educational research, a randomized control trial is the gold-standard model for evaluating a new method. Researchers, including Clay, had ethical concerns with this model when there was already a body of evidence for Reading Recovery's impact. Randomly depriving some children of this evidence-based intervention had serious consequences for their learning lives. While extensive national data had been collected from schools in England since 1992, providing descriptive information on the progress of every child who had received Reading Recovery, no experimental comparison had ever been carried out. It was vital to undertake a well-controlled study to assess the effectiveness of Reading Recovery and, when the opportunity to carry out such a study arose, it was put into action in schools serving areas of London with a low socio-economic demographic (Burroughs-Lange and Douëtil, 2007).

The essential questions explored by this research were:

(i)   Would Reading Recovery work even in underperforming schools, serving low socio-economic urban environments?

(ii) Would poor readers progress just as well without the more costly Reading Recovery intervention?

(iii) Would any gains wash out, or be sustained at least a year after the intervention?

The study was undertaken in ten London boroughs, using 42 matched primary schools, half of which used Reading Recovery and half of which made other provision for early literacy intervention. These schools were similar in size (average 355 on roll), and had similarly high levels of children entitled to free school meals (average 41 per cent compared to 14 per cent nationally) and children learning English as an additional language (average 49 per cent compared to 17 per cent nationally). They offered a tough testing ground for Reading Recovery. The literacy attainment of the lowest-achieving 6-year-olds and of the whole Year 1 cohort (1,166 Year 1 children in all) was compared at the beginning and end of the 2005–06 school year. The children were assessed on letter, word, and text reading skills, using standardized tests.

At the beginning of Year 1, the 292 lowest-achieving children were unable to read even the simplest texts, could recognize only a few letters, and could write only about six words correctly. At the end of Year 1, most of these low-achieving children had made little progress, except for the group of children who received Reading Recovery, who had now caught up with their average peers. From uniformly low starting points, children who received Reading Recovery gained on average 20 months in reading age and could write 45 words correctly. A teacher-report questionnaire showed improved behaviour and attitudes to learning in those children who had received Reading Recovery in Year 1, and a decline in these learning-related aspects for the matched sample of children who were falling further behind their peers (Burroughs-Lange and Douëtil, 2007). The follow-up study a year later found that at the end of Year 2, on average, the ex-Reading Recovery children were still achieving at the level expected for their age, while the children in the comparison group, who had not experienced Reading Recovery, were still well below age-related expectations (Burroughs-Lange, 2008).

Table 2.1: Word-reading age on British Abilities Scales II (end of Year 2 follow-up).

Group	Number	Mean	Standard deviation
Comparison	108	81.18 months (6.8 years)	16.23
Ex-Reading Recovery	77	93.21 months (7.8 years)	14.26

Note: Significant difference $p<.0001$, effect size 0.74

Source: Burroughs-Lange, 2008

Key Stage 1 National Curriculum assessments, carried out when the children were around seven and a half years old, showed that 86 per cent of ex-

Reading Recovery children achieved an age-appropriate level (Level 2+) in reading (84 per cent achieving this target nationally). In writing 83 per cent of ex-Reading Recovery children achieved Level 2+ compared with 80 per cent nationally (Burroughs-Lange, 2008). Classrooms where the lowest achievers had access to Reading Recovery reported an average four months' higher overall achievement in literacy at the end of Year 1, and there was still a three-month class-level advantage at the end of Year 2.

Three years later, when these children had reached the end of Year 4, a further follow-up study was undertaken. Altogether, 120 children in the comparison group and 73 ex-Reading Recovery children were traced, spread across the original 42 schools and 54 other schools. In National Curriculum assessment scores, the ex-Reading Recovery children were still doing significantly better than those in the comparison group who had received a range of other interventions. Ex-Reading Recovery children were significantly less likely than children in the comparison group to be identified as having special educational needs (Hurry and Holliman, 2009). In 2011, at the end of Key Stage 2 (11-year-olds), slightly more children from the original sample were traced, and assessed again.

Table 2.2: Mean scores at the end of Key Stage 2 National Curriculum assessments for English reading, and writing, and for Mathematics

	Reading (Max. 50)	Writing (Max. 50)	NC Level	Maths (Max. 100)
Comparison children (No. = 126)	Mean – 21.5 (SD – 11.43)	Mean – 21.38 (SD – 10.03)	Mean – 3.99 (SD – 0.79)	Mean – 53.78 (SD – 20.94)
Reading Recovery children (No. = 76)	Mean – 26.27 (SD – 9.29)	Mean – 25.0 (SD – 8.1)	Mean – 4.31 (SD – 0.64)	Mean – 60.77 (SD – 19.01)
Comparison children in Reading Recovery schools (No. = 50)	Mean – 26.6 (SD – 14.47)	Mean – 23.41 (SD – 11.57)	Mean – 4.26 (SD – 0.93)	Mean – 58.11 (SD – 25.15)

Table 2.2 shows that the ex-Reading Recovery children were still doing significantly better in reading (â=.191, p<.005), effect size (Cohen's d)

= .39) and writing (â=.162, p<.013, effect size (Cohen's d) = .33) than the comparison children in non-Reading Recovery schools. They were also scoring significantly higher in their maths test (â=.154, p<.036, effect size (Cohen's d) = .31). However, the comparison children from non-Reading Recovery schools were not doing significantly better than the comparison children from the Reading Recovery schools on any of the measures (reading, writing, or maths). Indeed the comparison children from Reading Recovery schools (i.e. those that were poor readers at six but did not receive the programme) were also doing significantly better in reading than the comparison children from non-Reading Recovery schools (â=.222, p<.002, effect size (Cohen's d) = .24) (Hurry, 2012: 9).

This suggests that the substantial gains that result from receiving Reading Recovery in Year 1 continue to deliver a significant advantage for those children at the end of the Primary phase, providing a surer footing for their transition to secondary school (Hurry, 2012: 1).

These follow-up studies provide convincing evidence that the effects of Reading Recovery are considerable and do not fade over time, but are still detectable three and five years later, reducing the difficulties experienced by the weakest children and transforming them into competent readers and writers. This experiment demonstrates the impact that Reading Recovery could make, even in contexts where raising levels of achievement are shown to be challenging.

Amplifying the impact of Reading Recovery: Every Child a Reader as a cost-effective approach for schools

For a number of years, some professionals who were familiar with Reading Recovery in different roles (for example, as teacher leaders or local authority advisers) had taken up positions within the National Literacy Strategy. In 2003, Jean Gross, Principal National Strategy Adviser for Special Needs, approached Reading Recovery's national leadership team to explore ways of supporting literacy for children in poverty, thereby also creating an opportunity to dismantle the barriers that had restricted the spread of Reading Recovery. There were a few models to draw on. Some teacher leaders had used Reading Recovery as a catalyst for wider-scale change in schools, instituting other interventions for children with less severe difficulties alongside Reading Recovery for the lowest-attaining. Their results demonstrated the potential for wider benefits from using the Reading Recovery teacher's expertise to serve more children.

The concept of layered literacy interventions was formalized as an efficient way to address the needs of all children. This capitalized on the professional capacity of Reading Recovery teachers as a source of expertise within a school, the power of the Reading Recovery intervention to overcome the difficulties of the very lowest-attaining children, and the possibilities opened up by a range of related interventions to meet the varying needs of other children. The name given to the initiative, Every Child a Reader, was no accident. From the start the aspiration was ambitious: that literacy should be an expectation for every child, and that the aim would be not only for every child to progress in learning to read but, even more challenging, to read and write at the level expected for their age.

Every Child a Reader was designed to help primary schools make sound decisions about deploying literacy interventions according to their pupils' assessed needs. It recognized that the provision of intensive intervention that is not needed is wasteful, but provision of an intervention that does not work for a particular child is more costly as it leaves potentially long-term difficulties still needing to be addressed. Hence the term 'layered intervention' was adopted to describe Every Child a Reader's approach and, over the six years during which it expanded into schools across England, this became a recognized image. The metaphor of layers is inclusive of all children but implies differing teaching environments that will make up the fabric of a schooling experience in which all children learn to read and write appropriately for national age-related targets.

Table 2.3: Every Child a Reader literacy intervention layers

READING RECOVERY – For the lowest achievers	
Better Reading Partnership (BRP) *Supported by Reading Recovery*	Focuses on establishing independent reading, aimed at children who can, with some appropriate support, become effective readers; involves reading, one-to-one, with the trained teaching assistant or volunteer for 15 minutes, three times a week, over a ten-week period.
Fischer Family Trust Wave 3 (FFT) *Supported by Reading Recovery*	Addresses both reading and writing; is delivered by an experienced teaching assistant, working one-to-one, for 15 to 20 minutes a day for 10 to 12 weeks, and is for children who do not yet have the skills to access the ELS programme (see below).

Talking Partners (TP) *Supported by Reading Recovery*	Structured oral language programme provided as part of an integrated approach: trained partners work with groups of three children for 20 minutes, three times a week, for 10 weeks, helping them to learn to listen more actively and to talk for a range of purposes.
Early Literacy Support (ELS) *National Literacy Strategy*	Taught by a specially trained teaching assistant in small groups using scripted, structured materials, aimed at children in Year 1 who have had access to classroom teaching and have not made sufficient progress.
QUALITY FIRST TEACHING – For all children, including:	
Letters and Sounds *National Literacy Strategy*	A phonics programme that concentrates on developing children's speaking and listening skills, phonological awareness, and oral blending and segmenting. Acts as support for engaging with a broad, rich language curriculum; links language with physical practical experiences in a print-rich environment; and provides abundant opportunities to engage with books.

These targeted interventions were found to work well in schools where Reading Recovery was in place to support their efficacy and to address more complex literacy learning needs. The number of teaching assistants in schools increased because of the workforce reform agenda, and schools increasingly deployed teaching assistants to work with the lowest achievers. Research was showing that in general teaching assistants were not effective in improving children's outcomes, potentially impeding progress in comparison with similar children left in the classroom (e.g. Blatchford *et al.*, 2009). In Every Child a Reader schools, using the Reading Recovery teacher's expertise for training, ongoing support, monitoring, and quality assurance created the conditions that allowed teaching assistants to become more effective.

Every Child a Reader in a primary school: A case study

This is a case of a primary school serving a culturally diverse population, close to a major city centre, where many families experience social and economic disadvantage, and is typical of those adopting Reading Recovery and Every Child a Reader.

In this school:

- almost half the pupils are from ethnic minority groups, mainly of Pakistani heritage
- around a third of pupils have a first language other than English
- an above-average number of pupils are identified with a learning difficulty or a disability
- more than half the pupils are eligible for free school meals.

In September 2008, the school committed funding to Every Child a Reader. The leadership team appointed a teacher with experience and expertise in early years to train as the school's Every Child a Reader/Reading Recovery teacher. Reading Recovery also provided training for another member of staff in the assessment tools of the Observation Survey, including running records of text reading. This 'link' teacher would also undertake exit assessments when children completed their Reading Recovery series of lessons, ensuring the reliability of the monitoring process. The Reading Recovery teacher together with the literacy coordinator and the Reading Recovery link teacher began to work together to form the Every Child a Reader team.

By 2012, Every Child a Reader was embedded across the school through a range of staff meetings and professional development training sessions, with aspects of Reading Recovery principles identified in the School Development plan.

For example, all children in Key Stage 2:

- had running records, which were used to check their reading progress and to target teaching or additional needs
- used a 'practice page' in writing classes, which enabled them to trial independent spelling strategies (e.g. analytic phonics and onset/rime)
- had all their books colour-labelled using the 'Book Bands' organization system for text levelling.

There was continual, informal, and planned discussion between the Reading Recovery teacher, class teachers, and parents to ensure that all concerned understood what children were learning and shared high expectations of them both in their intervention lessons and in class. The Reading Recovery teacher was included in pupil-progress meetings so that all information about targeted children was fully shared and understood. Everyone in the school knew about and came to value Every Child a Reader.

Immediate results

In 2008–09, the first year that Every Child a Reader was used in the school, its teacher was undergoing Reading Recovery training. That year eight children (five boys and three girls) received Reading Recovery. Five of those children were receiving free school meals. Six of the eight children made accelerated progress. The two Year 2 children in the cohort went on to achieve appropriate age-related outcomes in national assessments of their reading at the end of the school year.

Meeting more children's needs

Additional interventions in the school were carefully selected to meet the needs of the children. Noting the impact of this, the school and its governors made additional funding available. By the end of the third year the school had trained volunteers, teaching assistants, support aides, and some dinner ladies to work with children in interventions. These included Talking Partners, a reception intervention, Fischer Family Trust Wave 3, 'Ten minutes a Day' writing, Better Reading Partnership, and a number of adapted phonics catch-up programmes. All the children supported through these interventions were monitored closely, and the impact on their progress was measured with entry and exit data. This was also discussed at each child's pupil-progress meeting.

Bringing home and school closer together

Many parents of the children at this school had literacy issues of their own and may have had negative experiences of their own schooling. Among the added benefits of Every Child a Reader for this school, the headteacher identified the involvement of parents, the improvement of children's attendance and attitudes, and the development of their self-esteem.

This was brought about in part through parents and carers being encouraged to sit in on their children's lessons. This encouraged parents to share in their children's sense of success in Reading Recovery. The positive feedback that parents received from the school helped them feel more secure about coming into school and more empowered to support their child with learning at home.

Momentum for achievement

In October 2009, representatives from the National Primary Strategy and the Institute of Education, University of London (IOE) visited the school as part of a formal review process. The school's implementation of Every Child a Reader was deemed to be 'beyond exemplary', providing clear, strategic, and substantive support towards making a reality of the school's motto 'Together we can achieve'.

In May 2011, three years after it began the implementation of Every Child a Reader, the school was rated as 'outstanding' by Ofsted. The inspection report commented on the present and ongoing impact of the implementation:

> Across the school, pupils make particularly strong gains in reading. This is largely due to the emphasis placed on developing pupils' reading skills and the systematic programme of interventions for pupils who find learning difficult. These carefully planned programmes of one-to-one and small group support are effective in raising pupils' attainment and self-esteem. This means that pupils with special educational needs and/or disabilities feel positive about developing reading skills and also make the progress necessary to achieve as well as they can. By the time pupils reach the age of six, their attainment in reading is close to average and is above average by the end of Year 6.

Results at this school, one of many that implemented Every Child a Reader, bear out research findings that enabling children to become confident readers and learners early pays dividends in terms of their ongoing progress through the rest of their primary schooling (Burroughs-Lange and Douëtil, 2007; Burroughs-Lange, 2008).

Expanding the role of the Reading Recovery teacher

Relying on skilled teaching rather than a set of resources, Reading Recovery invests in the teacher so as to create change at many levels. This provides the school with an in-house literacy expert (Lyons and Pinnell, 2001) who can respond flexibly to learners' needs. It is this expertise that forms the basis of Every Child a Reader. Through Every Child a Reader, the Reading Recovery teacher becomes an agent of change (Fullan, 2004), enabling schools to meet the literacy needs of a larger number of children. This wider efficacy is also achieved through the quality of teaching rather than the methods or resources used.

The case study outlined above (one of many similar stories at other schools) showed that professional development at all levels (teacher leaders, teachers, teaching assistants, volunteers, school leaders, and local authority managers) played an essential part in building the successes of Every Child a Reader in the first three years (2005–08) and offered a template for its expansion over the next three years. This expansion required strategic management and detailed monitoring. An important part of developing the credibility and reliability of Every Child a Reader was the accreditation of professional development in Reading Recovery for trainer-coordinators, teacher leaders, and teachers through the IOE. Professional development was also provided by teacher leaders for those managing Reading Recovery in their local authorities. Professional capacity-building is the main driver of Every Child a Reader.

The start of Every Child a Reader in 2005 brought innovation in professional development. In order to ensure that Reading Recovery teachers had the expertise necessary to manage this approach to intervention, a specially designed short course, Reading Recovery in Primary Literacy Leadership (RRiPLLe), was established. Built around action research, it provided trained and experienced Reading Recovery teachers with a wider range of skills to apply to the task of whole-school literacy improvement. They were no longer only delivering one-to-one intensive teaching. Their task was also to identify children's literacy needs across a school cohort and devise a strategy for training, monitoring, and supporting others to enable children to achieve success in literacy and learning (see Chapter 4).

Broadening the reach: Expanding Reading Recovery to Every Child a Reader – The pilot phase (2005–08)

Every Child a Reader was initially set up as a three-year pilot project. It was supported most significantly by the KMPG Foundation, but also by other charities, including the Man Group Plc Charitable Trust, the Esmée Fairbairn Foundation, SHINE, the Indigo Trust, the JJ Charitable Trust, and the Mercer's Company. From the beginning the project had an eye to the 30,000 children identified annually in national testing who did not meet national targets at the age of 11. However, the pilot project focused on just ten local authorities across England, to determine what was possible if sufficient resources were made available to schools. One practical constraint on the rate of the project's expansion lay in how many new Reading Recovery professionals could be trained each year, beginning with existing capacity in 2005. There was also a substantial financial constraint on expansion, in terms of infrastructure costs to local authorities and of extra teacher salaries for schools. It was therefore vital to attract financial support from a broad swathe of prominent funders in the education sector. Not only was a critical figure needed so as to allow expansion to commence, longer-term commitment was also essential so as to sustain its growth by, for example, ensuring that teachers' salaries would be funded in future years. The evidence of Reading Recovery's success, and the exceptionally high returns on funders' investment, in terms of outcomes for children, provided both pressure and reassurance for the government to contribute financial support. Thus, the commitment from charitable trusts was match-funded by the Department for Children, Schools and Families, working with the Institute of Education.

The goal in 2005 and beyond was to reduce the incidence of underachievement in literacy, particularly for children from socially and economically disadvantaged backgrounds. The specific aims were:

(i)   to demonstrate the effectiveness of Reading Recovery as an intervention for children who would otherwise not learn to read

(ii) to explore the potential for Reading Recovery teachers to support tailored literacy teaching more broadly within a school, in order to have an impact beyond those receiving intensive one-to-one support

(iii) to secure sustainable and long-term investment in early literacy intervention (Every Child a Reader 2007: 3).

By the beginning of the 2005–6 school year, Every Child a Reader was ready to start, this being made possible by a unique collaboration between the IOE, charitable and business sectors, and the government.

Every Child a Reader adopted a strategic approach to raising literacy achievement in schools. It offered a means of organizing and managing a range of effective literacy interventions for children struggling to read and write at Key Stage 1. At the core of this strategy was the Reading Recovery teacher, who provided intensive teaching for the very lowest-attaining children, and professional support for less intensive interventions and for classroom teaching. The Reading Recovery teacher provided mentoring, practical support, quality assurance, professional development, and management for the range of literacy provision operating within the school, and extending to home/school projects with parents and volunteers.

By the 2008–9 school year, Every Child a Reader had become embedded in the National Primary Strategy. It is interesting that the catalyst for making Every Child a Reader a national programme came from the Treasury, on the basis that England could simply not afford to have 30,000 children *per year* entering secondary education and subsequently the economy with inadequate literacy for the 21st century.

The Department for Children, Schools and Families committed funding to Every Child a Reader for the three-year period 2008–11. This supported the programme's central infrastructure and national leadership, enabled new teacher leaders to be trained, and allowed existing regional teacher leaders to support consortia of local authorities. It also enabled schools to free up or employ a teacher to operate Reading Recovery and Every Child a Reader. Funds were allocated to local authorities on the basis of levels of poverty and underattainment, but the identification of schools with the highest level of need was a local decision. Many local authorities supplemented government grants in order to enable more schools to implement the programme.

The pace of expansion was constrained by the rate at which Reading Recovery personnel could be trained for new areas. To address this, while honouring the commitment to every child, local authorities were grouped into consortia sharing the expertise of teacher leaders. The intention was that, through consortia, schools with the greatest need could be identified and supported more quickly, without having to wait for their local authority's 'turn' to train their own teacher leader. Some consortia already had access to a trained teacher leader; those that did not were prioritized to receive a grant to train one.

Expanding Reading Recovery through consortia was not without difficulty. Some local authorities that had already self-funded a teacher leader found that they were now expected to share that person, thus reducing his/her capacity to support schools in the local authority that employed him/her. Authorities that had previously collaborated well now found themselves in different consortia. Some teacher leaders found that the considerable distances they were expected to cover severely affected their working and personal lives. From having strong relationships and a support network in their employing local authority, teacher leaders often struggled to build relationships and communications networks in a number of partner authorities. While local authorities that employed a teacher leader or had a history in Reading Recovery generally had support and management structures in place to run the programme, their consortium partners very often had little experience or understanding of the programme, making support for challenging schools more difficult. However, a few local authorities with large numbers of schools or that covered a large geographical area were designated as stand-alone and not gathered into consortia (see Chapter 5).

While attention to quality assurance and accountability for teaching were maintained, the involvement of external funders heightened the need for high-quality communication and dissemination of information about the initiative and its outcomes. Qualitative data on the experiences of being part of Every Child a Reader gave life to the quantitative impact data that were collected. Both needed to be interpreted for the many different groups involved: parents and governors, school and wider management professionals, investors, and government departments.

Outcomes of the rollout of Reading Recovery and Every Child a Reader

The implementation of Reading Recovery and Every Child a Reader saw exponential growth each year between 2008 and 2011, when they operated as part of the National Primary Strategy in England.

Table 2.4: Increase in children in Reading Recovery from 2007 to 2011

Academic Year	2007–8	2008–9	2009–10	2010–11
Number of Children	5,272	13,282	22,456	27,632

In spite of that rapid expansion, and the inevitably high proportion of inexperienced personnel operating at every level in the first few years, Reading Recovery maintained its effectiveness and even improved on outcomes (Stein *et al.*, 2008; Every Child a Reader, 2010, 2011, 2012).

In national assessments, schools in which Every Child a Reader had been implemented showed improved achievement levels of 1 per cent year on year – more than other (including more advantaged) schools. Every Child a Reader schools were among those highlighted as demonstrating best practice in Ofsted reports. For example, of an outer London primary school inspected in November 2011, Ofsted reported:

> Progress in English across the school has improved markedly, with better progress in reading because of the success of intervention programmes like "Better Reading Partnerships" and "Reading Recovery";

and of a Leicester primary school inspected in March 2011, this:

> Senior leaders have begun to redesign the curriculum in order to tackle low attainment and inadequate progress. For example, the Reading Recovery programme and other interventions are helping pupils to become confident readers.

For fuller examples of the impact of Reading Recovery on individual schools, on local authorities, and on consortia see Chapter 5.

Conclusion

This chapter has shown how, by 2003, there was government acknowledgement that the National Literacy Strategy alone was not reducing the incidence of underachievement in literacy. Recognition had grown that Reading Recovery offered some ways to solve this problem. Through annual reports and particularly through a well-controlled experiment – the study of schools in ten London boroughs (see pp. 40–43), showing the effects of Reading Recovery on children who received it and on the classes from which they were drawn – research had produced persuasive evidence of its effectiveness. More recent follow-up studies have shown that gains in literacy for children in schools with Reading Recovery and Every Child a Reader are maintained while, for children in schools without, they are not (e.g. Hurry and Holliman, 2009; Hurry, 2012).

The model of 'waves of intervention' needed fine-tuning and better management. An effective solution was to use a layered approach, through which the selection and delivery of interventions could be skilfully managed and monitored. Reading Recovery offered professionally trained expert teachers to assess the schools' needs and provide appropriate professional development for staff to meet those needs. It offered techniques for assessing and monitoring children's early literacy progress and knowledge of a variety of interventions suitable for a wider range of children than only those deemed hardest to teach.

The reach of Reading Recovery had to be broadened to capitalize on the potential of the Reading Recovery teacher in schools. This allowed the programme to address the high incidence of underachievement and to raise literacy levels overall. The pilot phase, the first three years of Every Child a Reader, was co-funded by government and charities and provided strong evidence of that goal having been achieved. For the following three years government took responsibility for funding and Every Child a Reader became part of the National Primary Strategy, while charities took on an advocatory and advisory role. By the end of the 2010–11 school year, the programme's national expansion was drawing very close to reaching 30,000 children in Reading Recovery and other Every Child a Reader interventions. Detailed evidence showed no reduction in their efficacy, an unprecedented achievement in such a rapid scaling up of educational innovation (Tanner *et al.*, 2011; Every Child a Reader, 2010, 2011, 2012).

But change at school level needs a chance to mature and time to mould itself to the particular ethos and needs of individual schools, so that further gains are expected over time, if funding for Every Child a Reader can be sustained. The following chapter looks at the contribution of theoretical grounding and practical pedagogy in achieving the literacy learning results of Every Child a Reader.

References

Blatchford, P., Bassett, P., Brown, P., Koutsoubou, M., Martin, C., Russell, A., and Webster, R., with Rubie-Davies, C. (2009) *Deployment and Impact of Support Staff in Schools*. London: DCSF.

Burroughs-Lange, S.G. (2008) *Comparison of Literacy Progress of Young Children in London Schools: A follow-up study*. London: Institute of Education, University of London.

Burroughs-Lange, S.G. and Douëtil, J. (2007) 'Literacy progress of young children from poor urban settings: A Reading Recovery comparison study'. *Literacy Teaching and Learning*, 12 (1), 19–46.

Bynner J., and Parsons, P. (1997) *It Doesn't Get Any Better*. London: Basic Skills Agency.

Every Child a Reader (2006) *Every Child a Reader: The results of the first year*. London: Institute of Education, University of London. Online. http://readingrecovery.ioe.ac.uk/reports/37.html

Every Child a Reader (2007) *Every Child a Reader: The results of the second year*. London: Institute of Education, University of London. Online. http://readingrecovery.ioe.ac.uk/reports/37.html

Every Child a Reader (2008) *Every Child a Reader: The results of the third year*. London: Institute of Education, University of London. Online. http://readingrecovery.ioe.ac.uk/reports/37.html

Every Child a Reader (2010, 2011, 2012) *Every Child a Reader Annual Reports*, 2009–10, 2010–11, and 2011–12. Online. http://readingrecovery.ioe.ac.uk/reports/37.html

Flood-Page, C., Campbell, S., Harrington, V., and Miller, J. (2000) *Youth Crime: Findings from the 1998/99 youth lifestyles survey*. Home Office Research Study no. 209. London: HMSO.

Fullan, M. (2004) *Systems Thinkers in Action – Moving beyond the standards plateau: Teachers transforming teaching*. London: Department for Education and Skills.

Godfrey, C., Hutton, S., Bradshaw, J., Coles, B., Craig, G., and Johnson, J. (2002) *Estimating the Cost of Being Not in Education, Employment or Training at Age 16–18*. DfES Research Report 346. London: DfES

Green, A., Preston, A., and Sabates, R. (2003) *Education, Equity, and Social Cohesion: A distributional model*. London: Institute of Education.

Hurry J. (2012) *The Impact of Reading Recovery Five Years after Intervention*. London: Every Child a Reader Trust.

Hurry, J. and Holliman, A. (2009) *The Impact of Reading Recovery Three Years after Intervention*. London: Institute of Education, University of London.

KPMG Foundation (2006) *The Long Term Costs of Literacy Difficulties*. London: Every Child a Chance.

Lyons, C.A., and Pinnell, G.S. (2001) *Systems for Change in Literacy Education: A guide to professional development*. Portsmouth, NH: Heinemann.

Parsons, S. (2002) *Basic Skills and Crime*. London: Basic Skills Agency.

Parsons, S., and Bynner, J. (2002) *Basic Skills and Social Exclusion*. London: Basic Skills Agency.

Rack, J. (2005) *The Incidence of Hidden Disabilities in the Prison Population.* Egham: Dyslexia Institute.

Scott, S., Knapp, M., Henderson, J., and Maughan, B. (2001) 'Financial costs of social exclusion'. *British Medical Journal,* 323, 28 July.

Stein, M.L., Berends, M., Fuchs, D., McMaster, K., Yen, L., Fuchs, L.S., and Compton, D.L. (2008) 'Scaling up an early reading program: Relationships among teacher support, fidelity of implementation, and student performance across different sites and years'. *Educational Evaluation and Policy Analysis,* 30 (4), 368–88.

Tanner, E., Brown, A., Day, N., Kotecha, M., Low, N., Morrell, G., Turczuk, O., Brown, V., and Collingwood, A. (2011) *Evaluation of Every Child a Reader.* London: DfE.

Chapter 3

The theoretical and pedagogical base of Reading Recovery

Sue Bodman and John Smith

Introduction

The preceding chapters have discussed the sociopolitical and curricular policy contexts from Reading Recovery's arrival in England in 1990 to the inception and implementation of Every Child a Reader, with Reading Recovery at its heart, in 2005. Over a six-year period (2005–11), this small-scale early literacy approach expanded to reach almost 30,000 children each year. These were the children most at risk of failing to learn to read and write.

As well as providing a contextualized historical perspective, this book's aims are focused on looking for explanations of why and how this expansion was possible without the loss of Reading Recovery's singular effectiveness. To do this, we examine the theoretical foundation of Reading Recovery. In this chapter, we describe and critically assess the theories of early literacy acquisition on which Reading Recovery is built and that shaped the ways in which literacy interventions are brought together in 'layers' to form Every Child a Reader. We also discuss and give examples of the role played by the pedagogy derived from this theoretical base, claiming that the particular relationship between theory and pedagogy plays a central role in Every Child a Reader's potential for transferability. Transferability is achieved by adopting criteria for malleability and durability and, importantly, by closely monitoring for integrity to the research-based evidence that relates to success. Structures for systemic support have enabled Every Child a Reader to build a school-wide strategy around early intervention.

This chapter begins by briefly contextualizing the theoretical landscape within which Reading Recovery was developed. Next, we describe and assess the complex theory of early literacy acquisition, linking aspects of the theoretical framework to formative assessment processes and pedagogies. We provide some examples of how teaching is honed to meet individual needs. To conclude, we offer some reflections on how the theory underpinning Reading Recovery has supported the development of a school-wide strategy exemplified in the model of Every Child a Reader.

A theory-based intervention

Reading Recovery is an early literacy intervention designed for those experiencing the greatest difficulty in acquiring literacy skills after about one year in school. A well-articulated theory supports its implementation. Here, we use the word 'theory' to mean a reasoned and evidenced hypothesis. A theory is formed by 'a related set of concepts used to explain a body of data and to make predictions about the results of future experiments' (Stanovich, 2010: 21). Theory makes possible predictions, which if they are fulfilled reinforce the viability and durability of that theory. The more that its elements are shown to offer clear prediction of what will happen in a given situation, the stronger the theory becomes. When we apply this idea to theories underpinning early intervention, we see that, in order to make cost-effective decisions about responses to educational need, we need durable theories to avoid life chances and valuable resources being wasted. The theory underpinning Reading Recovery has, from the outset of its development, provided a structural plan for designing a systemic response to need that will work flexibly within any education context (Clay, 1993: 60). This has been tested, across time and across context. As more children are successfully returned to the expected trajectory of literacy progress, or 'recovered' (Clay, 1982: 174), the more durable this theory can be considered to be.

Building a theory to support early intervention

Professional insight and the influences of research are both significant in the development of Marie Clay's own theoretical perspectives on early literacy acquisition. Her work as a clinical psychologist honed her observation skills in capturing and interpreting the oral reading behaviours of young children as they became literate. Her longitudinal systematic observations of the behaviours of high-, average-, and low-progress learners as they learnt to read gave rise to her view of reading as rapid communication between perceptual and cognitive activity in the brain. Perceptual activity involves picking up letter information and checking it with meaning and grammar information. Cognitive activity involves the decision-making needed to monitor semantic and syntactic sense and to take action if the reader reaches a point of difficulty.

Here, two things are significant to the development of the theory that underpins Reading Recovery:

(i)   the validity of observation as a tool for grounding teaching decisions

(ii)   an evidenced perspective on what low-progress learners need to learn in order to become successful.

Clay's interpretation of observation data and the subsequent development of a theory of early literacy acquisition were supported by two models of reading. Even though both models focus on skilled reading, they provided the principles that would underpin a theory of literacy acquisition. The interactive parallel processing system described by Rummerlhart (1994, cited in Clay, 2001) proposes that reading is governed and guided by areas of neurological activity in the brain that deal with or process information gathered from many sources (perceptual and cognitive). This processing of information from many different sources occurs simultaneously, as hypotheses are confirmed or rejected. When processing becomes more consciously checked, the reading rate is slowed. The model outlined by Singer (1994; Holmes and Singer, 1964) states that neurological, working systems provide three functions to deal with information. These functions are perception, interpretation, and output. While reading, the reader picks up information (perception), evaluates the range of information for match (interpretation), and makes a reading response (output). These functions have been termed 'strategic activity' within Clay's theory. Clay built initially on these existing models, proposing that the way in which we utilize available information (letter and letter-cluster knowledge, word knowledge, phonological knowledge, morphological knowledge, meaning, and syntax) can occur in any order dictated by economy of responding to the task's demands.

A model of the processes involved in skilled reading does not explain how we build the ability to read and write from early experiences with letters and print. The speed and automaticity with which we combine information in print with knowledge about language and the world is developed as we become more skilled. A developmental theory of early literacy acquisition is considered in detail in the next section.

A complex theory of literacy acquisition

A clear and well-defined theoretical framework underpins the intervention procedures used in Reading Recovery. It is articulated in texts for Reading Recovery personnel at all professional levels: teachers, teacher leaders, and national leaders[1] (Clay, 2001; 2005a; 2005b). This is unusual in guidelines and publications for teachers of children with literacy difficulties. Such materials often go no further than providing sequences of described and prescribed content (Wasik and Slavin, 1993; Clay, 2001). That is not to say that these teaching programmes are not founded on durable theories, but the underlying theories are not often laid bare for teachers to draw into their pedagogical decision-making; teaching materials more usually give a sequence and a practice to be followed. In contrast, the literacy acquisition theory that informs Reading Recovery is coherently presented to guide teachers' decision-making and pedagogic development.

Defining reading and writing

Clay offers definitions of reading and writing as 'message-getting' and 'message-giving' activities (2005a). This view clearly indicates the key role of meaning in the reading process (Clay, 2005b: 101). Meaning engages both conscious and unconscious attention during reading (Clay, 2001: 69); conscious attention is given through active monitoring of meaning ('Am I making sense of it?'). Unconscious attention ensures that the neural networks are engaged in assembling a system focused on picking up, working with, and making decisions on sources of information, with visual information from print and an understanding and application of the alphabetic code as essential to this process (Clay, 2001; Lyons, 2003).

Interactive literacy processing

Some researchers have aligned Reading Recovery's theoretical approaches with models and representations that do not acknowledge its complexity. For example, Reading Recovery has been positioned by some as a meaning-based intervention aligned with 'whole language' (Greaney, 2011: Tunmer and Chapman, 2004). These authors claim that Reading Recovery does not provide opportunities for the explicit phonological and phonics teaching that struggling readers require. This claim cannot be substantiated.

Greaney (2011) implies that Reading Recovery operates on the basis of skilled reading as a process in which minimal word-level information is used to predict and confirm word recognition. This implication is refuted by the long-standing promotion of fast perceptual processing of words in print that can be traced through Clay's work. For example, the core text (Clay, 2005a: 43) contains a section entitled *Fast perceptual processing* to support teachers to make sound pedagogical decisions and understand that 'everything we do in mature reading and writing will rely on fast accurate perceptions of language sounds (captured by the ear) and visual symbols (captured by the eye) as we read and write'.

Attending to sources of information

During literary processing fluent readers (and writers) must constantly bring together, combine in flexible ways, and actively monitor information from a variety of sources in order to derive meaning from the text (Clay, 2005b; Clay and Cazden, 1990; Rummelhart, 1994). These sources include:

- visual information – information contained in letter-sound correspondences that activate phonemic and phonological processes

- meaning information – from meaning existing within the text itself and the pictorial representations available to the reader and from the reader's experience of how the world works
- syntactic information – information gleaned from knowledge of how language is structured in oral and written contexts
- language information – information about how spoken language works and how book language differs from oral language experiences.

A range of sources of information is also implied in the Simple View of Reading (Gough and Tunmer, 1986). The two axes (word recognition and language comprehension) in the Simple View of Reading model are presented to exemplify a growing control over the interaction of their strategic use in improving reading ability. Cautions have been raised as to whether there has been sufficient attention to the cognitive activity implied when both these axes are employed (Stuart *et al.*, 2008: 59). Rose, however, makes clear that the simpler aspects of the model should not dominate teaching, with high-quality phonic work needing to take place in a language-rich environment (Rose, 2006: 2). Expansion of information used as we read contrasts sharply with explanations of the reading process as a 'psycholinguistic guessing game' (Goodman, 1967). While Reading Recovery instruction acknowledges the supportive role of meaning and comprehension in learning to read, it does not attempt to foster the 'whole-language' approach. Nor is Reading Recovery solely meaning-based, since 'Reading Recovery has been methodically designed to establish and secure that whole complex of lower-order skills on which reading so integrally depends' (Adams, 1990: 421). Clay saw the challenge of learning to read as creating a rapid exchange of information, both consciously and unconsciously, described as interactivity between areas of perception and knowledge, and processing of that perception and knowledge (Clay, 2001: 150). This interactivity is referred to as 'literacy processing'; 'psychological processes like perceiving, linking and decision making' (Clay, 2001:42). Knowledge of the alphabetic code and the ability to draw it into activity at every level is a fundamental aspect of this processing, but 'it is not a simple problem of what theorists, researchers and teachers call "phonics"' (Clay, 2005b: 123). When engaging in 'reading work' (Clay, 2005b: 101), the active learner 'directs attention, picks up and uses information, monitors the "reading", makes decisions, and activates self-correcting to revise a prior decision' (Clay, 2001: 128). The interaction between brain and eye (Clay, 2005b: 102) forges 'invisible patterns of oral language with visible symbols' (Clay, 2005a: 1).

Thus the theory of literacy learning that underpins Reading Recovery gives a pivotal role to attention to print, proposing that 'the visual must finally dominate' (Clay, 1972: 162). Meaning is acknowledged as the goal of reading: skilled readers need only to give minimal conscious attention to other sources of information in gaining meaning from printed text. Some influential critics of Reading Recovery have focused on this, stating that pupils are taught to guess without a thorough analysis of the alphabetic code information (Chapman *et al.*, 2001) and that they are 'encouraged to use context as the principal method of identifying words' (Singleton, 2009: 96). This is not the case.

Combining sources of information flexibly

Children learning in Reading Recovery are trained not to guess at words; 'to guess' is defined as 'to estimate or suppose (something) without sufficient information to be sure of being correct' (Merriam-Webster, 2012). This definition is the antithesis of the way in which skilled teaching prompts are used, as a central pedagogical feature, to scaffold the child's learning. The suggested sequence of 'Does it look right? Read right through the word to check' (Clay, 2005b) is a clear example of a teaching prompt to guide the child so as to ensure that enough visual information is drawn on in decision-making during literacy processing. The child is being asked to check that he/she has sufficient information about the alphabetic coding of the word to make a decision that also fits with its semantic and syntactic context. The word 'predict' is sometimes used by teachers; however, using Reading Recovery theory, the teacher is not using the word 'predict' to describe asking the child to make a decision, ahead of all the other information, on the basis of meaning alone. The teaching also encourages the child to identify their own independent reading strategies by prompts such as 'What was it you did on that page that helped you to work out the word?', so building self-monitoring and meta-cognition. Clearly, the immediate requirement for gathering print evidence in simple and transparent representations such as 'cat' or 'play' is to work through the word. Ensuring that children have the skills to do this is the focus of early teaching, in a variety of ways. Procedures for teaching how to attend to features of print are provided to support fast acquisition of the rules of the code: namely, to follow the rules of print and the alphabetic code, and to attend to words in a line in a left-to-right sequence and letters within a word in a left-to-right sequence (Clay, 2005b: 1–2).

Active emergent readers

Clay's theory of early literacy acquisition is a complex one, where the child learns to operate on texts by 'searching for particular information, finding, associating it, and linking it to prior experience, moving across visual, phonological, language and semantic information, checking how it is going together, backing up and looking for new hypotheses, self-correcting, reading on, using peripheral vision and syntactic anticipation' (2001: 114). The emergent literacy learner needs to develop skills to attend to print, to use print information, and to use phonic knowledge and language experience in order to read fluently, with enjoyment and understanding of what he/she reads. Clay's theory of literacy acquisition (Clay, 2001; 2002) describes the learner as constructing personal theories about how print and the alphabetic code work. Fluent processing is the goal of teaching at every stage of reading and writing complexity. Fluency provides evidence of a processing system working efficiently at that level. In other words, fluent reading is the output behaviour that allows the teacher to conclude that the neurological working system is able to pick up sources of information quickly, combine them and check them against each other, and make a decision as output. This signals the point at which to introduce new challenges. Clay's doctoral research clearly identified that after one year in school it was possible to separate those who were able to bring together a range of knowledge sources and process them efficiently in order to support reading and writing, and those who were not. The next section considers how theory has shaped the design of the assessment tools that allow the early identification of children most likely to fail to acquire an effective literacy processing system.

Assessing early literacy development: observing systematically

The reliability of the assessment tools used in identifying successful learners and avoiding expensive false positives is governed by several factors. These include: their appropriateness to the subjects; their sensitivity to critical features of what is being assessed; and their capacity for allowing comparison for attainment and progress. Literacy learning assessment can be organized in many different ways to measure different skills (Rodgers, 2012). For example, one could measure an age-equivalent performance by using a standardized word list (e.g. British Ability Scales III (Elliott, 2011)), capturing knowledge of the alphabetic code and knowledge of high-frequency words known as 'whole units'. This type of assessment focuses on a restricted number of processes needed to read and attempts to extrapolate information about progress in general. This is a fundamentally different approach from that taken in the identification of children for Reading Recovery. Clay (2001) rejected the hypothesis that the learner first concentrates on an aspect of reading activity, becoming fluent before moving on to the next aspect in a hierarchy of skills. Instead, the formative assessments attempt to capture how the learner is picking up on and making decisions about the range of information possible at any given point in time.

Observing closely

Systematic observation is critical to the process by which the teacher hones instruction so that learning is accelerated, leading to the learner 'pushing the boundaries of their own knowledge' (ibid.), and enabling them to catch up with their classroom peers. This requires the teacher to design instruction that is finely differentiated by using assessments that have scope for the detection and exploration of a wide range of individual differences. Reading Recovery teachers are trained to use *An Observation Survey of Early Literacy Achievement* (Clay, 2002) to assess each child's strengths and confusions in order to assist in making the decision to take a child into the intervention as the lowest achieving in comparison to others in their class.

An Observation Survey of Early Literacy Achievement

Each of the six assessment tasks in *An Observation Survey of Early Literacy Achievement* assists in developing insight into a young child's emergent literacy processing skills and reflects aspects of the complex process described above (Clay, 2005a: 13).

A 'Letter Identification' task is deployed to gain insight into how the learner perceives and labels letters, both lower- and upper-case. Responses are marked as correct or incorrect but, in addition to gathering information about letters correctly identified, the assessment creates a context for observing the acuity of the child's visual discrimination, the speed with which letters are recognized, any confusions (both auditory and visual) becoming established, and whether the child has patterns of labelling responses that are potentially unhelpful.

A 'Word Reading' task demonstrates not only how many words on a list of high-frequency words the child can identify, but also how the task is approached. The teacher observes the child operating on a word reading task in order to gather information about how that child is able to perceive the word and how he/she goes about looking at it in order to decode it from left to right. The learner may confuse the visual elements of written words that have similar orthography or find the task of identifying frequently seen words laborious. The task also checks whether the child is learning how to move words from a 'decodable' to a 'known' lexicon. All these elements are important in considering how the working systems (Singer, 1994) are being deployed.

A 'Concepts about Print' task is used to observe what the child knows about how spoken language is represented in print. An authentic context is created through the use of a little book specially designed for the purpose. The task is informal and collaborative, allowing for observation of how the child uses the rules of the alphabetic code ('Show me where to start reading.' 'What's wrong with the writing on this page?') alongside the language needed to benefit from instruction in letter and word learning ('Show me a letter; show me a word.' 'Show me a capital letter; show me the first word.').

A 'Writing Vocabulary' assessment prompts the child to write as many words as he/she can in ten minutes. A mark is given for accuracy, though the assessment also provides information about letter formation, directionality, phonemic awareness, known words in writing, and orthographic awareness. This is not a test of memory, since the teacher prompts the child with words that are likely to be within a young literacy learner's repertoire when he/she is unable to think of any to write.

In order to assess phonemic awareness, a 'Hearing and Recording Sounds in Words' task creates a standardized context for exploring the child's knowledge of phoneme–grapheme correspondences and of how spoken language is recorded.

A 'Running Record of Text Reading' is taken in order to observe how the child draws on and interrelates sources of information during the reading process. This observation opportunity is also used to identify an appropriate level of text difficulty for instruction (Clay, 2002). Locating a level of difficulty on which the child can operate with some independence and success is an important link to the teaching the child will receive. A wide range of levelled texts[2] are used throughout the teaching programme that the child receives, and also to ensure that children whose series of Reading Recovery lessons have been completed (or 'discontinued'; Clay, 2005a: 52) are able to operate at the literacy attainment norms for a particular classroom. The validity of using a text-reading level to predict continued progress has been established through longitudinal studies linking these assessment tasks to standardized literacy tasks (Hurry, 2012; D'Agostino and Murphy, 2004).

These assessment tasks are used in combination to consider the individual profiles of learners. Emergent readers and writers show considerable variation in the skills and understandings that they bring to the task, despite achieving remarkably similar quantitative scores. Observational evidence is used continuously as a tool to make inferences about the learner's 'within-the-head' processes; the next section considers how this underpins daily teaching in Reading Recovery.

Teaching and learning: The pedagogy of Reading Recovery

In Reading Recovery an individual pathway through literacy learning is designed for each child and repeatedly readjusted. Careful observation and recording of reading and writing behaviours form the basis of constant within-lesson assessment and analysis processes that allow the construction of individual literacy curricula. The young literacy learner is helped to develop skills to attend to print, and to use print information, phonic knowledge, and language experience in order to read fluently, with enjoyment and understanding of what he/she reads. Clay's theory of literacy acquisition (Clay, 2001; 2002) describes the learner as constructing personal theories about how print and the alphabetic code work. 'The constructive child is one who makes something of [instruction] and becomes a fluent processor of printed messages' (Clay, 2001: 301). A key assumption in the theoretical base of Reading Recovery is that there are many potential routes to early proficiency in both reading and writing (Clay, 2001: 93). This needs to be reflected in the design of lessons, so that there is a structure aligned with the theoretical base, but enough flexibility to respond to individual needs, building on each child's growing competencies. To effectively design lessons tailored to each child, the teacher incorporates various forms of formative assessment into each lesson, and reviews progress weekly. These ongoing and continuous assessment processes help determine what the child needs to learn next so that effective decoding, encoding, and comprehending in reading and writing are achieved in the shortest possible timeframe (Clay, 2005a).

Design elements in a Reading Recovery lesson

The sequence of components for Reading Recovery lessons allows for changes to be made for each child, day by day as his/her learning develops. In each half-hour lesson, the child typically reads four or five books and writes a sentence or two, with specific and embedded work on letters and words incorporated into the session. Opportunities for developing perceptual and cognitive processes are paramount. Research into the ways in which brain activity changes as we learn supports Clay's focus on interpreting behaviours as representing 'within-the-head activity' (Clay, 2005b: 103). A Reading Recovery lesson can therefore be considered an opportunity for changing the way that the brain works, so that neural networks pick up on, work with, and make decisions about information. The elements within the lesson are not separate and unconnected; rather, the learning needed to refine the way the child operates on text flows across the entire lesson. As in the 'confluence' of emergent processes that enable a child to learn to walk (Thelen and Smith, 1994: 90), or just as an adult perfects a golf swing (Lyons, 2003: 12), so learning involves a complex interplay of experience and knowledge. Future competencies develop on the back of earlier, simpler ones (Sirois *et al.*, 2008: 326), speeding up as repeated activations of information-carrying neurons in the brain increase the myelin coating along their axons and facilitate faster message transmission (Wolf *et al.*, 2009: 291). These newer understandings derived from neurological research sit well with Clay's descriptions of cognitive networks combining to build a 'reading brain', prompted and secured by exposure to opportunities for active meaning-making and problem-solving on texts.

Table 3.1: An outline of each component of the lesson structure

Lesson Component	Description of Activity
Familiar reading	Lessons begin with the child reading familiar texts. The child will have read these texts once to three times before.
Yesterday's new book, on which the teacher will take a running record	The teacher takes a running record as the child reads a new book. This will have been introduced and read through once in the previous lesson.
Letter and word work	The child works with letters and/or words using magnetic letters.
Composing and writing a message	A conversation prepares the composition of the child's message. Explicit teaching during writing may include work on letter formation, phonics, punctuation, grammar, language structures, and comprehension.
Assembling a cut -up story	The child then works on the reciprocity between reading and writing by sequencing and rereading their story, written on a strip of paper and then cut up by the teacher.
Introducing the new story	The teacher prepares the child for the new text.

Reading the new book	The child reads the new text with support to solve problems if needed. This new book will provide the text for the next lesson's running record.

Each of the lesson activities (Table 3.1) are designed to present a variety of problem-solving contexts in reading and writing with the purpose of creating and refining a system of strategic behaviours. Without specialist knowledge, it may be hard to see how these lesson components can be adapted to meet the specific needs of individual children. However, such fine-tuning can be made in many different ways, and at any given point in a sequence of Reading Recovery lessons: the level of text in both reading and writing is carefully judged to enable the child to self-monitor and problem-solve, applying what he/she knows as much as possible; the teacher creates opportunities for the child to develop print awareness at whatever level of text he/she is working; there are personalized opportunities to work on letter-sound relationships; the teaching interactions help the child to address an imbalance of attention on sources of information. Each part of every lesson is designed 'to target the cutting edge of an individual's learning' (Clay, 2005a: 20) and contribute to the formation of a 'reading brain' (Dehaene *et al.*, 2010).

We continue by considering some ways in which the potential for designing lessons creates opportunities for the teacher to craft contingent teaching responses to reflect the intertwining of theory and practice. Some brief examples from Reading Recovery lessons are now given to illustrate key points.

Building a responsive learning environment

A daily running record of the child's reading behaviours allows the teacher to consider progress in detail. The child reads a text that has been introduced by the teacher and that the child has read with some support during the previous lesson. The record is analysed through the perspective of a 'literacy processing view of progress' (Clay, 2001: 42) to determine how well a child is working on text. The teacher records accurate reading, errors, and self-corrections in order to make an analysis of how the neural networks, or working systems, are being activated to solve problems in reading and writing (Clay, 2001). The teacher considers progress from both quantitative and qualitative perspectives. Control on texts of increasing difficulty and use of visual information are assessed by recording accuracy with which words are read, providing a quantitative measure of progress. Evidence of how the child perceives information, links information, and makes decisions about that information provides a qualitative measure of progress.

A complex problem-solving process

Making a running record inevitably involves inspection of letters attended to, words read accurately, and processes of decoding from left to right. However, the complexity of making a running record is often overlooked. Formative assessment of text reading might be interpreted very differently within an alternative model of reading. For example, the dual route model (Castles, 2006) proposes two distinct routes to dealing with the printed word. In this model, reading is treated as a linear process, during which the brain decides whether to deal with the printed word by either a 'lexical' function, which retrieves words that have been read before, or a sub-lexical function, which maps individual graphemes and word segments on spoken segments to produce a pronunciation. In the latter function, meaning can only be accessed once a possible pronunciation has been worked out. This model does not propose an expectation of meaning in the reader. It does not see teacher analysis of evidence of the recursive brain activity that links many parts of the brain as we read, as fundamental to the reader's scaffolding of learning. With this model, assessment would be focused on which of the two possible routes the reader used to access the printed word and on a teaching response designed on the basis of one of these routes. Unlike Clay's theory, this model does not characterize the teaching task as helping the brain to develop ways of approaching the complexity of the task with flexibility, both consciously and increasingly automatically.

Making a running record of text reading is designed to capture how effectively the brain is receiving a complex range of information and working on that information. It is used to plan lessons contingently and to identify appropriate challenges in the selection of texts for the child to read and the creation of texts for him/her to write.

Ben

At the beginning of his Reading Recovery series of lessons, Ben typically used meaning and grammar as sources of information, and was also guided by a small number of high-frequency words that he knew. He neglected to use visual information if his reading made sense, or appealed to the teacher if meaning was lost during his reading. While reading the text for which a running record was being made, Ben read 'hole' for 'sand'; the word made sense because it corresponded with the picture of a snake laying its eggs in a hole and because it sounded like the structures he used in his spoken language. The running-record analysis pointed to the importance of showing Ben how to solve textual problems and ensure that he attended to visual information so that he could use what he knew about letters and words. The development of reading skills is shown when the child routinely uses more sources of information, including more complex information, in combination. Teacher prompts, 'a call for action to do something within the child's control' (Clay, 2005a: 39), need to help Ben continue to use his knowledge of the structure of language and his language comprehension skills, and now also to incorporate more visual information when he comes to an unknown word and to keep a check on whether his reading of words 'looks right' too. After the child has successfully read a phonically regular, known word (e.g. 'went'), the teacher might use the example as a model and explicitly demonstrate how sources of information are brought together in a way that Ben needs to use on new and unfamiliar words. The teacher might return to the word and say, 'Run your finger under the word and say it slowly [demonstrating a slow articulation of "went"]. Does the word look right and sound right? Good job: you thought about what looked right, sounded right, and made sense. We need to check all these when we are reading.' The running record allows the teacher to respond contingently to each child's needs. For Ben, the skill of attending to known letters in both reading and writing, in concert with his existing strengths of using meaning and language structure, was demonstrated by the teacher and then rehearsed and applied by Ben across the entire lesson. This is automating an early strategy.

Orchestrating decision-making

Across the lesson, the teacher is alert to signs of fluency – how the reading sounds. Stress, pace, pitch, and juncture are important signals regarding how information is picked up and worked on. Fluency is a 'window' on what the child is able to do independently – the 'cutting edge' of learning – so that teaching moves are powerfully contingent. For example, growth in reading speed implies that decision-making in the brain is occurring more efficiently. The reading of familiar texts creates a context for the efficient application of decoding and comprehension skills, reading with conscious attention to fluency, and sounding like a successful reader (Stanovich, 1986). This also builds 'reading mileage' and reinforces the activity between neural networks. Myelination allows effective processing to be achieved so that attention can be paid to phrasing and comprehension. In the following example, the teacher observes carefully so as to pinpoint helpful ways of working and redirecting attention to allow smooth and independent processing of text.

EMMA

Emma tracked words with her finger to monitor one-to-one correspondence. She was expert in doing this across a range of texts that she could read with high accuracy (no more than one error in every ten words). She always moved from left to right across the page. Her teacher observed that her finger moved quite slowly across the text and Emma sometimes had to reread to allow her finger to 'catch up' with her voice. With her progress in reading, finger-tracking was getting in the way of fluency and slowing up the efficiency with which she was able to pick up and combine information from a range of sources. At the beginning of every lesson, the teacher provided a book that Emma knew well and encouraged her to 'read it with just your eyes' (moving across the print 'without using your finger'). Emma was provided with positive feedback on the increased pace of her reading. Very quickly she was choosing to use her finger only if she wasn't sure whether she was reading accurately. Her eyes and her brain had learnt to scan across print from left to right, word by word, line by line. Now she could pay more conscious attention to 'sounding good', reading in a phrased manner and enjoying the experience.

The key role of print information

Work on letters and words may appear anywhere in a Reading Recovery lesson as appropriate, but a discrete component gives the child the opportunity to recognize and rehearse phonological and decoding skills that he/she can apply to known letters and words and apply them to solving new and unusual words. Fast visual discrimination between well-known and becoming-known letters is followed by work that explicitly teaches the rules and conventions of the alphabetic code and 'how words work', matched to the learner's own cutting edge.

HARRY

Harry knew 12 lower-case letters and the capital letters with which his forename and surname begin. He knew three of the letters in his name and was able to write the word 'then'. The other eight letters in his name that Harry knew were frequently occurring, easy to hear, and easy to distinguish. However, he did not use this letter knowledge to help in his text reading.

Harry's Reading Recovery lessons were therefore specifically designed to create opportunities for him to find those letters in a variety of texts that he was given for reading and writing. In some lesson components, the focus was on using them to support decision-making; in others it was used to bring together writing knowledge and reading knowledge. Within the letter-identification activities, Harry was introduced to a group of letters, chosen from his own 'known' collection, on a magnetic whiteboard. The group contained multiple examples of two or three letters, presented as a 'letter sort' activity. The letters were visually distinct and easy to identify (w, s, and t, for example) because visual discrimination between letters was still a challenge for Harry. Demonstration helped Harry to understand the task of sorting this array of letters into like sets. Both hands were used to get the hand, eye, and brain to work together speedily on this task. As he became more skilled, Harry was presented with known letters that were increasingly less visually distinct, so that he was required to make gradually quicker decisions about letters that were increasingly similar (o, s, and e, for example). New letters were then introduced into this 'known set'. Multisensory experience is much more successful than speech in perceiving and then recognizing at speed what are sometimes tiny differences between letters (h, r, and n, for example). Harry's knowledge of these new letters was then reinforced in his daily writing tasks, a powerful context of the physical production of the written word and the orientation of a child's attention to the visual features of print.

Reading and writing as interrelated processes

An authentic conversation between teacher and child provides an opportunity for oracy development. In the Reading Recovery lesson, such a conversation focuses on capturing and shaping language as oral composition for a story, a piece of writing that the child executes. The writing component involves explicit teaching, which may include work on letter formation, phonics, punctuation, grammar, language structures, and comprehension, all at a level of complexity tailored to the individual child's need. The child writes the story on a strip of card that the teacher then cuts up. Next, the child re-sequences and rereads the story, thus experiencing at first hand the reciprocity between reading and writing.

MORGAN

Morgan's message was cut into words for him to reassemble. He repeated the sentence to himself as he searched: 'When ... I ....pack'. Morgan's hand hovered over 'pyjamas' for a moment. He kept searching and found 'pack'. At this point he reread, as if to gather the meaning: 'When I pack my....'. He started searching again, saying the words slowly, searching for the letter sequences that matched his oral utterances. As the number of remaining words decreased, he began to work faster. When he had placed the final word, he went back to the beginning of the message and read: 'When I pack my suitcase, I will put in my pyjamas and my toys.' This activity gave Morgan the opportunity to 'relate reading to writing, writing to speaking, and reading to speaking' (Clay, 2005b: 81). Awareness and opportunity for the learner to use the interrelationships between these three language activities make for faster progress.

Learning how words work

Reciprocity, or the two-way flow of knowledge between reading and writing (Teale and Sulzby, 1986), contributes to the formation of a constructive view of learners and learning. The Reading Recovery lesson design creates instructional spaces to make explicit the common ground between the two contexts. When reading is taught side by side with writing, young learners can 'actively organize and learn from self-initiated experiences' (Clay, 2001: 15). Beginning with simple words and sounds that are easy to hear, a specific lesson component[3] establishes the link between the way sounds are heard, sequenced, and recorded by means of a written code.

CHICO

Chico was writing 'Father Christmas is bringing me a hot tub'. He was able to hear and record initial phonemes and knew around 15 high-frequency words; *is*, *me*, and *a* were among those 15 words. He sometimes did not indicate word boundaries by leaving spaces.

Chico recorded 'F'. The teacher quickly wrote in the remainder of 'Father' because this complex word did not offer profitable learning opportunities for Chico at this point (though using it had enormous motivational value). He wrote 'C' and again the teacher quickly filled in the rest of the word. He wrote 'is' quickly and easily. Chico said 'bringing' and looked at his teacher. He was guided to 'say it slowly'. This is a 'hard to hear' word, so his teacher modelled slow articulation to help him hear and identify the sequence of sounds. His teacher drew some boxes on the workspace above his writing page, creating a box for each phoneme. 'What can you hear?' Chico gave the first phoneme. His teacher knew he could write the grapheme, so she asked, 'Where will you write it?' Chico indicated the first letter position and wrote it in. He was prompted to say it slowly once again. 'What can you hear?' Chico responded with the phoneme 'i'. The teacher had observed that Chico could decode from left to right when reading, could hear phonemes, and knew which graphemes to use to record those sounds, so she made an important shift, now asking that the phonemes be attended to and recorded sequentially. She acknowledged that there was an 'i' phoneme, and asked, 'But what can you hear next – bringing?' She demonstrated, running her finger under the boxes as she slowly articulated the word. Chico recorded 'r' ... then the phoneme 'ing'. He asked, 'Is there another "ing"?' and recorded it when his teacher confirmed this. Chico then wrote the remainder of the sentence quickly and easily, without comment from the teacher. She then went back to the meaning of his whole message to elicit a further sentence about Chico's hopes for Christmas, while making a note to herself to look for opportunities in his text reading to reinforce his attention to a hard-to-hear consonant cluster that had just helped him in his writing.

Composing and writing their own messages and stories provide learners with a meaningful context for the development of phonemic and orthographic skills. Explicit teaching of the alphabetic code and how to use it to decode printed text runs through every Reading Recovery lesson.

Lifting processing to another level

Placing the new text at the end of the lesson means that the child's most recent literacy behaviours are still fresh in the teacher's mind as he/she introduces this new book and responds to the child's first reading.

The new book is introduced to the child. It is one that will interest him and stretch his emerging reading skills as he reads it.

OWEN

This was the third text that Owen had read at Reading Recovery Level 7. The previous day's running record had showed an accuracy rate of 97 per cent and the reading had sounded phrased and well paced. His errors showed that Owen did not always analyse words in every detail (for example, 'come' for 'came' or 'dad' for 'daddy') and did not notice these errors if the meaning was maintained. Owen's teacher had chosen a text that required Owen to make a precise visual analysis, as he would have to make fast decisions between several words that begin with the same grapheme ('big', 'boys', 'ball', 'back'). Up to the point of error, all those words could make semantic or syntactic sense. She decided to give a brief introduction as Owen's quantitative scores at this level of reading had been high for a few days. She wanted to see what he could do independently.

Teacher: I chose this story because I thought of you and how good at football you are. This is a story about a boy who is good at football *(placing the book on the table in front of Owen)*. The thing is, some of the other children think that because he's little he can't be good at football.
Owen *(turning through the pages)*: They won't let him play. It's like the little kids in the playground. They can't play with us.
Teacher: But hang on a minute, look at this page *(turning to a specific moment in the story)*. That looks like a brilliant kick to me. What do you think?
Owen: Oh yeah! He's good at football, like me!
Teacher: Let's read this story and find out if he can play with them.

Owen started to read. The first time he reached the phrase 'the big boys' he read 'the boys'. His teacher let him read to the bottom of the page and asked him to go back and check. 'You said "The boys"; does that look right?' Owen affirmed that it didn't. The teacher then wrote 'The boys' and 'The big boys' on a piece of paper and scaffolded Owen's anticipation of what he would expect to see in each version. Taking Owen back to the book, she said, 'Try that again and think what looks right.' Owen read all further examples of 'the boys' and 'the big boys' accurately. 'Ball' and 'back' posed no problems, indicating that he was now attending to all the letter information in the words.

The new text is carefully chosen to bring together many aspects of the child's current processing and acts as a 'testing ground for emerging strategies, consolidating some and [providing] an opportunity for learning others' (Clay, 2001: 227).

The Reading Recovery lesson: A summary

As illustrated in the six examples given above, every Reading Recovery lesson is designed to acknowledge and work with each learner's unique cognitive and perceptive landscape, shaped by past experiences at home and in school (Clay, 2001: 294). Each lesson component has the potential to make a powerful contribution towards sculpting the brain's architecture for skilled reading. Changing the shape of learning is difficult but not impossible. Other complex learning, such as learning to walk, demonstrates that learning is a highly individual process (Thelen, 1995) and that it is achieved by the merging of many skills. Although learning to read is different from learning to walk, developmental psychology is beginning to offer a strong argument that change and development are the result of the interaction between multiple factors, rather than of single causes, either environmental or genetic. The process of progressing upwards through successive levels of reading difficulty and of creating footholds along the way is unique and particular to each learner. Finding these footholds and using them to forge powerful pathways through an accelerative learning trajectory requires highly skilled, finely tuned teaching.

Quality of teaching is key

The fast pace of pupil progress in Reading Recovery has sometimes been attributed to factors associated with daily teaching and the one-to-one instructional context. Critics have suggested that one-to-one teaching must automatically improve a child's literacy, and that teaching in small groups is more efficient. An analogy might be made with the medical model. Patients are not generally treated in small groups; remedies are individually designed and applied, and as the severity of the illness increases so too does the expertise of the clinician. In education we can ignore this, often placing the most vulnerable learners with the least qualified – for example, teaching assistants or volunteers (Blatchford *et al.*, 2009). Clay, however, considered that it is the skill and speed with which the Reading Recovery teacher is able to capture, analyse, and respond to very small but consequential changes in literacy processing that facilitate the accelerated learning trajectories consistently observed in rates of pupil progress.

Experienced teachers who implement Reading Recovery follow a year-long professional development programme (see Chapter 4), to learn how to scaffold learning by finding 'the clearest, easiest, most memorable examples with which to establish a new response, skill, principle or procedure' (Clay, 2005a: 23). Teaching in Reading Recovery requires both a high level of expertise and a thorough understanding of the complex theory of literacy learning and of the importance of close observation and contingent teaching.

The importance of powerful professional development

From the inception of Reading Recovery, the quality of the professional development of teachers has been acknowledged as vital, both to enable them to work with this complex theory of literacy acquisition and to respond effectively to each child's particular mix of strengths, gaps, and confusions in their literacy learning. Teachers' understanding of these interactions is fostered through repeated collection and analysis of observational data on individual learning and teaching, and through opportunities for 'real-time' reflective critique that relates observation of children's performance to literacy theory (see Chapter 4). An infrastructure of professional development supports teachers to develop the depth of knowledge and skills required in order to build a curriculum for each individual child learning in Reading Recovery. The enquiry-oriented model (Lyons *et al.*, 1993) features a critically reflective discussion around the teaching of children in Reading Recovery.

The 'live-lesson critique' uses a one-way viewing screen (see figure 3.1). The observing teachers study and discuss the lesson as it is happening, shaping their observations towards insights into the child's control over reading and writing competencies. Close observation of children undertaking oral and literacy tasks builds a body of pedagogical knowledge for teachers. Engaging in the constructive critique of rationales for observed behaviour of teacher and child allows teachers to use their theoretical knowledge to provide finely tuned instruction.

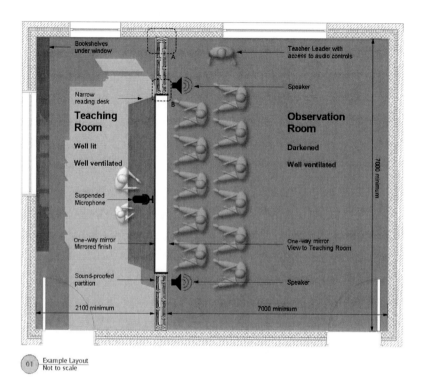

Figure 3.1: Diagram of the one-way viewing screen and facility

Reading Recovery teachers often mention that each child they have worked with in Reading Recovery has taught them something more about the process of learning. They enjoy and value the collective opportunities for critical reflection on practice that models what they can do in their individual lessons – praxis at work. From the inception of Every Child a Reader, it was apparent that the praxis that Reading Recovery teachers possessed would be essential to its development. To conclude this chapter, we suggest four key dimensions that have acted as a support for the development of Every Child a Reader (see Chapter 2).

Concluding remarks: Supporting the development of Every Child a Reader

In Every Child a Reader, literacy interventions are organized into patterns, or waves of response that are activated following the systematic formative assessment and tracking of children's needs and developing provision. How, then, was Reading Recovery able to provide the backbone to a school-wide strategy?

(i)   Empowered by theory

Every Child a Reader brings together a collection of established, evidence-based educational responses of varying intensity. These are driven by detailed assessment and analysis of learners' needs across the complex and connected spectrum of skills required for literacy. The theoretical base of Reading Recovery presents teachers with two intertwined but contrasting views of progress; one quantifies known letters, known words, level of difficulty of text read using any given criteria, and complexity of word reading, and the other attempts to make inferences about 'within-the-head' processes by systematically capturing and analysing literacy behaviours. The robustness of the theory has sustained other, lighter-touch interventions and allowed them to be implemented successfully, because schools have been given theoretical criteria by which to determine the interventions that best match the needs of particular children.

For example, Better Reading Partners (see page 44) draws on some of Reading Recovery's formative assessment practices to enable teaching assistants and classroom volunteers to improve two key things: the quality of focused interactions around texts; and the provision of reading material that is appropriate to each child's attainment. It is not an intervention for children demonstrating the greatest difficulty in literacy learning, but its theoretical base has been employed to support paraprofessionals in providing evidence-based teaching.

Every Child a Reader is no mere 'catch-up' remedy, raising low literary levels to an acceptable classroom average, nor is it a means of providing a rich literacy environment to stimulate innate abilities. More importantly, it seeks to change the future trajectory of literacy learning and 'assist the child to construct effective networks in his brain for linking up all the strategic activity that will be needed to work on texts, including but not limited merely to accumulation of items of knowledge' (Clay, 2005b: 44). The theory itself is why the 'layers' of intervention that make up Every Child a Reader successfully raise children's achievements.

(ii)   Constructive view of learning and learners

The pedagogy of Reading Recovery aims to change a 'literacy passive' learner into a 'literacy active' learner through 'simple tasks which call for complex learning' (Clay, 2001: 300). Formative assessment processes provide a window on perceptual and cognitive processing (ibid.). While the pathway followed by each child is uniquely constructed, there is clear evidence around when to intervene in order to create the greatest impact in the shortest time. Every Child a Reader is a recognized label for the organizing structure and mapping of these literacy interventions for wider 'reach'. These interventions may be implemented by a range of professionals and paraprofessionals. The pedagogy may be derived from different parts of the complex processes involved in learning to be literate. Reading Recovery's theoretical foundation and flexible practices have allowed schools to improve the reach and quality of lighter-touch interventions across the primary age range.

(iii)   Evidence for effectiveness

Support for Every Child a Reader has been provided by the systematic collection of data for the purpose of making decisions as to the cost-effective deployment of staff. Reading Recovery's effectiveness continues to be tested by stringent data-collection at the levels of school, local authority, and education system, and the same practice has been adopted by Every Child a Reader. This has been important in ensuring that the interventions' approaches are effective, both individually and in combination, and that they offer viable and cost-effective solutions for individual schools.

(iv)   Professional development model

The professional development dimension of Reading Recovery highlights the importance of teacher development being structured, differentiated, and sustained (Joyce *et al.*, 1987; Joyce and Showers, 1988). Within this general framework, the integration of modelling, simulated practice, feedback, and coaching are seen as key, transforming professional development opportunities from passive receipt of information to one of repeated and upward spiralling of understanding to support and 'power' the learning process (Carless, 2007). The effectiveness of these elements is also increased by discussions during individual teacher leader visits to Reading Recovery teachers in their schools (see Chapter 4). In Every Child a Reader, Reading Recovery teachers work alongside those providing other layers of intervention in school, to support, extend, and monitor their effectiveness, and provide feedback and feed forward for school planning.

Conclusion

This chapter has presented and evaluated the theoretical base of Reading Recovery. This complex theory of literacy acquisition is enacted through formative assessment practices and lesson-component design. The professional practice of the Reading Recovery teacher, made possible through deep understanding of early literacy acquisition and resultant pedagogy created through the Reading Recovery professional development model, has the capacity to propel the learning of an individual child, the professional learning of staff, and the future maintenance of successful literacy practice in the school as a whole. The theoretical base, the view of learning, and the professional development model have been instrumental in the successes of Every Child a Reader.

In the next chapter, the goals and processes of professional development for all those who play a part in the mosaic of Reading Recovery and Every Child a Reader are presented and evaluated in terms of their importance in achieving system change and improving outcomes for learners. The chapter shows how an understanding of the theoretical base and its practical iterations build and sustain this capacity in school and district professionals.

Notes

[1] For a description of the roles and responsibilities of Reading Recovery professionals, see page 83.

[2] Texts used in Reading Recovery are levelled numerically from 1 to 20 with Level 1 being most supportive of emergent readers and Level 20 representing more sophisticated texts for six- to seven-year-olds. Readily available books from a range of reading schemes, and of different types and genres are levelled into a fine gradient of difficulty through evaluation criteria and field trialling.

[3] Elkonin analysis (1973) underpins the Reading Recovery procedure of Hearing and Recording Sounds in Words (Clay, 2005b).

References

Adams, M. (1990) *Beginning to Read: Thinking and learning about print.* Cambridge, MA: MIT Press.

D'Agostino, J.V., and Murphy, J.A. (2004) 'A meta-analysis of Reading Recovery in United States schools'. *Educational Evaluation and Policy Analysis,* 26 (1), 23–38.

Blatchford, P., Bassett, P., Brown, P., and Webster, R. (2009) 'The effect of support staff on pupil engagement and individual attention'. *British Educational Research Journal,* 35(5), 661–86.

Carless, D.R. (2007) 'Learning-oriented assessment: Conceptual bases and practical implications'. *Innovations in Education and Teaching International,* 44 (1), 57–66.

Castles, A. (2006) 'The dual route model and the developmental dyslexias'. *London Review of Education,* 4 (1), 49–61.

Chapman, J.W., Tunmer, W.E., and Prochnow, J.E. (2001) 'Does success in the Reading Recovery program depend on developing proficiency in phonological processing skills? A longitudinal study in a whole-language instructional context'. *Scientific Studies of Reading,* 5 (2), 141–76.

Clay, M.M. (1972) *Reading: The patterning of complex behaviour.* Auckland: Heinemann.

– (1982) *Observing Young Readers: Selected papers.* Portsmouth, NH: Heinemann.

– (1993) *Reading Recovery: A guidebook for teachers in training.* Auckland: Heinemann.

– (2001) *Change Over Time in Children's Literacy Development.* Portsmouth, NH: Heinemann.

– (2002, 2nd ed.) *An Observation Survey of Early Literacy Achievement*. Auckland: Heinemann.

– (2005a) *Literacy Lessons Designed for Individuals. Part One: Why? When? And How?* Portsmouth, NH: Heinemann.

– (2005b) *Literacy Lessons Designed for Individuals: Part Two: Teaching procedures*. Portsmouth, NH: Heinemann.

Clay, M.M. and Cazden, C.C. (1990) 'A Vygotskian interpretation of Reading Recovery'. In Moll, L.C. (ed.), *Vygotsky and Education: Instructional implications and applications of socio-historical psychology*, 207–22. Cambridge: Cambridge University Press.

Dehaene, S., Pegado, F., Braga, L.W., Ventura, P., Nunes Filho, G., Jobert, A., Dehaene-Lambertz, G., Kolinsky, R., Morais, J., and Cohen, L. (2010) 'How learning to read changes the cortical networks for vision and language'. *Science, 330* (6009), 1359–64.

Elliott, C. (2011) *British Ability Scales III*. London: Granada Learning Group.

Goodman, K. (1967) 'Reading: A psycholinguistic guessing game'. *Journal of the Reading Specialist,* May, 126–35.

Gough, P.B. and Tunmer, W.E. (1986) 'Decoding, reading and reading disability', *Remedial and Special Education*, 7, 6–10.

Greaney, K.T. (2011) 'The Multiple Cues or "Searchlights" word reading theory: Implications for Reading Recovery', *Perspectives on Language and Literacy*, Fall, 15–20.

Holliman, A. and Hurry, J. (in press) *Children's Reading Profiles on Exiting the Reading Recovery Programme: Do they predict sustained progress?*

Holmes, J., and Singer, H. (1964) 'Theoretical models and trends towards more basic research in reading'. *Review of Educational Research,* 34, April, 127–55.

Hurry, J. (2012) *The Impact of Reading Recovery Five Years After Intervention*. London: Every Child a Reader Trust.

Joyce, B. and Showers, B. (1988) *Student Achievement Through Staff Development*. White Plains, NY: Longman Inc.

Joyce, B., Showers, B., and Bennett, B. (1987) 'Synthesis of research on staff development: A framework for future study and a state-of-the-art analysis'. *Educational Leadership,* 45, 77–87.

Lyons, C.A., Pinnell, G.S., and DeFord, D.E. (1993) *Partners in Learning: Teachers and Children in Reading Recovery*. New York: Teachers College Press.

Lyons, C.A. (2003) *Teaching Struggling Readers: How to use brain research to maximise learning*. Portsmouth, NH: Heinemann.

Merriam-Webster (2012) *The Merriam-Webster Online Dictionary*. Online. www.merriam-webster.com/dictionary/guess (accessed 10 January 2012).

Rodgers, E. (2012) 'Using Systematic Observation to Assess Early Literacy Development and Plan Instruction'. In Evan Ortlieb and Earl H. Cheek (eds), *Using Informative Assessments towards Effective Literacy Instruction*. Bingley, W. Yorkshire: Emerald.

Rose, J. (2006) *Independent Review of the Teaching of Early Reading: Final report*. Nottingham: DfES.

Rummelhart, D.E. (1994) 'Toward an interactive model of reading'. In R.B. Ruddell, M.R. Ruddell, and H. Singer (eds), *Theoretical Models and Processes of Reading* (4th ed.), 864–94. Newark, DE: International Reading Association.

Singer, H. (1994) 'The sub-strata factor theory of reading'. In R.B. Ruddell, M.R. Ruddell, and H. Singer (eds), *Theoretical Models and Processes of Reading* (4th ed.), 895–927. Newark, DE: International Reading Association.

Singleton, C. (2009) 'Intervention for Dyslexia: A review of published evidence on the impact of specialist dyslexia teaching. DCSF Report', May. Online. www.thedyslexia-spldtrust.org.uk/article/13/review-of-international-research-published-by-dr-chris-singleton (accessed 21 November 2011).

Sirois, S., Spratling, M., Thomas, M.S.C., Westermann, G., Mareschal, D., and Johnson, M.H. (2008) 'Precis of neuroconstructivism: How the brain constructs cognition'. *Behavioral and Brain Sciences*, 31, 321–56.

Stanovich, K.E. (1986) 'Matthew effects in reading: Some consequences of individual differences in the acquisition of reading'. *Reading Research Quarterly*, 21 (4), 360–406.

Stanovich, K.E. (2010) *How to Think Straight about Psychology* (9th ed.). Boston: Pearson/Allyn and Bacon.

Stuart, M., Stainthorp, R., and Snowling, M. (2008) 'Literacy as a complex activity: Deconstructing the Simple View of Reading'. *Literacy*, 42 (2), 59–66.

Teale, W.H., and Sulzby, E. (1986) 'Introduction: Emergent literacy as a perspective for examining how young children become writers and readers'. In W.H. Teale and E. Sulzby (eds), *Emergent Literacy: Writing and reading*. Norwood: Ablex Publishing Corporation.

Thelen, E. (1995) 'Time scale dynamics and the development of an embodied cognition'. In R. Port and T. Van Gelder (eds), *Mind in Motion*. Cambridge, MA: MIT Press.

Thelen, E. and Smith, L. (1994) *A Dynamic Systems Approach to the Development of Cognition and Action*. Cambridge, MA: MIT Press.

Tunmer, W.E. and Chapman, J.W. (2004) 'Reading Recovery: Distinguishing myth from reality'. In R.M. Joshi (ed.), *Dyslexia: Myths, misconceptions, and some practical applications*. Baltimore, MD: International Dyslexia Association.

Wasik, B.A. and Slavin, R.E. (1993) 'Preventing early reading failure with one-to-one tutoring: A review of five programs'. *Reading Research Quarterly*, 28 (2), 179–200.

Wolf, M., Gottwald, S., Galante, W., Norton, E., and Miller, L. (2009) 'How the origins of reading inform reading instruction'. In P. McCardle and K. Pugh. (eds), *How Children Learn to Read: Current issues and new directions in the integration of cognition, neurobiology and genetics of reading and dyslexia research and practice*. New York: Routledge.

Chapter 4
Experts gaining expertise
Susan Taylor, Janet Ferris, and Glen Franklin

Introduction

Change – in children, in teachers, in schools, and in an educational system – is at the heart of Reading Recovery. An established infrastructure provides professional development for all involved in effecting change through Reading Recovery and Every Child a Reader. The professional development model effects a process of change in attitudes and beliefs, as well as in expertise in children's literacy learning (Taylor, 2003). However, such changes do not happen spontaneously; to bring them about, planning is needed, the ultimate aim being acquisition of, and becoming comfortable with, perceptions of knowledge and skills that are flexible and usable in many contexts.

This chapter expands on the theoretical strengths of Reading Recovery discussed mainly in Chapter 3. Professional development in Reading Recovery empowers national leaders, teacher leaders (teacher-educators), and teachers to become effective decision-makers and problem-solvers (Taylor and Bodman, 2012). In this chapter we look at the principles of the professional development model used within Reading Recovery and at how these principles are transferable across professional development in other literacy interventions that support the wider reach of Every Child a Reader. Reading Recovery uses a 'three-tiered system' (Schmitt *et al.*, 2005) of professional development to establish and maintain consistent, positive results: national leaders trained and based in universities provide professional development for Reading Recovery teacher leaders; and teacher leaders work in regions and local authorities providing professional development for school-based teachers. All are experienced literacy professionals when they start their professional development programme in Reading Recovery, and as part of ongoing professional development, they all continue to teach children in Reading Recovery.

This chapter describes and critiques the professional development model and explains how these experienced professionals, who are already regarded as having expertise in their field, continue to learn and gain expertise through generative learning processes (Wittrock, 1990). We define generative learning and explore its role in effective professional learning

(Taylor, 2006). Similarly, at these three levels of professional development, the parallel curricula juxtapose critical reflection with a particular blend of learning environments, linking theory and practice in a cyclical manner.

One of the features supporting criticality comes from the teaching of children, which allows theories of teaching and learning to be tested and reformulated (Bruner, 1996). As professionals develop generative learning powers, they too are able to provide and facilitate deep-level learning in others. We have named this exponential learning power a 'living pyramid', and it is constructed through in-service professional development sessions. Communities of learners (Moore, 1997) are established during both initial and ongoing professional development. The pyramid supports professionals in providing wider benefits to regional and whole school teams through Every Child a Reader. With targeted support for children with literacy difficulties, the implementation of Every Child a Reader has resulted in more children benefiting from interventions derived from this unique professional development (see Chapter 2 and Chapter 5).

In this chapter, as the complexity of the professional development that supports a multilevel change process is described and critiqued, examples are drawn from a case study that includes four individual professionals and one school context:

- Gemma[1] is a national leader at the European Centre for Reading Recovery. Together with others in the leadership team, she is responsible for providing initial and ongoing professional development for Reading Recovery teacher-educators (teacher leaders), which is initially facilitated through a master's degree (MA) programme at the Institute of Education, University of London.
- Tom completed this MA programme and is now an experienced teacher leader. He provides initial and ongoing professional development for Reading Recovery teachers.
- Rachel was trained as a Reading Recovery teacher by Tom and, supported by him, now also works as an Every Child a Reader teacher in addition to her Reading Recovery role. In her Every Child a Reader role she supports professional development around literacy teaching within the whole school community, including teachers and teaching assistants.
- Sahira is one of the teaching assistants who has benefited from Rachel's professional support at North Street Primary School.

The range of vignettes and reflections used below to illustrate the change process were gathered from these professionals through semi-structured interviews. They are woven through the discussion of processes of change under the following headings: theories and assumptions in generative professional learning; testing professional learning by teaching; and adaptive expertise. Wherever possible, the professionals' own voices are used to illustrate both the conceptual ideas and the practical application of these concepts.

Theories and assumptions in generative professional learning

Adult learners interpret experiences in their own way, based on perceptions grounded in their culture. Mezirow (1997) defines these perceptions as meaning perspectives. He suggests that adult learners usually prefer to remain within their own meaning perspectives to avoid anxiety and loss of self-confidence, but this inhibits the flexibility that can develop as generative learning. Effective professional development curricula provide opportunities for adult learners to challenge their strongly held assumptions (Brookfield, 1986). Experts need to become fast, efficient decision-makers in novel situations. It is not possible to prepare professionals for every eventuality, and the unique nature of literacy difficulties experienced by each child in Reading Recovery calls for the developing of generative learning in Reading Recovery professionals (Taylor and Bodman, 2012). Below, we look at how this is developed by drawing on our case studies. We first consider Tom, the teacher leader in the case study setting.

During the initial year of his professional development to become a teacher leader, Tom assumed he would be 'imparting a body of knowledge to the teachers' but eventually realized that much more was needed. He needed to learn how to prepare teachers to become effective decision-makers in their teaching. His learning needed to become generative. He needed to learn how, as a teacher-educator, he could support the change process in the teachers he would train:

> The essence of the generative learning model is that the mind, or the brain, is not a passive consumer of information. Instead, it actively constructs its own interpretations of information and draws inferences from them.
>
> (Wittrock, 1990: 348)

Elaborate knowledge structures are necessary for interpreting new information; reasoning from these structures elicits what is known, thereby enabling problem-solving. Generative learning might be considered in terms of deeper levels of processing where the depth of processing can be thought of as the kind and number of elaborations generated to develop and use new organizational paradigms (Eysenck and Keane, 2000). Gardiner (1989) defines the generation effect as the superior learning that results from material that has been generated and acted upon by the learner. Learners immersed in generative learning environments generate sub-problems, sub-goals, and strategies for achieving a larger task. Generative learning depends on the 'generation of meaningful relations – among concepts and between knowledge and experience – on learning from teaching' (Wittrock, 1992: 531–2), so that people use generative learning processes:

> actively and dynamically to (a) selectively attend to events and (b) generate meaning for events by constructing relations between new or incoming information and previously acquired information, conceptions, and background knowledge. These active and dynamic generations lead to reorganizations and reconceptualizations and to elaborations and relations that increase understanding.
>
> (ibid.)

Gemma, a national leader, supported Tom and Rachel to construct and use new organizational paradigms so as to develop the deeper levels of processing associated with generative learning. This enabled them to build the more elaborate knowledge structures that are necessary for interpreting and organizing new information. Gemma supported this process by providing multiple learning experiences and cycles of constructive formative feedback. She and the other national leaders provided opportunities for Tom to reason from these elaborate knowledge structures so as to elicit what he and his colleagues on the teacher-leader course knew and could employ to aid problem-solving. Knowledge construction is a perceived active integration of new ideas or a hypothesis, where more elaborate structures are built by capitalizing on the learner's existing experiential knowledge and transformative learning experiences. For Tom and his teachers, one way that this cyclical and iterative process is supported is through active observation of a teacher and child engaged in a one-to-one Reading Recovery lesson on the other side of a one-way viewing screen (Figure 4.1).

This mediated learning context, with opportunities for cycles of formative feedback, supports the change process with parallels for both Tom becoming a teacher leader and for his teachers' learning in Reading Recovery. Here we explore Tom's learning at the one-way viewing screen during his professional MA programme. We then discuss how he provided and continues to provide the same support for his teachers after taking up the role of teacher leader. This professional development model adopts a constructivist approach to learning (Kroll, 2004; Perkins, 2006).

Figure 4.1: Active observation through the one-way viewing screen. Image courtesy of European Centre for Reading Recovery, Institute of Education, University of London.

The centrality of a one-way viewing screen in developing expertise

Gemma, a member of the national leadership team, facilitated the conversation around the observation at the screen of a teacher and child engaged in a lesson. This observation is not a passive activity; Gemma encouraged and eventually expected Tom and his colleagues to engage in active observation using language as a tool for mediating their learning. There has been criticism of Reading Recovery as being cult-like for the exclusivity of the language it uses (Woods and Henderson, 2002). Organizations within any discipline, including education, have their own particular discourses, which 'outsiders' might find difficult to engage with. But language and discourse have long been shown to be essential tools for effective learning (Vygotsky, 1986; Mercer, 1995; Wood, 1998; Wells, 1999).

Gemma's goal in the teacher leader role was to elicit tentative hypotheses from the group and for the group members to learn to challenge each other (Bruner, 1996). Thus multiple perspectives drawn from applying their previous experience and from their daily work in teaching children were brought to this observation of teaching and learning. These perspectives were articulated to the rest of the group and, prompted by Gemma, were used to reformulate new hypotheses and facilitate deeper processing and problem-solving, which in turn gradually generated new learning and thereby developed expertise. Through this hypothesis-forming, Tom and his colleagues learnt how to learn (Brookfield, 1986) as they created 'something generic that allows you to go beyond what you already know ... [and] permits you to know more than you ought' (Bruner, 1996: 129). As Gemma pointed out: 'They [Tom and his colleagues] were not likely to come to the same realization that they will do ... after their understanding has been probed.'

Nevertheless, the university teaching team noted that Tom and his colleagues seemed not to have developed generative ways of learning fully until they had moved into their new professional roles. It was perhaps the opportunities that they had to continue their critical stance as they engaged in practice, and having to solve problems and make decisions on the run, that supported them towards deeper-level processing. This process is illustrated in Figure 4.2, by the spiral professional learning path extending beyond the initial professional MA programme.

One might question why, in an age of rapid technological development, this professional development relies on teachers bringing children to a centre for a lesson behind a one-way screen. The use of videos or other electronic devices are presumed to reduce costs and obviate logistical and ethical problems about bringing children (albeit very few) to a Reading Recovery centre for a lesson. Early on in their professional development programme, Tom and some of his colleagues asked Gemma why they could not simply watch videoed lessons. At that point in their learning, they seemed unhappy with what they perceived as a stock response from Gemma:

> The observation [of video] tends to be more passive and therefore, if we value language as a tool for learning, then the learning is negatively impacted as a direct result of more passive activity. A video has only one set of 'eyes' and ... then we don't benefit from the multiple perspectives that we get from many people viewing the same teacher–child interactions simultaneously and offering up their tentative hypotheses for challenge and for theory to be built.

Tom responded by asking: 'Why can't we add multiple cameras then?' There are occasions during the professional development year on the MA programme when a video *is* used. For instance, the first time that Tom and his colleagues on the teacher-leader course were required to try to facilitate group conversation, to create a lower-risk learning environment and an opportunity for constructive formative feedback cycles (Bodman, 2006), a video of a lesson was played behind the one-way viewing screen. Tom and his colleagues found this experience a 'useful way of dipping one's toes in the water' but also found it 'artificial in some way', and when they reflected on the experience they noted that it 'was not as rewarding as a learning experience as when facilitating the conversation at the screen with live lessons'. Tom now robustly defends the value of live lessons and their importance in developing generative learning.

With Gemma's guidance, they came to realize that the teacher's physical presence means that the lesson is not observed in a hypothetical context. They observe the lesson of a teacher colleague who has worked over time and in depth with a child, and so are able to gain greater insight into why the child might have responded as he/she did. The live context, as opposed to a video, also means that the advice and solutions arising from the ensuing discussion are not hypothetical either. They can be tested in real time by the teacher going away from the discussion and implementing the guidance suggested, and later reporting back on its efficacy. In this way, discussion and inferences for teaching arising from the observation are both grounded and tested in reality.

Gemma also noted that watching live and videoed lessons resulted in differences when she asked Tom and his colleagues to reflect on their conversations at the screen and give feedback to teachers after the lesson. When the group watched a video, the conversation tended to focus more on negative criticism, rather than remaining tentative, supportive, and anchored in theory. By contrast, when they watched live lessons, their hypotheses were more tentative and focused more on constructive dialogue that gave feedback to the teacher to support *her* decision-making and problem-solving in helping move the child forward in his learning. Language used as a mediating tool for learning was more effective in the individual and shared construction of knowledge when live lessons, rather than videoed lessons, were observed.

Generative learning in Reading Recovery is achieved through developing a critical stance towards the integration of theory and practice, and of learning and teaching (Bodman and Taylor, 2010). Gemma and her colleagues developed and evaluated the spiral curriculum model for its potential to capitalize on the integration of theory and practice through a unique blend of learning environments. The spiral curriculum gave opportunities for multiple cyclical experiential events, thereby creating more capacity for generative growth.

A spiral curriculum for professional learning

A spiral curriculum organizes learning around concepts and themes that are inductively designed. In other words, Gemma assessed how and when each theme and concept was revisited depending on the ability of Tom and of his colleagues on the teacher-leader course to generate hypotheses and apply new learning. Themes and concepts were revisited at increasing levels of generality and abstraction with a focus on flexible transfer. Tom and his colleagues undertook the same programme of study with the same cycles of assessment for learning (Bodman, 2006) and fieldwork but each followed their own spiral learning path (Taylor, 2012; Figure 4.2).

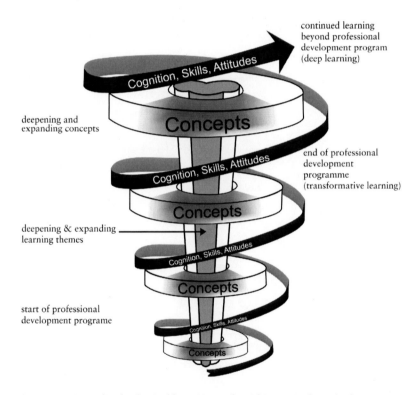

Figure 4.2: An individual spiral learning path within a spiral curriculum

As an experienced Early Years practitioner, Tom already had expertise in the field of literacy learning. He also had some knowledge of adult learning from his experience as a Primary National Strategy literacy consultant, albeit in delivering short or one-day professional training. In Figure 4.2 this prior knowledge and experience are represented by the spiral learning path extending below the programme's starting point. Although Tom's spiral learning path appears fairly regular, the model shown here is a simplified representation of Tom's journey. Risk and challenge, support and ever-rising expectations, demonstration and problematizing, individual and group critique, and critical reflection all played a key role in the pedagogical design and experience, together with cycles of assessment and feedback (Bodman, 2006). In fact, Tom's confidence was challenged early on as he realized that he still had much to learn about literacy learning. He needed to acquire more expertise to plan effective professional development for his teachers. These teachers will need to succeed in teaching literacy to those children who have confounded even the best efforts of good classroom teachers. This requires that they become not just good teachers of literacy, but be able to overcome the complex and various difficulties of the very lowest-attaining children. Environments where their own professional learning is challenged help trainee teacher leaders like Tom to gain the expertise they will need.

Brookfield (1986) suggests that challenge is essential for effective generative learning to develop and in this context the role of cognitive dissonance in developing generative learning continues to be explored (Taylor and Ince, 2012).

In the first term, Gemma introduced several concepts and themes related to both literacy learning and adult professional learning: constructive dissonance, critical reflection, and scaffolding – for example, working within the zone of proximal development (Vygtosky, 1986). Concepts are generic and can be applied to many disciplines. Themes are programme-specific and include learning how to tutor (how conversational critique is facilitated at the one-way viewing screen) and using teaching for learning (see below).

Gemma explained that 'we sort of light-touch things the first time around and gradually keep re-visiting in greater depth'. She recognized that:

> it may not be an easy journey ... and they have to travel on faith a bit ... they have to suspend their irritation of not having it all until you get them to a point ... where they start to feel how this relates to this and this relates to that.

The purpose of introducing dissonance into professional development is the triggering effect it has on reflective problem-solving, stimulating the search for resolution or the formulation of higher-level questioning. Gemma's management of dissonance in learning focused on enhancing change, growing from her sense that, as she puts it, she holds 'a bigger perspective of where we need to get them to and where they go from here'.

The professional curriculum, and learning and assessment within it, are organized to use dissonance as a tool for achieving generative learning (Taylor and Bodman, 2012). Despite course introductory materials and introduction of its curricular patterns, Tom had not really begun to understand this learning process. He certainly felt challenged and at times irritated by not being given the 'right answers'. He thought that the best way to learn was to be given information that he would assimilate, remember for the future, and teach to others. He had not yet discovered the power of generative learning through problem-solving.

Tom and his colleagues participated in daily fieldwork, teaching children in Reading Recovery as well as attending and observing experienced teacher leaders working with their teacher groups and individually. Related readings around a range of themes were introduced into workshops and seminars. They helped Tom and his course colleagues to make theory–practice links. Initially, Tom could not see the interrelationship between themes and between concepts, nor between and across themes and concepts. Eventually, Tom noted 'a sense of everything pulling together as the year went on', and later acknowledged how 'the seeds were sown in the autumn'. In Figure 4.2, we can see the merging and deepening of themes and concepts. Tom described this by saying 'there's a real sort of knitting together of it all'. He became less 'worried if we don't grasp things the first time'. He noted how the course experiences were intertwined and stated that 'we have changed over a short period of time in what we're thinking about as professionals and [regarding] the impact on our practice'. By the end of the initial professional development year, Tom acknowledged how he had now 'got a good enough working understanding to up and run with my own group of teachers and support them with their learning journey'.

Teacher leaders develop awareness that professional learning is better if it is both transformative and generative, and that is achieved not by imparting knowledge but through co-construction. Reflecting back on his learning journey, Tom was excited at the prospect of working with his own group of teachers. Although he felt he only had 'a minimum proficiency', he believed he and his colleagues were 'at the stage where we can go out and be let loose on a group'. He realized that his learning was not complete and he could accept that it might never be. This is indicated by the spiral in Figure 4.2, continuing beyond the end of the programme.

It is to be expected that generative learning processes develop over time and may not be complete by the end of a professional development year. But, having learnt how to learn, teacher leaders can use generative learning as a strengthening professional characteristic. This is more clearly observed in teacher leaders once they have taken up their new professional roles.

Having moved away from only wanting the 'right' answers, Tom realized that his programme had prepared him to problem-solve and make fast and robust decisions in most eventualities. He had become aware of the power of cycles of feedback in supporting learning (Bodman, 2006). He was aware that he too would need to effect such a change in the cognition, attitudes, and beliefs of his teachers. He had developed empathy, knowing that his teachers might become irritated and challenged at points along their similarly parallel journeys.

In the next section, we consider the significance of generative learning for all professionals through their continuing to teach children in Reading Recovery.

Testing professional learning by teaching

Fundamental to Reading Recovery worldwide is the recognition that all its professionals continue to learn through teaching children (Lyons *et al.*, 1993) wherever these professionals are within the three-tiered system identified earlier in this chapter.

Teaching of children by national leaders is seen as an essential part of their complex role (Schmitt *et al.*, 2005). Through teaching children, national leaders maintain contact with 'the fundamental level of education in Reading Recovery' (Lyons *et al.*, 1993: 6). Maintaining this teaching commitment is not always easy. Every Child a Reader increased the number of teacher leaders in the field fourfold, from 20 in 2005 to 82 by 2011 and with an additional 20 teacher leaders in the initial professional development course that year. National leaders became responsible for more than the professional development programme for new teacher leaders and the day-to-day support for those experienced. They also supported the implementation of the lighter-touch interventions within Every Child a Reader, which served far greater numbers of children. Additionally, they offered professional support at local authority level, particularly in disseminating national outcomes and in recruitment into new regions as the results from Every Child a Reader attracted more interest. National leaders such as Gemma spent a great deal of time travelling. The rollout of Every Child a Reader with its increased demands had impacted on the time available to teach children. However, Reading Recovery professionals see the teaching of children as key to their ever-evolving expertise and, as such, all strive to retain what opportunities they can to develop their own understanding through teaching struggling young learners as well as adult professionals.

The model of learning used in Reading Recovery professional development has been described as 'enquiry-based', with teaching, learning, and assessment (feedback) interwoven through a 'reflective/analytic experience' (Pinnell, 1997: 9). Gemma teaches three children in Reading Recovery. She was puzzling over Ben, a little boy she had worked with. Ben achieved average or above-average outcomes on all aspects of the exit assessments at the end of his lesson series and was reading at an age-appropriate level. He had gained in self-esteem and confidence. His parents were thrilled with his progress. Yet Gemma noticed that he had written 'wef' when asked to write 'with', seemingly relying on his strong phonic knowledge and his London accent to hear and record the sounds he heard. Gemma's first reaction was one of surprise. She had spent time working with him on ways to help him recall this high-frequency word, but her efforts had apparently been unsuccessful.

Gemma reviewed exit data from the other children who had completed Reading Recovery under her tuition. It seemed that, although these children were able to write over 40 words unaided, most of them were regularly patterned, three- or four-letter words (European Centre for Reading Recovery, 2012). The data showed that even words that were phonically regular but more orthographically complex (such as 'night') were more often spelt in a more phonically regular form (such as 'nit' or 'nite'). This posed a challenge to Gemma's teaching and identified a need for change (Cranton, 1996). Through her teaching of children, Gemma had realized that, although his literacy learning had allowed Ben to make rapid progress in reading and writing, she had not yet provided him with sufficiently refined tools to support his working on irregular or low-frequency words. Gemma considered whether she had really been supporting his independent problem-solving through the feedback she had provided. Critical self-reflection now challenged her thinking and understanding. It was something that she was pondering when she paid Tom a routine visit.

Tom was working with an experienced group of teachers in a continuing professional development session. His focus for the session was developing spelling skills in writing. Like Gemma, he was concerned about children's over-reliance on phonemic recoding for low-frequency or irregular spelling patterns. Clay (2005) describes a sequential approach to teaching spelling in Reading Recovery as part of the writing process. At first, teachers help children analyse words into an order of sounds, and to represent these sounds as letters in a correct left-to-right sequence. They use a technique adapted from Elkonin (1971, cited in Clay, 2001) to demonstrate the process of linking sounds to letters: in the child's writing book, the teacher draws a small elongated rectangle divided into boxes, one for each phoneme segment, prompting the child to say the word slowly and write the sounds he can hear in the boxes (Figure 4.5 illustrates the use of sound boxes to write the word 'trap').

Reading Recovery teachers will judge when a child has secured this early understanding and will make the transition to using spelling boxes instead of sound boxes, drawing one box for every letter rather than for each phoneme (Figure 4.4 shows an example of using spelling boxes to write the word 'are' as an awareness activity towards learning the word for fast recall). Clay cautions that:

> It is not sufficient for the child to become competent with the phonemic analysis; he has to expand his view of the task. Both sounds and spellings have to be thought about.
>
> (Clay, 2001: 72)

All young writers need to be aware that there are regular and irregular features of English words (Cain, 2010). Making this shift helps the child to realize that what he knows in reading and how he self-monitors in reading can be used to self-monitor and check orthographic patterns in spelling, and thus to support independent control of learning to spell by using generative learning.

Tom had noticed that his teachers seemed not to make much use of spelling boxes to support their children's development of orthography. As preparation for the session, he and Gemma returned to the theory underpinning the teaching of spelling for struggling learners (Clay, 2005).

With Gemma observing, Tom facilitated active observation and hypothesis-theorizing and testing by observable evidence at the one-way viewing screen as described earlier, while Rachel taught on the other side of the screen for her teacher colleagues. Tom guided the teachers and helped them to collaborate, participate, and actively observe. This allowed them to discover their own rationales and interpretations of children's literacy behaviour and the teaching decisions that they, as well as Rachel, made (Moore, 1997).

During the writing component of the observed lesson, the child needed to write the word 'lots'. This is a difficult word to write phonemically as the consonant 't' is not clearly articulated owing to the inflectional ending 's'. The child being taught predictably wrote 'los', whereupon Rachel added the 't' for her (figure 4.3).

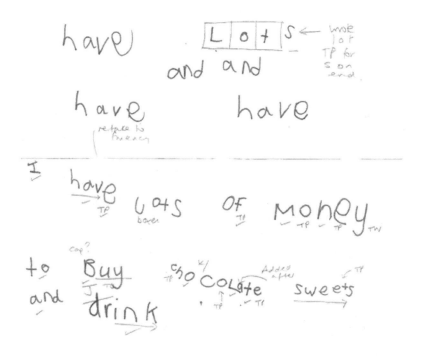

Figure 4.3: Rachel working with Simon

In the subsequent discussion and feedback, Tom directed the teachers to Clay's text (2005) for guidance on the use of spelling boxes, providing the child with a box for every letter rather than focusing solely on segmenting the sounds in a word. This teaching technique enables teachers to demonstrate the exceptions to regular recoding. Children need to learn about both phonology and orthography. Several of the teachers found it difficult to move their cognitive theory away from phonology at this point: one teacher commented: 'But he couldn't *hear* it!'. By exploring with Tom how using spelling boxes might have helped the child work through the word and make a decision about the placement of letters, the group left with new or revised understanding and a generative principle. Rachel appeared keen to develop this aspect of the lesson in her teaching.

During his next visit to Rachel, Tom noticed that, even after the seemingly revelatory experiences in the professional development session, Rachel did not use spelling boxes in the writing component of her lesson despite several opportunities where this might have been appropriate. It seemed that Rachel's practice had not been transformed nor become generative, and for Tom as her teacher leader, the question was 'why not?' (Williams, 2001).

Visits to observe Reading Recovery lessons in school are followed by a shared discussion (a further opportunity for a feedback cycle) about the lessons. With Rachel, Tom revisited the section in Clay (2005) to consider how using spelling boxes might help support the child's independence in writing. Tom left the school feeling that he had not really engaged with the issue in a way that elicited a change in understanding for Rachel. Tom was now being drawn into critical self-reflection in order to support his teachers. This could be considered as the critical behaviour of Tom's own generative professional learning development.

The European Centre for Reading Recovery's *Standards and Guidelines* (2011) stipulate that to maintain their accredited status teacher leaders teach a minimum of two children through a complete lesson series each year. However, Tom, like Gemma, was also finding it difficult to honour this teaching commitment as part of his teacher-leader role. Teacher leaders are highly experienced teachers of children with literacy difficulties. Moreover, they often come to Reading Recovery from a teacher-educator background, such as a consultancy role. Teacher-leader professional development builds upon this previous experience and expertise (Taylor, 2010) with its focus on adult learning. Teacher leaders generally work in the same local authority as the one in which they have previously been employed. Since the financial crisis of 2009, local authorities have cut back on staffing levels. This has resulted in a market-led economy where teacher leaders are expected to devote more of their time (and expertise) to other duties, leading professional development outside their teacher-leader role, as well as training and monitoring other interventions as part of Every Child a Reader (see Chapter 5).

Tom was aware of this pressure on his time. Yet, while reflecting upon his experiences with Rachel, he also noted how his own expertise was being challenged. His own teaching of children was a way for him to move forward in his own understanding, thereby becoming more able to support Rachel. After his visit to Rachel, Tom was teaching Kayleigh, who wanted to write the word 'are'. In her story, she wrote the letter 'r' then looked at Tom and said, 'I know it's "r", but what's next?'. Tom drew three boxes on the work page of her writing book and asked, 'Where will you write the "r"?'. Kayleigh put it in the middle box and then, looking at Tom quizzically, she asked, 'And is it "a" first?' before proceeding to write the first letter. Then she wrote another 'r' in the third box, but before Tom could intervene she said, 'Oh no, it's an "e"' and changed it herself (Figure 4.4). Tom then scaffolded

Kayleigh's learning in a process to 'take this word to fluency' so she could write 'are' automatically in the future.

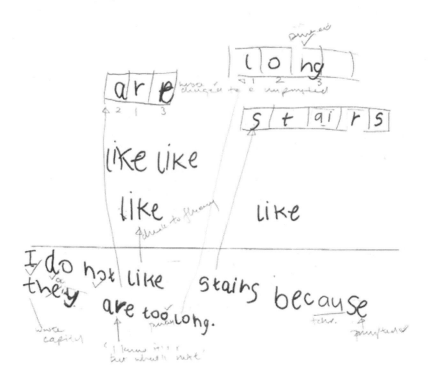

Figure 4.4: Tom working with Kayleigh

After the lesson Tom reflected on his teaching decisions and wondered whether Kayleigh had tapped into her partial recall of the visual image of a word she could read. The spelling boxes assisted her in recalling the sequence of letters. This small change in his practice seemed to have been effective for Kayleigh. However, it did not really address his greater concern about why the teachers in his group seemed reluctant to use this strategy in their teaching.

Gemma also continued to tussle with the spelling problem in her own teaching. Sarah, a Year 2 child, wanted to write 'its'. Drawing three boxes, Gemma explained clearly that she had drawn one for each letter. Sarah placed 'i' in the first box and began to write 's' in the second. Gemma intervened, asking 'Where will you need to write the "s"?' Sarah said the word again slowly, pointed to the third box and wrote the 's' in it. Then she looked at what she had written. 'Oh, I know,' she said and added a 't' to the middle box (Figure 4.5). By placing explicit focus on orthography at this point, Sarah was able to visualize the word she knew ('it'), which included the letter that had been hard to discern within the sounds ('iz') she heard herself say (Clay, 2005). For Gemma, this small incident was a turning point in her understanding – an example of generative learning in action.

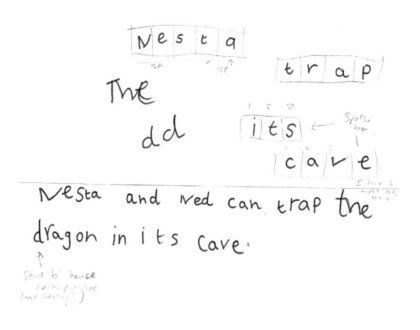

Figure 4.5: Gemma working with Sarah

These three Reading Recovery professionals, albeit with different experiences and working with different children, were puzzling over the same teaching and learning problem and coming to see the situation through a different lens. Franklin (2010a) posited that these small, seemingly insignificant teaching challenges can become what she termed focusing incidents. These focusing incidents trigger a reflective loop around theory, practice, and observation, with critical reflection operating at its hub. The potential is for reflective loops to contribute to the generative learning spiral curriculum. However, this cannot be assumed.

Cunningham (2008) warned of the inherent danger of reflective loops going round and round interminably with no spin-off into practice and learning. Simply reflecting upon an incident is not sufficient to elicit generative learning. Reflection may not lead to change and, even if it does, it may not necessarily be a change for the better. Moreover, there is the danger that reflection can lead to 'ego-damage' (ibid.: 171), which has the potential to close down the learning process (Franklin, 2010a). In their review of models of adult learning, Tusting and Barton (2003: 46) conclude: 'Reflective learning enables people to reorganize experience and "see" situations in new ways.' What Gemma, Tom, and Rachel had 'seen' and critiqued had offered new perspectives on teaching decisions. Previous approaches to teaching spelling had not offered the children an opportunity for independence nor for each child's generative learning to be developed.

Reflecting actively on their lessons, Gemma and Tom knew that there was more that could have been done to help the children they taught attend to unique features so that they could link it to something they already knew and begin to apply new knowledge independently in other situations. In this way the teaching and cycles of feedback enable children to develop learning that is generative, paralleling that of the professionals in Reading Recovery. The teacher's responsibility, therefore, is not solely to help the child get a particular word right in a particular instance. Rather, it is to strengthen that child's independent problem-solving capacity when encountering new learning in the future (Clay, 2005).

For Rachel, her experience of professional development, with critique of live lessons, discussion with colleagues, and support from her teacher leader, had not been sufficient to transform her practice to this level. Although Rachel did not overtly state her concerns, it is possible that at this point the model of professional development within which Reading Recovery operates was not yet accessible to her. Teacher leaders work to ensure that teachers are not led to over-dependence on the teaching procedures recommended in the course texts, and that they are given sufficient opportunity to critically analyse the praxis of literacy in Reading Recovery (Woods and Henderson, 2002). Rachel was facing an issue that challenged her previous understandings and beliefs about literacy learning. Although this can be uncomfortable for an experienced learner (Fullan *et al.*, 2005), resolving such discrepancies can lead to new learning (Cranton, 1996).

Professional development in Reading Recovery takes into account the responsibility of the individual learner for propelling their learning into new action (Franklin, 2010b). In a natural search for easy answers, there is a danger of inculcation that does not result in transformed practice or generative learning. While Tom and the other teachers in the group can discuss, observe, theorize, and challenge, ultimately it is Rachel herself who must be able to make 'an informed and reflective decision whether to act or not' and if so in which way (Mezirow, 2009: 22).

After the initial year of intensive professional development in Reading Recovery, Reading Recovery teachers not only continue with this professional development themselves but also provide it for others in their own contexts. One of the aims of the Every Child a Reader initiative is to explore the potential for Reading Recovery teachers to support tailored literacy teaching more broadly within a school, thus having an impact beyond those children receiving one-to-one support. The next section illustrates the professional development that Rachel provided for the school team at North Street Primary School. In particular we look at the support that Rachel gave to Sahira, one of the teaching assistants, as well as how action research, as professional development, supported the wider benefits to the whole school community.

Adaptive expertise

Adaptive expertise (Timperley, 2011) is the term used to explain how the principles of effective professional development in Reading Recovery are harnessed for the wider remit of Every Child a Reader. The Every Child a Reader concept of layers of intervention involves the Reading Recovery teacher working directly with the hardest-to-teach children but also using her continually developing expertise to support and mentor other personnel (professionals, para-professionals, and parents) to raise standards of literacy across a whole school. Often, it is teaching assistants who deliver lighter-touch interventions (see Table 2.3, p. 44). Despite Blatchford *et al.* (2009) noting the limited success of teaching assistants in supporting learning and raising standards in literacy, within Every Child a Reader there is evidence (Tanner *et al.*, 2011) to show that, through the principles of professional development redeveloped within Every Child a Reader, teaching assistants can also be empowered to transform, and become critically reflective of, their own practice. Through Every Child a Reader, the professional development of teaching assistants, of whole school teams, and of parental involvement becomes a more localized mechanism for effecting change depending on need (Bodman and Taylor, 2012). The next section explains how this worked in one local setting.

Tom works in a local authority with over 250 primary schools. Many of the children in the ambit of this authority are in the lowest 20 per cent in the UK who do not achieve appropriate levels of literacy by the age of 11. With only 40 trained Reading Recovery teachers, and with each teacher working with about eight children each year, it is not possible to make a significant impact on literacy outcomes for all. With Every Child a Reader, Tom helps the Reading Recovery teachers become literacy experts within their schools. This role entails supporting and advising on selecting the literacy interventions that will be most appropriate and have the greatest positive impact.

In some local authorities it is the Reading Recovery teacher leader who facilitates professional development for teaching assistants. But Tom does not have this capacity in such a large authority. To address this dilemma, Tom uses the living pyramid model of professional development where experienced Reading Recovery teachers such as Rachel are helped to gain further expertise to develop training for teaching assistants. This offers the potential for more children to benefit, resulting in a wider positive impact on literacy achievement within the local authority.

The living pyramid model

Reading Recovery professionals often refer to the three-tiered system of professional development outlined at the start of this chapter. Every Child a Reader created a fourth tier, expanding the professional development model to include another layer of support for personnel such as teaching assistants and volunteers, who are mentored by Reading Recovery teachers. Thus the number of children who benefit from the expertise of Every Child a Reader teachers is increased. The next part of this chapter explains how the living pyramid model worked in Tom's context.

Tom trained as a facilitator for three of the lighter-touch interventions described in Chapter 2: Better Reading Partnership, Fischer Family Trust Wave 3, and Talking Partners. This training helped Tom gain a view of how to respond to learners' broader needs, allowing him to give better support to Rachel and his other Reading Recovery teachers.

National trainers of these lighter-touch interventions work closely with Gemma at the European Centre for Reading Recovery. At first Tom piloted the living pyramid model with one of these interventions, Fischer Family Trust Wave 3. This allowed him to set up an infrastructure for eventually implementing other lighter-touch interventions. Fischer Family Trust Wave 3 is based on Reading Recovery principles. It is delivered by experienced teaching assistants who work one-to-one with Year 1 or Year 2 children for 15 to 20 minutes a day over 10 to 20 weeks. The intervention is targeted at children who need individual support but who are not in the bottom 5 per cent, unlike those identified as needing Reading Recovery. The national trainer for Fischer Family Trust Wave 3 trained 20 of Tom's Reading Recovery teachers, including Rachel, to become trainers of teaching assistants for this intervention. The training consisted of three days of professional development based on the underlying principles of Reading Recovery professional development, with strong theory–practice links. Afterwards, the Reading Recovery teachers formed local clusters to work together to deliver professional development in local venues. The 20 teachers worked in groups of four, in five venues spread across the local authority. During the autumn term each venue invited 15 schools to send teaching assistants for professional development. By the end of that term, 75 more schools were involved. That meant 75 more teaching assistants each working with at least two children; approximately 150 more children were benefiting from the expertise of Rachel and her teacher colleagues. During the spring term, more training took place, expanding the expertise and increasing the numbers of children reached exponentially.

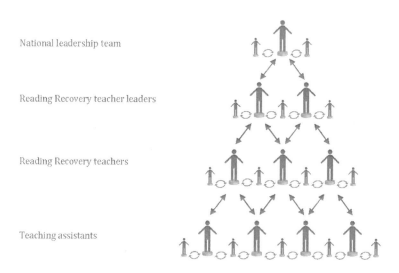

National leadership team

Reading Recovery teacher leaders

Reading Recovery teachers

Teaching assistants

Figure 4.6: A living pyramid model of professional development

Rachel, with three other Reading Recovery teachers, then facilitated three days training to 15 teaching assistants from nearby schools. She also visited four teaching assistants in their own school contexts immediately after the training. During these visits she helped them analyse assessment data and plan individual programmes for each child. Later that term, Rachel again visited each of the four teaching assistants that she was mentoring to observe their lessons and provide feedback cycles to support their teaching and learning (Bodman, 2006).

Rachel also worked collaboratively with her three colleagues to plan and prepare continuing professional development for the teaching assistants. In the same way as teachers' and teacher-leaders' learning is never finished (Lyons *et al.*, 1993), neither is it for the teaching assistants within this model of supporting generative learning. These sessions were held locally on a half-termly basis and were planned to ensure fidelity to the programme (Rose, 2006) and to maintain its efficacy. Engaging in regular professional development supports professionals at every level to keep up to date with their knowledge and pedagogical skills and demonstrates a commitment to learning (Harris, 2005). The teaching assistants preferred professional development in local venues. Tom was able to provide this as he had organized his team of expert teachers to support professional development across the authority.

Sahira, an experienced teaching assistant who works at North Street Primary School, attended three days of professional development. Rachel supported Sahira to assess and select the children who would benefit most from the Fischer Family Trust Wave 3 intervention. Targeting the right intervention for the child is a key concept of Every Child a Reader (European Centre for Reading Recovery, 2012). Once children had been selected, Rachel worked with Sahira to analyse assessment data and plan individual programmes for each child.

Sahira had worked for many years with children who struggle in literacy but had had little previous professional development to support her in her work. The professional development provided by Rachel was a transforming experience for Sahira (Mezirow, 2000). Previously, the interventions Sahira had delivered were scripted but now Sahira found that she was empowered to offer flexible teaching. She was experiencing a greater sense of 'preparedness' (Blatchford *et al.*, 2009). Sahira noted that 'for the first time in my work as a teaching assistant I was beginning to know what to do with the children I work with'.

On her second visit to observe Sahira teaching George, a Year 1 pupil, Rachel noticed that Sahira's practice had changed from emphasizing lists of words to be learnt and spelt correctly to supporting George towards independently developing ways of solving words he will need to use in the future. Clay (2001) refers to an additive model of learning, in which credit is given for numbers of words learnt, and a transformative model, in which the pay-off is greater as learning is more generative. Sahira saw the link between George's progress and the professional development and support through feedback cycles that she had received. Rachel also attributed George's progress to Sahira's greater flexibility and preparedness. For a number of years, Sahira had 'worked with children like George without having the subject knowledge, skills, and confidence to know what to do'. This awareness reinforced her transformation, indicating that she was developing further expertise.

The living-pyramid model of professional development adopted in Every Child a Reader has meant that more children in Tom's local authority have benefited exponentially from the expertise of Reading Recovery teachers.

However, those pressures mentioned earlier meant that not all teacher leaders had the time, support, or local infrastructure to implement the other layers of intervention in their areas. Therefore the potential for change and for making a wider impact on children's literacy was being lost.

Experiencing a model of professional development that interwove theory and practice had prompted Sahira to critically reflect not only on what she was doing but why (Williams, 2001). For Sahira, the scripted interventions that she had previously delivered felt like having a doctor's bag without knowing how to use it, but with Rachel's expertise and ongoing mentoring she felt empowered to give the right level of support to the children she worked with. As Sahira explained, 'I now ... know more than just what to do, I know why I am doing what I do'.

Timperley (2011) refers to this as the difference between using routine expertise – learning how to apply a core set of skills – and adaptive expertise – identifying where known routines do not work and being flexible enough to adapt and seek new approaches.

To evaluate the effectiveness of the professional development of teaching assistants, Tom collected data on the progress of children who received the intervention. He found that, whereas children in Reading Recovery as expected made four times the average rate of progress, children who received the lighter-touch intervention made twice the rate of progress, which was appropriate as these children had less ground to make up (Ferris, 2008; Brooks, 2007, 2013).

The aim of any intervention should be to raise children up to the standard expected for their age (Brooks, 2007, 2013). However, it was not only the layers of intervention that supported children's progress but also the whole school's commitment to a process of change, with shared goals and shared desire for continued professional development and problem-solving for teaching and learning (see Chapter 5).

Action research as professional development

Rachel had continued to develop her expertise through continued learning from teaching and from ongoing professional development. She valued the role of problem-solving in learning and, as part of her Every Child a Reader role, took a further opportunity, through action research, to make a positive impact on progress across the school community. Tom, having undertaken extended professional development by the leadership team at the European Centre for Reading Recovery, was supported by Gemma and members of the National Literacy Strategy to facilitate an MA-level module delivered within the local authority. Known as RRiPLLe (Reading Recovery in Primary

Literacy Leadership) and reflecting the wider benefits of Every Child a Reader, this module was the vehicle for engaging in a school-based action research project (see Appendix 4). Tom formed an action research group in his region, drawing on local literacy leadership expertise in his locality, with the added benefit of local regional ownership of the change process (Reason and Bradbury, 2006; Wilson, 2009).

In support of the action research project, capacity-building for whole school teams was improved by professional development sessions throughout the year. In conducting a needs analysis across the school as a preliminary to planning her action research, Rachel had a pretext for talking to many school staff, and others involved in school, soliciting their views on literacy. Through this she was able to identify key collaborators in her school team, and develop shared ownership of the change initiative. By gaining management support, Rachel enabled school teams to see the potential of using her in this way as a change agent (Fullan, 2001).

The headteacher of North Street Primary School said: 'For the first time in all my years as a headteacher I can go to my governing body and tell them this is what we spent and we have the data to show exactly what we have for our money!'

Summary

In this chapter we have argued that a goal for professional development intended to bring about positive changes requires that generative professional learning be the expected outcome for participants. This is also economically efficient because of its self-perpetuation of attention to further improvements. We have described and shown through case studies how the professional development model in Reading Recovery supports generative learning through continued integration of theory and practice, and cycles of assessment and feedback within its unique curriculum design. The 'practice' is the seminal role of teaching children for learning at every 'tier': in short, experts gain expertise through opportunities to develop generative learning with individual and group engagement towards critical reflection and improved practice. We have shown how adopting a living pyramid model through Every Child a Reader with the pivotal role of Reading Recovery provides the structure, theoretical grounding, ongoing commitment, and support for individual and organizational improvement. This professional model with its integral quality assurance processes has had a positive impact on many lives (see Table 2.4, p. 52) and in many contexts.

Chapter 5 builds on this responsive concept of the role played by professional development in school improvement. It considers the importance of capacity-building across Reading Recovery and Every Child a Reader professionals in the effective scaling up of Reading Recovery early literacy intervention into Every Child a Reader.

Notes
[1] All names are fictitious. Vignettes and quotes express the thoughts and perceptions expressed by Every Child a Reader professionals.

References

Blatchford, P., Bassett, P., Brown, P., Koutsoubou, M., Martin, C., Russell, A., and Webster, R., with Rubie-Davies, C. (2009) *Deployment and Impact of Support Staff in Schools*. London: DCSF.

Bodman, S. (2006) 'The Power of Feedback in Professional Learning'. Unpublished EdD thesis, Institute of Education, University of London.

Bodman, S. and Taylor, S. (2010) 'Developing generative learning: Spirals of action and assessment'. Paper presented at the TARC International Conference on Learning and Teaching, Malaysia, October.

Bodman, S. and Taylor, S. (2012). 'Every Child a Reader: A local mechanism for raising literacy standards'. Paper presented at A Child's World Conference, University of Aberystwyth, June.

Brookfield, S.D. (1986) *Understanding and Facilitating Adult Learning*. Milton Keynes: Open University Press.

Brooks, G. (2007) *What works for Pupils with Literacy Difficulties? The effectiveness of intervention schemes*. Sheffield: Department of Children, Schools, and Families: 294.

– (2013) *What Works for Children and Young People with Literacy Difficulties? The Effectiveness of Intervention Schemes*. 4th edition. Bracknell: Dyslexia-SpLD Trust.

Bruner, J. (1996) *The Culture of Education*. Cambridge, MA: Harvard University Press.

Cain, K. (2010)*Reading Development and Difficulties*. Oxford: Wiley-Blackwell.

Clay, M.M. (2001) *Change Over Time in Children's Literacy Development*. Portsmouth, NH: Heinemann.

– (2005) *Literacy Lessons Designed for Individuals. Part One: Why? When? And How? (LLDfL, Part 1)*. Portsmouth, NH: Heinemann.

Cranton, P. (1996) *Professional Development as Transformative Learning: New perspectives for teachers of adults*. San Francisco: Jossey-Bass.

Cunningham, B. (2008) 'Critical incidents in professional life and learning'. In B. Cunningham (ed.), *Exploring Professionalism*, 116–89. London: Institute of Education, University of London.

European Centre for Reading Recovery (2011) *Standards and Guidelines*. London: ECRR, Institute of Education, University of London.

– (2012) *Every Child a Reader (ECaR) Annual Report 2010–11*. London: ECRR, Institute of Education, University of London.

Eysenck, M.W. and Keane, M. (2000) *Cognitive Psychology: A student's handbook*. Hove: Psychology Press.

Ferris, J. (2008) 'Adapting and evaluating a professional development model to meet the needs of teaching assistants delivering a one-to-one early literacy intervention'. Unpublished report submitted as part of MA: Literacy Learning and Literacy Difficulties. London: Institute of Education, University of London.

Franklin, G.C. (2010a) 'From Looking to Seeing to Learning: An exploration of how the challenge of teaching children might provide Reading Recovery Trainers with a focusing lens for critical reflection and thus promote transformative learning.' Unpublished assignment submitted as part of EdD (International). London: Institute of Education, University of London.

– (2010b) 'The Responsive Professional: The challenge to the individual learner in the collegiate approach to professional development in the Reading Recovery Teacher Leader training programme in England'. Unpublished assignment submitted as part of EdD (International). London: Institute of Education, University of London.

Fullan, M. (2001, 3rd ed.) *The New Meaning of Educational Change*. London: RoutledgeFalmer

Fullan, M., Cuttress, C., and Kilcher, A. (2005) 'Forces for leaders of change'. *Journal of Staff Development*, 26 (4), 54–64.

Gardiner, J.M. (1989) 'A generation effect in memory without awareness', *British Journal of Psychology*, 80 (2), 163–8.

Harris, A. (2005) *Improving Schools through Teacher Leadership*. New York: Open University Press.

Kroll, L.R. (2004) 'Constructing constructivism: How student-teachers construct ideas of development, knowledge, learning and teaching'. *Teachers and Teaching*, 10 (2), 199–213.

Lyons, C.A., Pinnell, G.S., and DeFord, D.E. (1993) *Partners in Learning Teachers and Children in Reading Recovery*. New York: Teachers College Press.

Mercer, N. (1995) *The Guided Construction of Knowledge: Talk amongst teachers and learners*. Clevedon: Multilingual Matters Ltd.

Mezirow, J. (1997) 'Transformative learning: Theory to practice', in P. Cranton (ed.) *Transformative Learning in Action: Insights from practice. New directions for adult and continuing education*, 74, 5–12. San Francisco: Jossey-Bass.

Mezirow, J. (2009) 'Transformative learning theory', in J. Mezirow, E.W. Taylor and associates, *Transformative Learning in Practice: Insights from Community, Workplace and Higher Education*, 18-31. San Francisco, Jossey-Bass.

Mezirow, J. and associates (2000). *Learning as Transformation: Critical perspectives on a theory in progress*. San Francisco: Jossey-Bass.

Moore, P. (1997) 'Models of Teacher Education: Where Reading Recovery teacher training fits'. Online. www.readingrecovery.org/development/archives/moore.asp (accessed 18 February 2010).

Perkins, D. (2006) 'Constructivism and troublesome knowledge'. In J.H.F. Meyer and R. Land (eds), *Overcoming Barriers to Student Understanding: Threshold concepts and troublesome knowledge*. Abingdon: RoutledgeFalmer.

Pinnell, G.S. (1997) 'An inquiry-based model for educating teachers of literacy'. In S. Swartz and A.F. Klein (eds.), *Research in Reading Recovery*. Portsmouth, NH: Heinemann.

Reason, P. and Bradbury, H. (eds) (2006) *Handbook of Action Research*. London: Sage.

Rose, J. (2006) *Independent Review of the Teaching of Early Reading: report.* Nottingham: DfES.

Schmitt, M.C., Askew, B., Fountas, I., Lyons, C., and Pinnell, G. (2005) *Changing Futures: The influence of Reading Recovery in the United States.* Worthington, Ohio: Reading Recovery Council of North America.

Tanner, E., Brown, A., Day, N., Kotecha, M., Low, N., Morrell, G., Turczuk, O., Brown, V., and Collingwood A. (2011) *Evaluation of Every Child Reader.* London: DfE.

Taylor, S. (2003) '"From Teacher to Tutor": A Critical Case Study in Re-structuring Professional Identity and Learning', Unpublished IOE focused study as part of EdD programme. London: Institute of Education, University of London.

– (2006) 'An Advanced Professional Development Curriculum for Developing Deep Learning', Unpublished EdD Thesis. Institute of Education, University of London.

–. (2010) MA: Literacy Learning and Literacy Difficulties, programme handbook 2010–11.

– (2012) 'A spiral curriculum to develop generative learners'. Paper presented at the eighth International Conference of Education, Institute of the Eastern Aegean with the University of Athens, Samos, Greece, July.

Taylor, S. and Bodman, S. (2012) '"I've never been asked that before!" Preparing Teachers for any eventuality?' In O.S. Tan (ed.), *Teacher Education Frontiers: International perspectives on policy and practice for building new teacher competencies.* Singapore: Cengage Learning Asia Pte Ltd.

Taylor, S. and Ince, A. (2012) 'Towards critical reflection to develop generative learners: The use of cognitive dissonance in effective professional learning'. Paper presented at the eighth International Conference of Education, Institute of the Eastern Aegean with the University of Athens, Samos, Greece, July.

Timperley, H. (2011) *Realising the Power of Professional Learning.* New York: Open University Press.

Tusting, K. and Barton, D. (2003) *Models of Adult Learning: A literature review.* London: NIACE.

Vygotsky, L. (1986) *Thought and Language.* Cambridge, MA: MIT Press.

Wells, G. (1999) *Dialogic Inquiry: Toward a sociocultural practice and theory of education.* Cambridge: Cambridge University Press.

Williams, B. (2001) 'Developing critical reflection for professional practice through problem-based learning'. *Journal of Advanced Nursing*, 34 (1), 27–34.

Wilson, E. (ed.) (2009) *School-based Research: A guide for education students.* London: Sage.

Wittrock, M.C. (1990) 'Generative processes of comprehension'. *Educational Psychologist*, 24 (4), 345–76.

– (1992) 'Generative learning processes of the brain'. *Educational Psychologist*, 27 (4), 531–41.

Wood, D. (1998, 2nd ed.) *How Children Think and Learn: The social contexts of cognitive development.* Oxford: Blackwell.

Woods, A. and Henderson, R. (2002) 'Early intervention: Narratives of learning, discipline and enculturation'. *Journal of Early Childhood Literacy*, 2 (3), 243–68.

Chapter 5

Creatively responding to the imperative of scaling up Every Child a Reader

Penny Amott, Val Hindmarsh, and Helen Morris

Introduction

By the end of the pilot (2005–08) the scope and focus of Every Child a Reader (ECaR) had expanded rapidly. Over the next three years, following an injection of government funding and in collaborative leadership with the National Strategies, 139 English local authorities (LAs) and 2,427 schools became involved, providing direct intervention for 28,123 children, close to the goal of reaching 30,000 children targeted as at risk of attaining below National Curriculum Level 2 (age appropriate) at the end of Key Stage 1 (age 7).

Education systems are dynamic, with constant change, influenced by policy, by social or economic drivers, and by research. When research indicates robust outcomes of particular approaches, the biggest challenge is to scale them up while maintaining fidelity to the principles that contributed to their success on a smaller scale. Political interest in reform is being driven by the emergence of a globalized economy and by the impact and demands of the information society (Drucker, 1994). With considerable pressure on national economies, an additional challenge is the need to ensure that improvements are also cost-effective.

Large-scale reform in education, usually focusing on the achievement of universal literacy and numeracy, became an aspiration in English-speaking countries with large populations as education took political centre stage in the 1990s (Fullan *et al.*, 2001a). Enacted at national, state/provincial, local authority/school district, or individual school levels, such reform is designed to bring about 'shifts in structural, financial or organisational dimensions of schooling' (Earl *et al.*, 2003: 6). Reform is generally 'directed at changing classroom practice and pupil learning in a myriad of ways that involve new learning and behaviours for the majority of teachers' (ibid.: 7), although teachers and pupils often have very little control over the reform process itself (Moss, 2009: 156).

An early large-scale reform was the National Curriculum, introduced as a result of the Education Reform Act of 1988. In England it was followed by the National Literacy Strategy and National Numeracy Strategy, 'top-down' initiatives with a brief to raise achievement. Alongside these reforms in the 1990s, other statutory reforms were introduced: national testing provided a means of measuring pupil performance and a greatly expanded inspection system raised the profile of accountability, using both pupil outcomes and teacher performance measures to evaluate and compare schools. Interaction between the educational goals of developing the curriculum and the policy goals of raising attainment and improving delivery provided the context for the implementation of Every Child a Reader. Policy at the time aimed for improvements in society driven by education, creating the demand for coherent intervention for pupils deemed to be falling behind; this was an opportunity for Reading Recovery to be scaled up so as to have a wider impact. Strong ideological and financial backing for its expansion came from the New Labour government. However, such backing could be at risk of causing the distorting effects that result from tying professional practice too closely to a political agenda, so making meaningful reform less likely (Moss, 2009: 171). Creating conceptual reform in a context of growing accountability required creativity and determination. 'Scaling up', or scalability, is the mechanism by which an externally developed design for school restructuring, which has been successful in a small number of school settings, can expand to be applied to many (Stringfield and Datnow, 1998: 271). Scaling up using this expansion and replication approach is based on a rational argument and view of change; however, in the real world of schools, reforms may fail to function as expected since schools are 'complex organisations embedded in a disorderly environment of multiple and often conflicting pressures and expectations' (Hargreaves and Hopkins, 1991: 8).

In this chapter we examine the scaling up of Every Child a Reader in England, using principles from research into educational system change as a theoretical framework. We discuss responses to the challenge of maintaining and enhancing quality, and of working innovatively with a range of partners while simultaneously undergoing rapid expansion. We draw on key documents and data, including perspectives gathered from a representative range of stakeholders during interviews[1] with participants who were selected as representative of others in similar positions and across the range of roles in Every Child a Reader. They include Reading Recovery national leaders, teacher leaders, local authority link managers, and teachers, along with key personnel from the Primary National Strategy and national intervention leaders. We have used their own names here (with permission).

This qualitative approach was deliberately taken so as to present Every Child a Reader in ways that resonate with the experience of other participants; however, we also draw on national and local reports and on the Department for Education's evaluation of the initiative (2011), which employed a more quantitative approach. We also present vignettes (drawn from interviews and case studies) exemplifying how Every Child a Reader was enacted in a school and in local authorities, and we use these as illustrations on which to base our discussion. It may be important to note that interviews took place at a key point, when Every Child a Reader was at a peak in its growth (autumn 2011) and in the context of political change and of an economic climate likely to present new challenges for sustainability. In the conclusion to this chapter, we review factors contributing to and impeding the maintenance and growth of Every Child a Reader, and propose principles that may inform the scaling up of other educational reform initiatives.

Background

Following the pilot phase of Every Child a Reader (2005–8), there was an exponential rise in the numbers of pupils and schools served, and of teacher leaders and teachers trained. Through the rollout (2008–11), the number of pupils reached by Every Child a Reader continued to grow, with a parallel increase in teachers and teacher leaders undertaking Reading Recovery professional development (Table 5.1).

Table 5.1: The growth of Every Child a Reader from 2005 to 2011

	ECaR pilot phase			ECaR rollout phase		
	Year 1 05–06	Year 2 06–07	Year 3 07–08	Year 4 08–09	Year 5 09–10	Year 6 10–11
Local authorities	26	26	31	107	128	139
RR teacher leaders	24	28	42	52	86	101
Schools	61	236	489	1,149	1,656	2,427
RR teachers	73	249	520	1,183	1,750	2,493
RR pupils	542	1,838	5,276	9,610	14,918	21,038
Pupils in linked interventions	Data not collected			3,400	8,208	7,085

In addition to Reading Recovery teachers and teacher leaders who led the innovation in schools and local authorities, large numbers of teaching assistants were involved in delivering associated interventions such as Better Reading Partnership,[2] Fischer Family Trust Wave 3,[3] and Talking Partners.[4] Link teachers in schools supported the development of a coherent approach to assessment, teaching, and mapped provision of literacy intervention. Headteachers committed their schools to professional development and intervention provision. Eventually, Every Child a Reader was available to all English local authorities and many took up the opportunity.

Figure 5.1 shows the geographical spread of Every Child a Reader throughout England by 2010–11. Percentages indicate the proportion of schools implementing the programme in each local authority.

Figure 5.1: The spread of Every Child a Reader in England in 2010–11. Detail: Greater London. These images are based on data provided through EDINA UKBORDERS with the support of the ESRC and JISC, and use boundary material which is copyright of the Crown, the Post Office, and the ED-LINE Consortium.

Growth concerns a system's capacity to accept increased volume without negatively impacting on that system's integrity or outcomes. In the case of Every

Child a Reader, this process of scaling up involved reaching larger numbers of the target group (the lowest-attaining children) in a broader geographical area (across England in areas already served by Reading Recovery, and in local authorities with no prior Reading Recovery implementation). This was achieved by adapting the concept and expanding the remit of an already effective programme: 13 years of evaluation and data generation from those children in the UK that were the hardest to teach had demonstrated that Reading Recovery could achieve consistent success with this constituency (Douëtil, 2005).

A conceptual reform

Many large-scale reforms rely on linear approaches (Moss, 2009: 157). Research influences the initial design (Coburn and Stein, 2010) but, once a programme has been developed and trialled, the goal of expansion is met through replication (Figure 5.2). 'Practical tools' such as work schemes and lesson plans are used to alter classroom practice as a means of shifting practitioners' thinking, relying on dissemination and privileging a 'breadth' notion of scale, that is, the number of teachers 'adopting' the approach (ibid.). The assumption is that transferring the right knowledge to the right place will alter practice and therefore outcomes (Taylor *et al.*, 1997, in Moss, 2009), downplaying the role of deep professional learning and teacher agency.

Figure 5.2: A linear relationship between research and practice (based on Coburn and Stein, 2010: 5). Reproduced by kind permission of Rowman & Littlefield.

Achieving consistency and fidelity is a continual challenge to such reforms as they are scaled up, giving rise to accountability processes that do not successfully drive reforms (Fullan, 2011). The approach followed by Every Child a Reader relied more strongly on what Fullan (ibid.) proposed as the 'right drivers': capacity-building, collaboration, a focus on pedagogy, and the development of a whole system, noting that they are effective because they work directly on changing a culture (values, norms, skill, practices, relationships). 'By contrast, the wrong drivers alter structure, procedures and other formal attributes of the system without reaching the internal substance of the reform – and that is why they fail' (ibid.: 5).

 'Practical tools' in Every Child a Reader play a limited role. Research-based professional development offered practitioners opportunities to inform and shape the initiative and draw in the evidence of their experience of practice. This approach aligns closely with Coburn and Stein's second paradigm, taking into account the learning that practitioners undertake as they enact the innovation (see Figure 5.3). It is a *conceptual* model, focusing on shifting teachers' cognitions and increasing their knowledge, and so enabling them to make responsive, practical decisions day by day (ibid.).

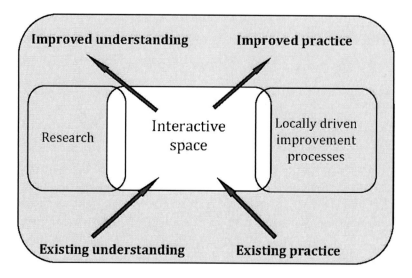

Figure 5.3: How research-based conceptual understanding comes together with practical knowledge and experience in an interactive space (based on Coburn and Stein, 2010: 8). Reproduced by kind permission of Rowman & Littlefield.

Scaling up is acknowledged to be daunting and complex: often being underestimated, the co-constructed nature of an implementation process is a common reason for its lack of success (Datnow *et al.*, 2002). As it was rolled out, Every Child a Reader evolved, as a balance between research-informed practice and practitioners' experience, and as local knowledge was sought and was fed into the scheme's ongoing development. Since educational change tends to 'unfold in unpredictable and non-linear ways through the interaction of individuals in different settings and conditions of uncertainty, diversity, and instability' (ibid.: 11), successful reforms include the contributions and responses of participants. Every Child a Reader has operated largely as a conceptually based reform in both the teaching and leadership strands, which were critical to successful scaling up: A communicative space developed where practice and research interact, leading to evaluation for constant improvement and development rather than reliance on a set scheme. At the heart of this approach are integrated local, national, and international communities of practice around intervention and early literacy provision.

Dimensions of scale in educational reform

Four critical dimensions of scale – depth, sustainability, spread, and transfer of ownership (Coburn, 2003) – draw together key concepts from the research canon on school improvement. In this chapter, those dimensions will be used to examine the scaling up of Every Child a Reader.

Depth

The depth of a reform is indicated by stakeholders' understanding and enactment of its core principles. In the history of large-scale interventions, 'deep learning', or being 'able to articulate both what they [leaders or teachers] do and why they do it' (Hill and Crévola, 1999, cited in Fullan *et al.*, 2006), seems to have been a significant factor contributing to success and known to be associated with pupils' increased attainment (Earl *et al.*, 2003). Continuing professional development is central to depth and to maintaining fidelity as the innovation spreads to more settings.

Sustainability

Sustainability relies on the potential for flexibility and adaptation within the reform, made possible through *depth* of conceptual understanding (Coburn, 2003). Despite early positive outcomes in 'adoption' (linear) models, success is unlikely to be sustained without the additional 'deep cultural change required for continuous improvement' (Fullan, 2001: 1). Sustainability is closely aligned with depth. The potential for sustainability is a factor in generating early commitment and resourcing for an innovation, with strong evidence acting as proof of concept. Sustainability is also an outcome as reform moves to scale.

Spread

Spread is apparent in wider adoption of the reform, and more importantly it is reflected in the spread of principles within a school, class, or district (Coburn, 2003). It relies on communication and reception of the concepts underlying the innovation, and on creating conditions for growth through resourcing. Lateral interactions support spread (sharing best practice across consortia or school clusters, or developing local leadership training) as participants use and develop tools for self-review, data-gathering, and analysis to inform further development. Spread of an innovation can pose risks for fidelity to core principles that had contributed to success in the small scale. However, depth of conceptual understanding and effective preparation of participants can guard against this.

Transfer of ownership

Transfer of ownership is critical, enabling the 'knowledge and authority' of a reform to be successfully shifted to the level of teachers and schools, contributing to sustainability and further spread (Coburn, 2003). Thus there is a prerequisite to prepare professionals by giving them an array of skills (leadership, administrative, and educative), which enable them to lead the scaling-up efforts. This is essential to ensuring that the innovation fulfils its goals. Transparency, greater involvement, modelling, and capacity-building are key features of leaders seeking to assist others in large-scale reform (Fullan, 2001). Although each dimension offers a discrete lens through which change and scaling up can be viewed, these dimensions are closely interrelated (Figure 5.4).

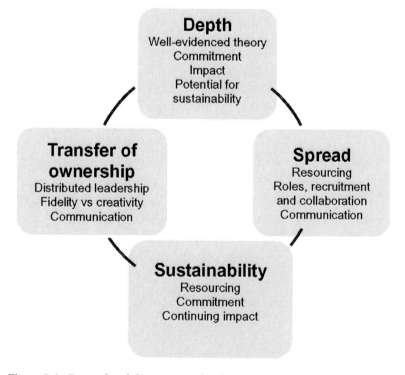

Figure 5.4: Four related dimensions of scaling-up reform
(developed from Coburn, 2003). Reproduced by
kind permission of Rowman & Littlefield.

Depth of conceptual understanding of a reform and its relevance to the needs of its stakeholders affects potential for sustainability. Conceptual understanding contributes to fidelity as ownership is transferred outwards from the centre. Likewise, ownership contributes to sustainability as well as spread, when practice is shared. Preparing leaders at every level with deep theoretical understanding impacts on commitment to sustain the innovation, while sharing good practice and positive outcomes contributes to spread of innovation.

Having examined our interview and documentary data through these four dimensions, we found some stronger connections between the concepts and practices that exemplified these dimensions. All four are related:

- *Depth* and *sustainability* are mainly characterized by the concepts and goals of scaling up.
- *Spread* and *transfer of ownership* largely relate to the process of scaling up involving additional settings and participants.

We now use these related dimensions to examine the growth of Every Child a Reader, beginning with the challenges and successes of creating and sustaining deep conceptual response to the reform.

Scaling up Every Child a Reader: Depth and potential for sustainability

Going beyond surface structures and processes, deep change alters stakeholders' beliefs, norms, and pedagogical principles to establish long-term, dependable impact (Coburn, 2003). Sustainability arises from the capacity to 'evolve to incorporate improvements, respond to new data, and yet remain consistent with the underlying principles' (Earl *et al.*, 2003: 6). It is directly linked to depth and 'may be the central challenge of bringing reforms to scale' (Coburn, 2003: 6). Short-term results are necessary to convince politicians and budget-holders of the efficacy of an innovation, but thorough groundwork must be laid down for sustained engagement. Barber (2004: 2) suggests creating

> a virtuous circle where public education delivers results, the public gains confidence and is therefore willing to invest through taxation and as a consequence the system is able to improve further. It is for this reason that the long-term strategy requires short-term results.

Where complexity such as that involved in Every Child a Reader exists (large pupil numbers, professional development to a greater depth and on a larger scale, and communication among many stakeholders) and where it is politically expedient to garner rapid success through short-term gains, pressure on the reform is considerably increased: 'The goal is not simply change, but lasting change' (Coburn, 2003: 1). Shifting or opposing political expectations, adjustments in key personnel, alterations to funding arrangements, and competing initiatives, as well as the pace of growth of the innovation itself, and the imperative to sustain high-quality outcomes – each of these poses a challenge to sustainability. Achieving both depth and sustainability is vital to successful reform, and those dimensions in Every Child a Reader are explored here through four themes:

(i)   strength and clarity of the theoretical model

(ii)   balancing fidelity and creativity

(iii)   evidence of impact

(iv)   commitment.

(i)   Strength and clarity of the theoretical model

A key factor in sustaining Every Child a Reader as one solution to the under-attainment of literacy is its nature as a principle-based reform with the moral imperative that every child has the right to literacy (UNESCO, 2010). Its outcomes demonstrate consistently high levels of success in meeting that goal. Figure 5.5 indicates the steady improvement in the Key Stage 1 SATs of all pupils in Every Child a Reader schools compared to all pupils in schools not involved in the programme. The latter schools had reached a plateau at 74 per cent in each year, when Every Child a Reader schools had year-on-year improvement from 60 per cent to 69 per cent, demonstrating the wider impact of the approach beyond those children accessing intervention programmes. During the rollout, Every Child a Reader schools were those specifically targeted by the Primary National Strategy due to their persistently poor outcomes. Thus their starting points differed considerably from those of non-Every Child a Reader schools.

Every Child a Reader could develop responsively and flexibly because of the intensity of the Reading Recovery professional development model and a shared understanding of intrinsic core principles among most stakeholders.

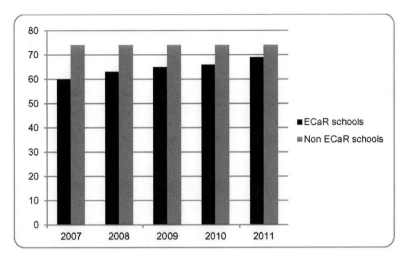

Figure 5.5: Reading outcomes at Level 2b+, comparing all schools with Every Child a Reader and all non-Every Child a Reader schools (DfE)

PROFESSIONAL LEARNING: TEACHER LEADERS

'Deep learning' is associated with increased pupil attainment (Earl *et al.*, 2003) and is achieved only through continuing professional development appropriate to the constituency and the challenge. Of the trainee teacher leaders taking the Reading Recovery teacher leader professional master's degree course at the Institute of Education, University of London, 100 per cent reported on the thoroughness of their preparation (DfE, 2011). Reflecting on the year of professional development, Alison,[5] commented: 'The inquiry model has enabled me to construct deeper knowledge and understanding of literacy learning.' Extending the theme, Rosina[6] considered that the course 'was geared towards developing flexibility, tentativeness of thought, and independence as a teacher leader, but ultimately as an independent learner'. Although the overwhelming response of teacher leaders to the Reading Recovery aspect of their professional development was favourable, some teacher leaders participating in the Every Child a Reader pilot considered themselves to be less well prepared for the wider role of Every Child a Reader itself (ibid.). In subsequent years, Reading Recovery national leaders addressed this issue by placing greater emphasis on the wider school improvement role during initial teacher-leader preparation and shaping continuing professional development to address these learning needs. All teacher leaders were offered training to implement the wider intervention programmes – Better Reading Partnership, Fischer Family Trust Wave 3, and Talking Partners (see Chapter 2).

PROFESSIONAL LEARNING: TEACHERS

The professional development programme for Reading Recovery teachers is similarly 'highly regarded' by '97 per cent of teachers' (DfE, 2011: 89), though the evaluation found that 'some teachers did not perceive that they had [been] adequately prepared ... to support the development of whole school literacy practice' (ibid.: 86). Measures put in place to address this apparent need (see above) included support for teacher leaders to focus more on this aspect of professional preparation when working with their teachers directly and through national biennial conferences at the Institute of Education. Greater emphasis was placed on provision mapping, monitoring intervention, and closer collaboration with class teachers and parents. Most Reading Recovery teachers have developed specific expertise in their roles, as Judith,[7] a local authority line manager notes: '[they are] expert practitioners, a home grown expert; they know, they will understand, they will be able to help wherever the child is in the reading journey.' The differing experience of the wider role may be due as much to individual practitioners' knowledge, skills, and credibility in their professional contexts as to the professional development received. While deep understanding of Reading Recovery's rationales and underpinning theory contributed to the preparation of most practitioners, the newer concept of Every Child a Reader was still being developed and may thus have been less easy to 'own' at the pace required to scale up.

PROFESSIONAL LEARNING: TEACHING ASSISTANTS

While the core intervention, Reading Recovery, must be led by a trained teacher, the linked interventions are designed to be delivered by teaching assistants. In a large-scale study, Blatchford *et al.* (2009) found that teaching assistants may have a negative impact on pupil outcomes if they are given insufficient support and development. However, a positive outcome of Every Child a Reader was the quality of professional development received by teaching assistants, better preparing them to lead literacy interventions and improving the quality of their contribution to classroom support as evidenced through pupil outcomes. The professional development approaches in the teaching assistant-led interventions are aligned with the Vygotskian principles within Reading Recovery professional development: 'Talking Partners uses direct observation to develop critical reflection and a spiral approach to learning by revisiting, consolidating, and extending key concepts' (Clare[8]). Better Reading Partnership and Fischer Family Trust Wave 3 were both developed by teacher leaders drawing on Reading Recovery principles with a goal of meeting the needs of pupils who could not access or did not need a teacher-led intervention.

An initial evaluation of Fischer Family Trust Wave 3 (Fischer Family Trust, 2004) reported positive outcomes, but highlighted that 'the knowledge and experience of both teaching assistant and the supporting teacher are critical factors. The programmes that were overseen by Reading Recovery teachers showed greater gains in book levels and writing vocabulary' (ibid.). A further evaluation (ibid., 2009) included reflections from teaching assistants concerning the transfer of their learning from the intervention into work with other children. Clare describes a similar impact on teaching-assistant professional development in the Talking Partners intervention: 'TAs [teaching assistants] become reflective practitioners with improved understanding of how children learn.' Through their work with children in interventions, many teaching assistants also develop a keener awareness of the ways that pupil data are used to track attainment and how the outcomes from interventions contribute to the wider picture. The extent of the impact of their work on pupil outcomes is affected by how well their teaching is monitored and supported, and is thus dependent on a school's leadership and on its commitment to developing the mentoring role of its Reading Recovery teacher.

Achieving deep conceptual understanding at leadership levels within local authorities proved a greater challenge, with less regular contact and continuous changes of those in key roles in many local authorities. Briefing meetings, reports, and case studies did not always reach the intended people or were not prioritized in the constant flow of material from the Primary National Strategy. Where support at those levels was successfully garnered, it was usually as a result of teacher leaders and link managers being proactive in checking that information had been received. This will be explored further, in the section on spread and transfer of ownership, below.

(ii)   Balancing fidelity and creativity

Interventions are rarely delivered as planned (Elias *et al.*, 2003). Since early impact is an imperative (Barber, 2004), leaders must be vigilant in preventing drift from the programme's principles and procedures threatening to upset the balance between fidelity and innovation:

> This will involve making clear the key principles that all schools are expected to meet or follow but, just as importantly, emphasising where schools can, on their own or with other schools, work out what makes most sense for their pupils.
>
> Earl *et al.*, 2003: 24

Despite well-evidenced rationales for reform, it is possible for a policy to 'lose its way as it unfolds in new settings or becomes subject to new conditions'

(Moss, 2004: 127). However, fidelity is safeguarded if changes are not as substantial as to reach the 'point of drastic mutation' that can dilute the policy's core purpose, integrity, and effectiveness (Hall and Loucks, 1978: 18). This involves careful balance, since schools improve most rapidly when they do not break the mould but rather begin to 'own' an innovation, creating their own developments within an existing framework (Hatch, 2000). High-quality continuing professional development can guard against reinvention or failure to operate within a programme's boundaries. By monitoring any changes for impact and unintended consequences, aware professionals can counter sources of risk of undermining confidence and effectiveness. Since Every Child a Reader created space for innovation rather than relying on the replication of a method, a challenge was to maintain its high positive outcomes while allowing for creative responses and continuing development.

Rather than accountability measured solely through data or relying on high-performing individuals, 'the key to successful reform is to make the energy of educators and students the driving force'; this energy comes from 'doing something well that is important to you' and 'which makes a contribution to others as well as society as a whole' (Fullan, 2011: 3). The 'energy' in Every Child a Reader came largely from the moral imperative to improve the literacy levels of the lowest attainers in order to improve their life chances; this was a goal widely shared in briefings, documents, and press statements, and linked to developing government policy about the rights of 'every child'. However, gaining conceptual understanding of Every Child a Reader at the highest levels in local authorities, where key decisions were made about finance and roles within the local authority, was a challenge when other imperatives were equally pressing and driven by accountability of inspection and comparison of performance data between local authorities. Where the potential was recognized at high levels in a local authority, as for example in Sheffield, the reform was seen as a way to meet existing needs:

> Reading Recovery came at just the right time because Sheffield also had a strong commitment to equity and empowerment. It was very opportune, because it offered a proven methodology, to address the needs of the hardest-to-teach. It also offered a convincing model of professional development and a knowledge-base which we recognized that we needed.
>
> Steve Anwyll, NLS leader and LA manager [9]

The initial year of professional development for teacher leaders and teachers contributed to fidelity of the Reading Recovery aspect of Every Child a Reader through opportunities for deep learning, although the time invested also offered a challenge: during the rollout phase, the year spent preparing teachers and teacher leaders in Reading Recovery seemed to limit their wider role in other interventions. On the other hand, the investment of time to secure deep understanding created a strong foundation for scaling up. Sue (a Reading Recovery National leader[10]) proposes that 'the length of time spent on professional development and capacity building inured the teacher leaders to some extent [to]some of the other pressures that [militate] against innovation'.

Professional collaboration is central to Every Child a Reader, inevitably producing a variation in local responses as 'people working together through multiple interpretations of an object offer potential for that object to be transformed or expanded and that in turn can lead to new tools and new ways of socially organising a practice' (Ellis, 2011: 40). In each of the different Every Child a Reader settings, creative responding feeds back in the manner described in Coburn and Stein's conceptual model (2010). As teacher leaders and teachers and their colleagues devise new responses to new problems, these are mediated by both their theoretical understanding of the innovation and the practical experience of leading Every Child a Reader in their local areas. Examples of such creative responses are found in the development of support materials and training for teachers on the teaching and assessment of reading, work with parents on sharing reading with children, development of a 'reading school ethos', or building local partnership with libraries and initial teacher-training providers.

(iii) Evidence of impact

Consistent collection of pupil data for analysis, monitoring, and accountability purposes is valuable in large-scale reform as an indicator of success, a contributor to sustainability, and a gauge of fidelity to core concepts. Pupil test data continue to be the main measure of achievement either at key points in time, such as the end of key stages and before and after intervention programmes (Datnow et al., 2002). In Every Child a Reader, the collection, analysis, and publication of both short- and long-term data have contributed to sustainability beyond the pilot programme.

EARLY IMPACT

Improving teaching quality and pupil outcomes through the implementation of the National Literacy Strategy highlighted 'the long tail of under-achievement' (Ofsted, 2004: 6; Mullis et al., 2003). In response, schools sought effective ways to address the needs of those pupils who had not progressed sufficiently, despite targeted class teaching. As pupil data became widely available, schools came under pressure to improve outcomes for particular pupils and needed to find robust means of doing so. Anne,[11] a headteacher who had previously been a Primary National Strategy leader, notes:

> One of the main goals of the [Primary] National Strategy was to identify programmes that would help narrow the [achievement] gap between children entitled to free school meals and those from more affluent backgrounds. Every Child a Reader did this particularly well. The data show the majority of children made gains in their learning well above what would be expected. They made accelerated progress and gaps were substantially reduced.

Systematic, rigorous, and comprehensive collection of Reading Recovery data, with outcomes for all children, is reported on a dedicated data website, consistently demonstrating potential to effect comprehensive and significant change for the most vulnerable pupils (Every Child a Reader *Annual Reports*, 2006 onwards). Often it can take until the second year of a reform before success is noted, making it difficult to achieve commitment from participants, but the impact of Reading Recovery in the years prior to the launch of Every Child a Reader had already demonstrated success of the core concept in terms of achieving consistent and significant pupil outcomes (Douëtil, 2005). One-to-one Reading Recovery tuition over four to five months (an average of 38 hours) enables children to make a gain of 24 months on average – five times the normal rate of progress (Every Child a Reader, *Annual Report, 2009–10*).

Government policy at the beginning of Every Child a Reader's rollout was influenced by the aim of giving every child access to basic skills, by providing a receptive context for early intervention aimed at the lowest-attaining pupils (Moss, 2009). These pupils had not been supported by the National Curriculum or Primary National Strategy approaches. By contrast, the outcomes of Reading Recovery acted as a powerful incentive for offering a package of support that delivered a wider impact on greater numbers of pupils through layered interventions and professional development for class teachers (see Chapter 2). Martin,[12] a primary school headteacher, comments on the central role Every Child a Reader played in his school's improvement:

> Every Child a Reader is now impacting throughout Key Stage 1 as teachers work with the Reading Recovery teacher. It has led to more consistent practice and a real purpose to intervention programmes in other year groups, better resources and planning and a better understanding of assessment. We now have a well-prepared team to equip children with effective reading skills.

The Primary National Strategy (2007–08) had access to data pointing to schools and local authorities with the greatest difficulties in reducing numbers of low-attaining children. In collaboration with the Reading Recovery's national leadership, Primary National Strategy leaders were able to identify where Every Child a Reader was most needed. However, where schools and local authorities were specifically targeted to take on the initiative but lacked capacity for innovation or did not achieve 'buy-in' from high levels of management, Every Child a Reader struggled to reach its potential for systemic change. The decision to offer only partial funding for the role of Reading Recovery teacher was a strategic move: it was intended to generate greater commitment from schools, and of course allowed the available budget to reach more schools.

Encouraging data from Every Child a Reader influenced educators' views. Observation of children's individual lessons by decision-makers at national levels was also significant. Nationally recognized politicians (e.g. Gordon Brown[13] and Alan Johnson,[14] who visited Lauriston Primary School, Hackney, East London, in May 2007) and trustees of supporting charitable trusts (e.g. Sir John Cass, chairman of trustees of the KPMG Foundation, in May 2006) observed Reading Recovery lessons that made such a deep impression on them that they often made Reading Recovery a part of their public presentations on pupil achievement. This high-profile attention and interest in knowing more strengthened external perceptions of the programme and contributed to funding being made available for its sustainability.

When layered interventions were added during the pilot phase of Every Child a Reader, the aim of the Primary National Strategy data requirement was simply to capture the numbers of children being supported through each programme as a result of rapid scaling up. There was little time (or funding sought) to adapt the national database to enable collection of additional impact data from these interventions, though this has since been achieved. In retrospect this was short-sighted; though the goal was to reach greater numbers of pupils with intervention, efficacy is of importance. Qualitative and outcome data from these programmes in local authorities were shared nationally through case studies, contributing to schools' decision-making about selecting suitable programmes. Brooks' publication (2007, updated 2013) with information and critique of evidence on the efficacy of a wider range of literacy interventions, is also extensively utilized by schools in selecting intervention.

While immediate impact was important, sustained improvement was crucial to the integrity of Every Child a Reader. Data need to be collated and disseminated efficiently in order to generate significant depth of change in beliefs and attitudes in school and to ensure that impact at local authority level is not lost. David,[15] a local authority senior manager, spoke about the impact on individual children ('The data show almost all of them making brilliant progress') and noted that feeding back their data to the teachers, schools, and local authority had been successful in sustaining the approach in Barking and Dagenham, East London. After implementing Reading Recovery, a school in Newham, East London, reported a dramatic increase of 30 per cent more children achieving reading at Level 2+ (Every Child a Reader, *Annual Report, 2009–10*). As the Every Child a Reader approach became embedded in the school, providing intervention for more children, the following two years showed a further 9 per cent and then 8 per cent rise in positive results, meaning that 98 per cent of children in Year 2 achieved age-related expectations.

In addition to data reports from Every Child a Reader schools, local authorities used end-of-key-stage assessments and pupil-tracking systems to monitor outcomes at individual, year group, school, and local authority level, providing layers of accountability. Figure 5.6 shows an example of this from a case study of Sheffield schools, indicating that Every Child a Reader schools in the city outperformed all other Sheffield schools in the percentage rise of pupils attaining Level 2 in reading and writing. The same report noted that 'Reading Recovery, operating within Every Child a Reader schools, consistently raises attainment of the most vulnerable children with 76% making two years of progress in reading during their 20 week programme of approximately 50 hours of teaching' (Every Child a Reader, *Case Studies*).

Although national data were initially shared to promote Every Child a Reader, with rapid scaling up, schools were quickly able to access and utilize their own data. Anne, a headteacher (see page 124), remarks on how such data can impact on commitment to sustain the programme:

> [Schools] could see the direct impact on the children and we were increasingly getting data that showed those schools were getting results above other schools. It was a 'buy one get one free' because it also improved behaviour so that children could access the curriculum, it improved their confidence ... not just a child who was able to read and write better.

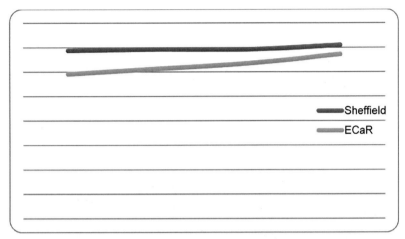

Figure 5.6: Percentage of children attaining Level 2b+ in Sheffield schools in Key Stage 1 SATs

Qualitative data featuring school and local authority case studies, published through annual reports and electronic newsletters, served two purposes as Every Child a Reader expanded. Sharing successful practice offered further proof of concept and, through the voices of children, parents, teachers, and headteachers, other schools and local authorities shaped their practice. The DfE's *Evaluation of Every Child a Reader* (2011: 169) is largely positive about the intervention's impact on schools based on qualitative measures:

> Participants in the study named five main areas in which they perceived the programme had had an impact: attainment and performance, wider pupil outcomes, improvements in wider literacy practice, the professional development of teaching staff and increased take-up of the programme in local areas.

With a national focus on Key Stage 2 outcomes, and pressure on schools to 'boost' the performance of Year 6 children, the challenge was to demonstrate a sustained gain in return for the cost of offering early literacy intervention. Follow-up studies of the London schools comparison research (Hurry and Holliman, 2009; Hurry, 2012) indicated that former Reading Recovery children were reading significantly better than comparison children at the age of nine, and becoming secure Level 4b readers at the age of 11 in 78 per cent of cases. Hurry notes that it is rare for interventions to demonstrate sustained gains over such a timespan. Richard,[16] a London teacher leader, tracked pupils who had received the intervention, through to Year 6 (age 11): An extract from his account is given in the box.

THE IMPACT OF READING RECOVERY ON CHILDREN IN THE LONDON BOROUGH OF HACKNEY

In the London Borough of Hackney children identified as the lowest-attaining and who are placed into Reading Recovery are considerably more likely, even compared with the lowest-attaining children elsewhere in the UK, to be entitled to free schools meals (58 per cent), to come from ethnic minority groups (72 per cent), and to speak English as an additional language (60 per cent). However, Hackney has implemented Reading Recovery since 1992 and the programme has played a vital role in changing children's lives, supporting a whole-school approach to raising standards and developing enhanced professional learning and understanding in school staff members in relation to early literacy difficulties. In a longitudinal study carried out in ten schools from 2006 to 2011, the cohort receiving Reading Recovery in 2006–07 was traced throughout their primary years. At the end of Key Stage 2, at age 11, in 2011, five years after the end of their Reading Recovery programme, 83 of the 92 children who completed the Reading Recovery programme in Year 2 went on to achieve National Curriculum Level 4 or higher in their National Assessments in reading. This represents a 90 per cent success rate. Not a single child who had completed their Reading Recovery programme in this cohort achieved below Level 3. These are the results for the very lowest-attaining six-year-olds living in an area of poverty and disadvantage.

Every Child a Reader Annual Report 2010–11

Towards the end of 2012, Key Stage 2 data from a sufficiently viable sample of former Reading Recovery pupils became available for the first time since the launch of Every Child a Reader. National Curriculum Level 4 is accepted as an age-related expectation for Year 6 pupils, and pupils eligible to receive Reading Recovery (that is the lowest-attaining of their year cohort) are those predicted to fail to reach Level 3 in Year 6. Of the 374 pupils whose data was reviewed, 95 per cent were assessed at Level 3 or above in reading, and 78 per cent reached Level 4 or above. In writing, 98 per cent were assessed at Level 3 or above, and 69 per cent reached Level 4 or above. These outcomes exemplify the early goals for Every Child a Reader and highlight the challenges posed by the time needed for outcomes of early intervention to become apparent.

IMPACT ON PEDAGOGY

Impact is not limited to pupils, but includes those practitioners working towards the goals of a reform. Deep change influencing teachers' beliefs and their understanding of pedagogy is harder to measure than surface change in the classroom, but it is the impact of improved understandings and renewed pedagogy that develops practitioners' expertise and enhances pupil achievement. Deep change engenders 'sustainable improvements [that] continue year upon year, from one leader to the next. They are not fleeting changes that depend on exemplary leaders' efforts and that disappear when leaders have left.' (Hargreaves, 2005: 2) In identifying those professional development approaches that make the greatest impact on pupil outcomes, Hattie (2009) largely describes the professional development model within Every Child a Reader. He notes the power of spreading development over an extended period of time; the importance of leadership of professional development by experts; and the fact that the development should aim to deepen knowledge and extend pedagogical skills in ways that impact on student outcomes and challenge teachers' prevailing discourse and conceptions. He also points to the impact that results when professional development stimulates discussion between colleagues that is focused on student learning, and to the need for all these aspects to be supported by school leadership. If these are the factors that have the most profound impact on student outcomes, they suggest that a commitment to professional learning should have priority over linear replication models, which do not empower teachers in decision-making about learning.

(iv) Commitment

Sustaining innovation depends on continuing commitment in the face of political and leadership changes and the advent of new approaches or new commercial products, for as long as there is proven efficacy. Embedding Every Child a Reader within school and local authority systems has both demanded and supported a high level of continued commitment. By creating capacity for growth and by getting the right people in place, including teacher leaders and Reading Recovery teachers, the potential for sustainability is increased. Hatch (2000) advocates the creation of a critical mass of adherents to establish an innovation firmly, but notes that the length of time required for this is generally underestimated.

COMMITMENT TO RESOURCING

Capacity for growth has been influenced by several factors deliberately planned from the start. These include consistency of personnel, with leaders who understand and own the concept, a balance of central funding for stability (from government and business), and local matched funding (for continued growth and ownership). Early support for Every Child a Reader from business and charity leaders and the Institute of Education was a lever in securing funding and raising the profile of the goals of Every Child a Reader. Jean[17] (Every Child a Chance Trust Director, 2006–09) recalls the vital importance of behind-the-scenes activity in supporting the reform; for example, by investing in the report *The Long Term Costs of Literacy difficulties* (KPMG Foundation, 2006; 2nd edition, Every Child a Chance Trust, 2009) and associated communications, by networking and lobbying, by re-emphasizing the cost benefits of investing early in children who appear to be struggling with literacy learning, by promotional events such as the Every Child a Reader school awards (2009 onwards), and through marketing to headteachers. Implementing reforms that have the greatest power to influence student learning is expensive (Pressley *et al.*, 2006, cited in Hattie, 2009), and dedicated government funding for the pilot and subsequent rollout of Every Child a Reader was an expression of high-level commitment, which in turn engendered commitment at local authority and school levels.

There is a risk that those children most in need of effective early intervention are dependent on the vagaries of funding. Dedicated funding indicates a recognition that 'even in the best systems there will still be low-attaining children, so if you want that commitment to every child being a reader and writer, you will, year on year, need to invest in it' (Sue, Reading Recovery national leader). While politicians tend to make pragmatic choices and constantly seek new initiatives that can demonstrate that they are driving forward the pace of reform (Moss, 2009), Hopkins (2001: 177) argues for funding to be attached to programmes with a proven track record: 'There is a strong case for the systematic development nationally of programmes that work and address educational challenge.'

COMMITMENT AT A PERSONAL PROFESSIONAL LEVEL

Personal commitment is a distinct feature of how those involved in Every Child a Reader speak about it, and it is strongly linked to outcomes: headteachers, teacher leaders, and teachers commit to Every Child a Reader because of their direct experience of its effectiveness. Jean (see page xxi) reflected on how headteachers' beliefs regarding the lowest-attaining children changed and how they became advocates of the reform when they saw the children's transformation. 'This was why [in the early years of the implementation] we chose respected headteachers, successful headteachers who could communicate,' she said. Local area knowledge from within the National Literacy and National Numeracy strategies and Reading Recovery local authority managers, where in place, provided invaluable knowledge of the network of influence that could be tapped through attracting well-respected leadership.

LOCAL AUTHORITY COMMITMENT

Regardless of how well personnel are prepared for and supported in their roles, when they move on the sustainability of an intervention is threatened (Hatch, 2000). Where there is much to be learnt that is new or where turnover is high, it can be assumed that problems will escalate, often as a result of poor communication due to the loss of the local knowledge base (ibid.). During the rollout of Every Child a Reader, the stability of teacher leaders and link managers in schools was remarkably high. However, there was often a rapid turnover of local authority link managers, which caused problems in communication. One teacher leader stressed the difficulties of repeatedly having to explain her role to new senior personnel in a partner local authority in her consortium. This became such a frequent occurrence and necessitated so much extra work that she considered that it impeded the growth of Every Child a Reader across her consortium. Competing work priorities, or failure to understand or to have the goals of Every Child a Reader clearly explained, were all factors in the failure to win the support of some link managers. In situations like these, the capacity of the teacher leader to manage and promote Every Child a Reader became even more critical. The example from Nottinghamshire (see box) demonstrates how a combination of effective use of pupil data, commitment, and understanding of the concept of Every Child a Reader at all levels in the local authority led to the reform acting as a key strand in their approach to school improvement. Attaining such a coherent approach has been threatened in recent years by the centralization of education and the reduction of local authorities' ambit. In the example from Nottinghamshire,[18] however, Every Child a Reader acts as a coherent concept to bind together professional development and support for school improvement.

> THE ROLE OF LEADERSHIP IN MAKING EVERY CHILD A READER A
> SUCCESSFUL APPROACH TO WHOLE SCHOOL IMPROVEMENT
> Support right through to the highest level makes ECaR successful in Nottinghamshire, and we also work effectively in a consortium. ECaR is seen as both an intervention and a school improvement tool. Marion's role as a [local authority] link manager has been absolutely crucial: Marion believes in Reading Recovery and ECaR and its

potential for changing children's lives. She is a well-respected member of the LA [local authority], leading on professional development for headteachers and has also been a literacy consultant. If we didn't have Marion, there could be issues – she has been a powerful leader of ECaR. The closing-the-gap agenda has focused our work and we feed ECaR data into that. Our data has always been strong and I think that has been a big factor in getting continued political support – I think you have to be tenacious about data ... it drives everything.

Our headteacher networks have been very powerful – headteachers in established schools meet twice a year and our new ones meet every term and they have been very supportive with fantastic attendance. Marion is always there. The Deputy-Director always comes along to the end-of-year meeting when we do our reviews. He knows about children, he's been out and observed ECaR children at the beginning and end of their programmes and if he's talking about achievement and narrowing the gap, he often talks about Dylan [a pseudonym], a successful ECaR child he has observed.

The schools' forum and LA finance people are supportive of ECaR and want to keep it going. Marion meets with the finance team regularly and they know why it is so important to keep the ECaR funding ring-fenced. In Nottinghamshire ECaR is about professional development for all schools and all staff. It's about teachers using running records, teaching assistants being more skilled to support reading, about interventions, about Book Banding. We have also developed our own one-to-one intervention 'Switch-on'. Governors and parents are important and we are always trying to keep sight of the big picture. When I have 10 seconds to explain it to someone, I quote our data and talk about the power of ECaR being that two-pronged approach – whole school development and an individual pupil focus.

Jose, a teacher leader in Nottinghamshire

The commitment of teacher leaders, local authority leaders, and headteachers, secured through efficacy and the strong theoretical foundation of Every Child a Reader, contributes significantly to its depth and sustainability. In the next section we examine the spread and transfer of ownership of Every Child a Reader and consider how a reform is developed and deepened through contributions from stakeholders.

Scaling up Every Child a Reader: Spread and transfer of ownership

The dimension of **spread** is not limited to notions of size and geographical breadth. More importantly, it is also linked to changes in practice – the 'potential to spread reform related norms and pedagogical principles **within** a classroom, school, and district' (Coburn, 2003: 7, our emphasis). Spread depends on the capacity of a reform to **transfer ownership** to stakeholders, and it is reliant on time for participants to 'buy in', adapt, and contribute to the development of the reform. Principles contributing to an innovation's success on a small scale must be translated successfully to a larger scale, requiring distributed models of leadership collaboration and effective communication. Focus on Every Child a Reader acts as a lynchpin in a creative implementation that is owned locally and extends within the individual systems of local authorities and schools, enhancing and expanding over time through contributions from participants. Spread and transfer of ownership in Every Child a Reader will be examined through the following themes:

(i)   distributed leadership and roles

(ii)   recruitment and collaboration

(iii)   communication.

(i)   Distributed leadership and roles

Effective large-scale reform calls for resolute, tenacious leadership (Fullan, 2010). Within Every Child a Reader, a centrally resourced innovation, systematic and strategically driven use of local leadership networks powered up already existing and new learning communities to operate collaboratively within a strong framework of accountability, as exemplified in Fullan's tri-level model of scaling up innovation (2005b).

NATIONAL LEADERSHIP

During the rollout phase (2008–11) the government part-funded Every Child a Reader. It was represented organizationally by Primary National Strategy national and regional managers. They worked with Reading Recovery national leaders from the Institute of Education to plan and monitor the progress of the innovation and support the accountability measurement and quality assurance. To increase capacity to provide professional development for the required number of teacher leaders, three new national leaders were trained in 2007–08 and four more in 2009–10.

The year of professional development required for national leaders' qualification in Reading Recovery created a dilemma in a period of rapid scaling up, and put a relatively small team under pressure, although all national leaders underwent in-depth preparation for carrying out their roles. The Primary National Strategy model of regional support was given a mandate. To permit greater access for potential teacher leaders across the country, teacher-leader professional development was also offered to groups in locations outside London – in Manchester (2007–09) and in Leeds and Birmingham (2010–11) – once the new national leaders joined the teaching leadership team. Having national leaders based in regional areas also increased the capacity of the team in supporting more intensive fieldwork as Every Child a Reader expanded further from its central hub in London.

TEACHER LEADERS, LINK MANAGERS, AND HIGH-LEVEL LEADERSHIP IN LOCAL AUTHORITIES

Teacher leaders act as agents of change, and as such are vital to the scaling up of Every Child a Reader. Trained through the Institute of Education to become literacy experts, and employed by local authorities, teacher leaders could be positioned in any one of a number of leadership teams: primary, literacy, special educational needs or inclusion teams, or school improvement, depending on the local authority's organization and emphasis. Their status and potential to create an environment for change was variable and largely determined by established networks and by their status in former roles (such as that of consultant) in the local authority.

The level of commitment by the local authority link manager to raising the profile of Every Child a Reader in schools also made a difference. In successful implementations, teacher leaders contributed to professional development for school leaders and teachers on aspects such as provision mapping of intervention, early literacy acquisition, literacy assessment, and class literacy provision. In implementations where teacher leaders were restricted to their role in Reading Recovery, they were less able to integrate their work into the wider school improvement agenda.

The national focus on lower-attaining pupils placed a spotlight on leadership and management and on the understanding of the principles of pupil assessment, provision mapping, tracking, and monitoring. Prior to Every Child a Reader, a National Literacy Strategy document *Managing Wave 3 Literacy Interventions: Good practice guidance for local education authorities* (DfES, 2003) had been introduced, but principles had not generally been well understood or taken up. In many localities a real shift came when teacher leaders coached Reading Recovery teachers and school personnel to develop local responses to the 'three waves' model. Reading Recovery's strong theoretical basis provided a foundation for school personnel to understand the implications involved in preventing the lowest literacy attainers from falling behind their peers.

At local authority level, a strategic leader, usually as only one part of a wider role, acted as the link manager and supported the teacher leader. The status and strengths of this role-holder often determined the strength or weakness of an implementation. During the rollout, regular national briefings and professional development sessions were held for link managers. Over time, some local authorities were represented by different link managers at each of these meetings, which eroded consistency and hindered strategic understanding and responses within the local authority. Where the role of link manager was maintained by one person with an understanding of and commitment to the goals of Every Child a Reader, the implementation usually remained strong, as in the example of Marion in Nottinghamshire (see p. 132).

Involvement at directorate level within local authorities was rarely successful. No forum was created for local authority directors or others with strategic control over the functioning and structures of the local authority and with responsibility for budgets. There was an assumption on the part of teacher leaders that the Primary National Strategy, through its regular contacts with local authorities, would approach this level of leadership; however, it was rarely the case. In many local authorities where the 'tail of underachievement' was a major concern, relationships with the Primary National Strategy were strained, and national and regional directors were not always in a position of influence. Success in engaging high-level local authority leaders to participate in Every Child a Reader became more critical in 2010 when, following a change of government, the ring-fence on funding was removed. Where knowledge and understanding of Every Child a Reader existed at higher levels in local authorities, the maintenance of dedicated funding enabled schools to continue and ensured that the role of the teacher leader was retained in staffing structures. However, national changes to the reach of decision-making of the schools forum and increasing pressure on local authority and school budgets have forced a reduction of provision or a diluted professional development model in some local authorities, threatening sustainability and further spread. In some cases the reverse has occurred as creative responses to maintaining Every Child a Reader have been made, often as a result of schools taking a teacher leader onto their staffing structure and funding the salary through the school improvement support that the teacher leader offers to neighbouring schools.

Although the concept of Every Child a Reader was realized gradually, when the model is embedded effectively in a school, it permeates all aspects of school management and classroom provision, acting as a tool for improving literacy outcomes through a layered intervention approach. Gill,[19] national leader for Better Reading Partnership wave 2 intervention, articulated this concept as:

> having a trained and highly skilled Reading Recovery teacher, who would impact not only [on] the lowest achieving pupils in literacy but manage and support other 'lighter touch' interventions, along with other professionals in school, thus enabling the school to choose and monitor interventions and track pupils effectively.

The trained Reading Recovery teacher forms the nucleus of the Every Child a Reader school team, along with teaching assistants who become qualified to lead layered interventions. He/she is central to the change process. As in the case of teacher leaders, Reading Recovery teachers bring a range of skills and experience to the role. During local recruitment, strategic leaders considered that 'observable and general teaching experience that demonstrated an aptitude for the role, a willingness to learn and in some cases level of teaching experience' (DfE, 2011: 77) was more important than familiarity with Early Years practice, or with providing one-to-one pupil support, despite Reading Recovery insistence that teachers have prior Early Years experience (European Centre for Reading Recovery, 2012). To ensure teachers' suitability for their position of influence, headteachers were advised to take seriously their selection of a teacher for professional development in Every Child a Reader, as the success of the school's implementation hinged on that appointment. That this advice was sometimes ignored may have been due to a lack of understanding of the potential for the role or to preconceptions about the capacity needed for teachers leading interventions, a role more commonly taken by teaching assistants, implying less need for teaching skill. Some headteachers selected teachers who were apparently failing in the classroom, or used the part-time nature of the Every Child a Reader post to accommodate requests for part-time work into their staffing structures.

Five components contributing to capacity-building in schools are identified by Newmann *et al.* (cited in Fullan, 2001): an increase in teachers' knowledge base; the development of a professional learning community; programme coherence; the availability of technical resources; and leadership from the headteacher and governing body. The example of one school (see box) demonstrates the power of wise decision-making by Jayne,[20] the headteacher, who discerned the leadership potential of the school's Reading Recovery teacher and grasped the opportunity to share her expertise more widely. Elmore's (2000: 15) emphasis on the leader's role to 'enhanc[e] the skills and knowledge of people in the organization, creating a common culture of expectations around the use of those skills and knowledge' is clearly demonstrated in this school.

KS1 READING STANDARDS LEAP FROM 45% (L2) TO 84% (L2) IN TWO YEARS

In 2005, I took over an inner city school [Barlow Hill Primary School, Manchester] with desperately low standards. Staff morale was low, turnover was high, and my teachers lacked subject knowledge – they didn't know how to teach reading and writing. Many of our pupils are asylum-seekers living in a local refuge. Others speak little English when they arrive at our school. They are often the children of medical students at the university. What attracted me about Every Child a Reader was the opportunity to work with specialists. In my previous schools I dabbled with early interventions – a bit of this and a bit of that, but I'm convinced that schools come a cropper because they go for the teaching-assistant model. I think the most vulnerable children need specialists. I've always thought that.

After I had decided on Every Child a Reader, I selected a really outstanding teacher in school to train in Reading Recovery. This is because I knew that the role would involve influencing other staff and raising the profile of reading, so I was prepared to take a risk and lose this teacher from the classroom context. The governors were firmly behind me. Working to Every Child a Reader principles in this school is non-negotiable. We wanted to use something we knew would work.Increasing standards in literacy learning has become the priority right through school. We did this through guided reading enriched by Reading Recovery pedagogy and differentiated across ability groups in class.

We have built a confident and collaborative school learning community by keeping the main messages simple, providing a rolling programme of continuing professional development especially for newly qualified teachers. Assessment, monitoring, and evaluation systems have been key to our school's success. Look at our KS2

> results! Staff have learnt from demonstration lessons and coaching
> and feedback. These methods have increased knowledge and keep
> teachers fresh. It's quite easy to prioritize something when you see
> the results in pupil outcomes. We took one initiative – Every Child a
> Reader – and did it properly.
>
> The whole school is in this for the long haul. That means
> dedicating time for long- and short-term planning and prioritizing
> funding to support Every Child a Reader, e.g. book orders and
> retaining a Reading Recovery teacher, even though it's difficult. The
> reason I'm an advocate is that it clearly works – if you can make it
> bigger and wider, the impact is great.
>
> Jayne, Barlow Hill Primary School headteacher

The evidence of distributed leadership in Jayne's approach – including the
high expectations of the teacher leader's specialist input and the potential
of the trained Reading Recovery teacher, the support of the governing body,
and an ethos of accountability throughout the school – contributed to the
rapid increase in literacy standards. This school's response to Every Child a
Reader also emphasizes how sufficient dedicated funding over several years
enabled a headteacher, who was already convinced of the potential impact, to
implement the changes and developments confidently.

Managing the transformation from a role as purely a 'Reading Recovery
teacher' working with the lowest-attaining pupils, to an 'Every Child a Reader
intervention leader' who strategically introduces, oversees, and monitors
layered literacy interventions in school, is fundamental to a school's success
with this reform. The potential for a response like Jayne's in Every Child a
Reader schools is not always nor easily realized. Sustainability of Every Child
a Reader is threatened where Reading Recovery teachers, perhaps due to a
dearth of experience or being in a part-time post, have insufficient seniority
or support to engender collegial respect and effect wider school improvement.
Where the Reading Recovery teacher is supported by a link teacher, ideally a
member of the senior management team, implementations of Every Child a
Reader are strengthened and deepened.

During the rollout, a means of providing additional professional
development opportunities for school-based personnel was developed. Action
research approaches to learning were found to be valuable (Elias *et al.*, 2003;
Kemmis and Smith, 2008), and the Reading Recovery in Primary Literacy
Leadership (RRiPLLe) module was designed to support school teams in

using action research as a method of school improvement (see Appendix 4). The module was accredited by the Institute of Education at master's degree level and focused on supporting Every Child a Reader teachers to develop a school improvement intervention with colleagues in their school context, supported by the teacher leader. After the first year the module had limited uptake, partly due to the additional demands that it made on teacher leaders' time. However, teachers who did engage with it benefited from an increase in their confidence, allowing them to take on leadership roles within a range of school contexts. Some went on to become Reading Recovery teacher leaders, or to take up posts as deputy headteachers. The module has now moved to a blended learning model that can be accessed more easily from anywhere in the country.

Elmore (2000: 15) highlights the key role of leadership in:

> enhancing the skills and knowledge of people in the organisation, creating a common culture of expectations around the use of skills and knowledge, holding the various pieces of the organisation together in a productive relationship with each other, and holding individuals accountable for their contributions to the collective result.

The investment of a year's preparation, with consistent and deep professional development for national leaders, teacher leaders, and teachers, initially constrained the timeframe of wider impact. However, this professional development contributed to fidelity and consistency in the 'spread within' and capacity for rapid transference of ownership of the innovation. Teacher leaders received comprehensive initial and ongoing professional development and, having invested heavily in preparing for the role, they consistently remained in post. Among those in other roles such as headteachers and link managers, who had fewer opportunities to engage with the theory underlying Every Child a Reader, there was greater variation in response to opportunities for ownership and the frequent changes in the role of link manager impacted on commitment at local authority level.

(ii)   Recruitment and collaboration

When funding and government support for the scaling up of Every Child a Reader became available, the challenge was to meet the goal that, wherever a child was located, they could access the intervention they required. A spreadsheet was developed by Primary National Strategy and Reading Recovery national leaders to identify the following: numbers of 'at risk' readers in local authorities, using Key Stage 1 SATs data from the previous year; the number of Reading Recovery teachers necessary to address that need; the number of teacher leaders necessary to train and support those teachers; and the number and location of new teacher leaders required for this task. Consortia of local authorities were created to promote partnership and share provision across a number of adjacent local authorities. Their collaborative work was fundamental to establishing capacity for spread of the concept by enabling the activation of Every Child a Reader in local authorities and schools that would otherwise have no access to a teacher leader.

RECRUITMENT

The recruitment of new schools during the rollout was usually managed at local authority level by the link manager and the teacher leader, based on funding allocation and additional local information about schools' data and leadership. A tension sometimes existed about whether to recruit schools that were keen to take up Every Child a Reader but having lesser need, or to recruit schools identified as having greater need but whose leadership was less able and or less committed to Every Child a Reader. Various models evolved for the recruitment of schools. However, as David (see p. 126) noted, successful implementation of Every Child a Reader was dependent on the senior leadership team recognizing the potential role for the Reading Recovery teacher. The focus in his local authority was therefore on recruiting schools that would commit to the programme. David explains how funding supported recruitment:

> One of the strengths of ECaR is that schools were funded centrally as part payment towards the Reading Recovery teachers' salary. This was great for recruiting new schools in the local authority, but it was also a limitation as some leadership teams saw it as only funding a 0.5 post and failed to recognize the need for time to fulfil the broader ECaR role.

There was a snowball effect, particularly for local authorities new to Reading Recovery, and as outcomes from pilot schools in Every Child a Reader were disseminated through meetings and reports and by word of mouth it became easier to recruit new schools. Part-funding for the teacher role was an impetus for schools, but Anne (see page 124) also pointed to the way in which pupil outcomes and the professional development model supported recruitment:

> The majority of schools really wanted to get into it for the genuine reason of wanting to have someone in their school highly trained

in early reading and writing skills. They could see the direct impact on the children who had been in the programme and we were increasingly getting data that showed ECaR schools were getting results above other schools.

While in some areas demand exceeded provision and the spreadsheet was modified flexibly in response, in other local authorities it proved difficult to recruit sufficient schools to meet the predicted demand. Anne emphasizes the importance of finding schools with the capacity to benefit from Every Child a Reader:

> One of the things that came out very strongly was that you needed to have strong leadership and management to be able to put ECaR in place and roll it out through the school properly. Schools had to be in a healthy enough place to be able to take it on.

COLLABORATION IN CONSORTIA

Collaborative work offers the possibility of discovering new ways of working to further enhance current practice. 'People working together through multiple interpretations of an object potentially allows for that object to be transformed or expanded and that in turn can lead to new tools and new ways of socially organising a practice' (Ellis, 2011: 40). In the event of problems or miscommunication, fast feedback loops enable progress at local levels and provide opportunities for discussing challenges and joint problem-solving (Moss, 2009). Commenting on the rollout of the Primary National Strategy, Ellis (2011: 39) notes 'how effective the learning/ work can be if knowledge and expertise [are] allowed to feed back into the enterprise'. Effective consortia are built on established working relationships and commitment to Every Child a Reader across all partner authorities, drawing on the leadership skills of the teacher leader (sometimes more than one in a local authority or consortia of local authorities) and link managers to support successful collaboration. A variety of models pertained to this (Figure 5.7). The complex consortia groupings were based on approximate geographical regions, existing relationships between local authorities, and the numbers of teachers requiring professional development. Existing teacher leaders had a key role to play within the consortia, supporting neighbouring local authorities to begin putting Every Child a Reader in place while their own teacher leaders were still being trained.

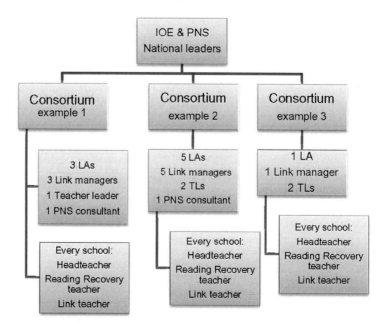

Figure 5.7: The variety of consortium structures existing in Every Child a Reader

Two specific challenges influenced the successful working of consortia. The first related to teacher leaders' capacity to work with the number of teachers allocated. The spreadsheet operated on a maximum figure of 45 teachers per teacher leader. Some considered that the strength of their implementations lay in working with fewer teachers and schools, while for others travel across the geographical spread of the consortium was unrealistic and too time-consuming. Where local authorities in a consortium were geographically close, it was relatively easy for the teacher leader to work across two or more local authorities; for example, in the West Yorkshire consortium, the teacher leader in Bradford led professional development in Wakefield and Leeds while teacher leaders in those local authorities were in training. However, when greater distances were involved, the ways of working across local authorities envisaged by the Primary National Strategy and Reading Recovery national leadership were less practicable. The second challenge lay in the issue of establishing Every Child a Reader in local authorities where teacher leaders were not employed, requiring them to build effective working relationships quickly with the identified link manager who had often been delegated to the role as an additional aspect of an already heavy workload. Given that link managers sometimes had poor knowledge of Every Child a Reader, despite having a teacher leader in their team, where the whole concept was new, it was more problematic. Sue (see p. 123) explains:

> The teacher leader had to identify someone in the other LA who was interested to become a direct link. Of course, until people see what is possible with this intervention, it is hard for them to believe that you can achieve that. It often depended on where the teacher leader was placed in those authority hierarchies ... some of them had it a lot easier than others in the network level they could operate at.

Sometimes the consortia grouping did not echo the natural relationships already established between local authorities, making it more difficult to achieve effective collaboration. In some cases, Primary National Strategy league tables of local authorities by pupil outcomes may also have engendered a competitive environment that militated against collaboration. This was the first national attempt at engineering working partnerships in which human resources could be shared across local authority boundaries, and it did not always result in the useful and mutually beneficial working relationships that were the original goal. Anne describes the problems of getting consortia up and running:

> At the time people weren't used to working across LAs. It was the first toehold into consortia working and the principles behind it. If there had been a greater history of that, it might have been better because the principles might have been understood. What we were doing was changing practice and changing mindsets and ways of working – we were doing the whole lot at the beginning.

The difficulty of getting consortia working effectively was also noted by Sue, who reflects:

> I can recall in a meeting, someone from the DfE saying 'Why aren't the consortia working?' and I remember saying 'It's early ... this is a big thing that you are trying to change here. Invite me back in a year's time and I will show you where it is working and what they are doing.

Many consortia did develop effective collaboration, as shown by regular consortia meetings, clear structures within and between local authority partners, and the sharing of outcome data and good practice, with a focus on meeting children's needs. Joy,[21] a teacher leader, explained how her local authority was keen to work in this way, providing leadership for the consortium that helped to strengthen the outcomes in each area. Other teacher leaders noted how headteachers with more established implementations of Every Child a Reader could encourage others in the consortium and support development of the strategy in their schools. Approaches developing in schools were shared and fed back into the development of Every Child a Reader.

The geographical spread of Every Child a Reader is evident in the numbers of pupils reached. However, the conceptual spread of Every Child a Reader and the transfer of ownership is demonstrated by the ways in which schools, local authorities, and consortia partners worked together creatively to develop local responses driven by the goal that every child could become a reader. While consortia were new and posed challenges to learning by participating, they also provided a forum for sharing practice and developing innovative local responses that went beyond local authority boundaries. Examples of creative practice were shared with the national network, supporting newer consortia in their collaboration and demonstrating that the approach was beneficial to the transfer of ownership of Every Child a Reader.

(iii) *Communication*

Effective communication is crucial to the success of large-scale educational reform (Earl *et al.*, 2003). The establishment of professional learning communities that meet frequently in consortia or in schools, supporting the construction and interpretation of common messages, can forestall the potential negative impact of such reform. However, these learning communities consist of many organizational layers: government, Primary Strategies, Institute of Education National Leadership, local authorities and local authority consortia, schools and teachers. The complexity of these layers, together with the numbers of pupils involved and the slow pace at which messages were delivered and shared, combined to make effective communication difficult, with an ever-present danger of appearing inconsistent in relation to aspects of the initiative or the educational programme itself.

Communication underlies the spread of pedagogical principles on which a reform is built. It is vital to maintaining momentum and to deepening teachers' understanding and ultimately as an aid to sustainability. Over the lifetime of a reform or innovation, messages may change and there will inevitably be new developments. It is imperative for all to be kept informed and to ensure that 'the language of reform invites participation and ownership' (Earl *et al.*, 2003: 25). Effective communication is fundamental to spread and devolved ownership. In Every Child a Reader, communication systems included newsletters, electronic news circulars, and website development. Data reports were prepared and disseminated, including Every Child a

Reader annual reports. The *Every Child a Reader Toolkit* (DCSF, 2008) was further developed and disseminated to all schools through the secure area of the Primary National Strategy website. This contained additional guidance and resources for local authority managers and teacher leaders, about implementation and the workings of consortia. In addition the collection of data on all children in Reading Recovery, and on the many children supported by Wave 2 interventions, using web-based data, enabled comprehensive reports to be prepared at school, local authority, and national levels.

Another level of communication was provided through meetings and professional development at leadership levels. Biannual meetings were held for link managers and their teacher leaders. The regional events and the annual residential professional development opportunity for all Reading Recovery teacher leaders provided a communication space for discussion and practice sharing. Link managers commented that they found it useful to meet with other people in similar situations and to be kept abreast of what was happening at a national level. They valued access to high-profile guest speakers such as Jo Clunie (KPMG Foundation, 2006), Nick Pearce (IPRR, 2007), Jean Gross (2007), Nick Peacey MP, and Joan Baxter (Audit Commission, 2009); and literacy researchers Professors Greg Brooks (2008), Morag Stuart, and Kathy Sylva (2007); Maggie Snowling (2008), Jane Hurry (2010), Peter Blatchford (2010), and Roger Beard (2011), who all shared their expertise, prompting discussion at meetings. Despite the high profile of speakers, there was irregular attendance from link managers. David comments: 'One of the problems was that not all the line managers turned up. The Reading Recovery teacher leaders would be there but when the time came to talk in the consortium, it [might be] just me plus the Reading Recovery teacher leaders.'

Clear communication of programme outcomes, best practice, goals, and expectations has been a feature of effective local authority and school implementations (see text boxes on pp. 128, 131, and 137). Sharing with the wider school community, including parents and governors, created understanding about the expectations and outcomes of Every Child a Reader. Since the reduction or removal of local authority infrastructures of support and challenge in many areas as part of recent government policy, innovative communication processes are developing. In at least one implementation, a virtual learning environment connects all schools for sharing data and support for school-based professional development, and updates for school leaders. In many local authorities, conferences on early reading have been aimed at whole school development, including support for school leaders to evaluate their provision and prepare for inspection and pedagogic support for both classroom and Reading Recovery teachers. Some innovative schools are becoming hubs of good practice, employing teacher leaders and inviting neighbouring school leaders and teachers to professional development using the Every Child a Reader approach. A few have formalized this aspect by becoming 'teaching schools'.

Conclusion

In this chapter we have aimed to ground the scaling up of Every Child a Reader in educational change theory, crystallizing the concept by drawing on the experiences and reflections of representative participants. We have used four dimensions of educational reform – depth, sustainability, spread, and transfer of ownership – as lenses through which to explore factors contributing to the scaling up of Every Child a Reader and to examine the challenges posed by rapid expansion. We now return to these again and propose some principles for success in similar educational reform.

Much reform in the current educational climate is led by what Fullan (2011: 5) describes as the 'wrong drivers': accountability (test results, inspection, league tables); a focus on individual teacher quality rather than on group solutions; investing in technology at the expense of pedagogy and instruction; and employing fragmented rather than systematic strategies. Fullan notes that history shows that reforms propelled by these drivers are likely to fail. By contrast, the four 'right' drivers – capacity-building, group work, pedagogy, and developing whole systems – are effective 'because they work directly on changing the culture of school systems (values, norms, skill, practices, relationships)' (ibid.). Coburn and Stein (2010) also point to the potential for success of conceptual reforms that engage stakeholders and leave space for creative responses to the problems that arise from practice, while drawing effectively on theory and research. From our examination of the scaling up of Every Child a Reader, we note core principles that resonate with both of these viewpoints and that may prove to be powerful foundations upon which to develop and scale up similar educational reforms:

- Movement towards a widely accepted goal, recognized as having merit by a wide range of stakeholders, with benefits not only for children, must drive the reform.
- A strong theoretical basis is essential, with well-communicated concepts and a clear definition of the line between fidelity and creativity based on evidence and outcomes whose quality is assured through data and monitoring.

- Professional learning is critical, with a strong focus on pedagogy, bringing together theory and practice in ways that enhance both instruction and further development of the reform.
- Establishment of an integrated system is important, with stakeholders at all levels empowered to take action and experience a sense of ownership, and able to contribute to creating the reform as well as participating in it.
- Distributed leadership models contribute to depth and sustainability and build capacity within the developing system so that they can function with less control from the centre.
- Creating a culture of collaboration facilitates the sharing of skills, knowledge, and resources, fosters innovation, and enables more creative responses than might be possible in a linear reform.
- Acknowledging that deep and sustained conceptual reforms need more time than linear reforms to develop and become embedded, and that consistent resourcing of funds and participants is essential to providing a longer timescale.

Every Child a Reader is no longer an innovation; it is an educational approach that has been successfully implemented at scale and that continues to evolve. This example of a collaborative national enterprise is arguably unique in meeting the challenge of rapidly scaling up, while maintaining quality of outcomes for children. Deep professional learning has acted as a lynchpin for a creative response to the opportunities of Every Child a Reader by participants in many schools and local authorities, as a result of shared conceptual understanding and ownership of the approach. This largely prevented the emergence of unhelpful adaptation that could have taken practice past the point of 'drastic mutation' (Hall and Loucks, 1978: 18) and weakened its impact. Conceptual ownership was strongest for those participants, mainly teachers and teacher leaders, who accessed the more extended models of professional development. Where there has been less investment in professional learning for participants such as headteachers, link managers, and link teachers, the challenge to generate long-term commitment and support has been greater.

Transfer of ownership from the pilot stage onwards was consistent, allowing local knowledge to be used to tailor the approach and generate creative practice, which was fed back into the national implementation through case studies, publications, and professional development. Compared to the top–down, or linear, approaches of other large-scale reforms that affected pedagogy but that did not reach the lowest-attaining pupils, Every

Child a Reader has demonstrated what can be achieved when there are sound core principles and opportunities for responding at local level (Earl *et al.*, 2003).

Where leaders have developed, or have come to develop, vision and commitment, Every Child a Reader can play its part as a sustainable programme of school improvement addressing underattainment. Sustainability depends on the successful choreography of leadership, commitment, and deep understanding of the concept and theory of Reading Recovery and Every Child a Reader. 'Authentic school improvement strategies actively search out the most appropriate strategy in response to the learning needs of students' (Hopkins, 2001: 175), and the commitment and vision of leaders from those in schools and those at the highest political levels can ensure the future of successful innovation.

Returning to the definition of sustainability explored earlier in this chapter, Every Child a Reader has 'evolve[d] to incorporate improvements, respond[ed] to new data, and yet remain[ed] consistent with the underlying principles' (Earl *et al.*, 2003: 6). As pupil outcomes have been consistently strong, it could be assumed that the virtuous circle described by Barber (see p. 117) has been created. Due to the high quality of professional development for teachers and teacher leaders, this is not a low-cost intervention. But it is the long-term investment in professional development, enabling deep and sustained change in teachers' understandings and pedagogy, that assures successful and sustainable outcomes for children. Every Child a Reader has demonstrated success using the 'right drivers' (Fullan, 2011), and it could become a central strand of what is permanently available, in addition to and in support of quality class provision, to ensure that lower-attaining children learn to read and write.

Every Child a Reader continues to be relevant in the current economic climate. However, there remains a twofold challenge – tackling under-attainment, which is often linked to deprivation, and providing enough capital to sustain an infrastructure that can achieve that goal. Economic constraints are the greatest threat to the implementation's sustainability. Early research by the KPMG Foundation (2006; 2009) has shown the long-term, widespread savings of early literacy intervention. More recently, Allen (2011: ix) has urged that the 'current government and those that come after it no matter what political colour, must carry early intervention still further until real inter-generational change has been achieved'. Despite that research and Allen's challenge, consistent resourcing for Every Child a Reader is proving problematic and may become the single limiting factor of future development, since single schools cannot implement the reform without the support of a national and local infrastructure.

Notes

[1] Data to exemplify a range of perspectives were generated from various sources. Semi-structured individual, face-to-face, email, or telephone interviews were conducted by the authors between September 2011 and February 2012 with those involved in national and local authority leadership. The specific roles played by these participants in Every Child a Reader are outlined in the notes below. Other data were derived indirectly from the Evaluation of Every Child a Reader (DfE, 2011) and reported in the same form as that document.

[2] Better Reading Partnership is a catch-up intervention for pupils who have begun to read, but not efficiently and often with little understanding. It is a short intensive programme (consisting of three 15-minute sessions a week for ten weeks) led by teaching assistants. Successful average progress in reading age is plus six months in Key Stage 1 and plus nine months in Key Stage 2.

[3] Fischer Family Trust Wave 3 is an intervention for Year 1 pupils who are not developing early literacy skills and cannot access group catch-up intervention such as Early Literacy Support. The programme is delivered on a daily basis by a teaching assistant supported by a teacher. The aim is to enable sufficient progress in reading and writing for children to access a Wave 2 intervention and/or continue to progress through whole class/group teaching.

[4] Talking Partners (consisting of three 20-minute sessions a week for ten weeks) is a short-term intervention led by teaching assistants and designed to improve speaking and listening skills.

[5] Alison was a teacher-leader participant in the MA: Literacy Learning and Literacy Development programme 2010–11, whose written comments are used here with permission.

[6] Rosina was a teacher leader participant in the MA Literacy Learning and Literacy Development programme 2007–08, whose written comments are used here with permission.

[7] Judith is a local authority link manager, interviewed in January 2012.

[8] Clare is the national lead for Talking Partners, interviewed in January 2012.

[9] Steve was a national leader of the National Literacy Strategy and a local authority manager in Sheffield, interviewed in December 2011.

[10] Sue is a Reading Recovery national leader, interviewed in November 2012.

[11] Anne is now a headteacher, but was previously a Primary National Strategy leader for Every Child a Reader, interviewed in November 2011.

[12] Martin is an Every Child a Reader headteacher, interviewed in November 2012.

[13] Prime Minister from 2007 to 2010.

[14] Secretary of State for Education and Skills from 2006 to 2007.

[15] David is a local authority link manager, interviewed in October 2011.

[16] Richard was one of the first Reading Recovery teacher leaders in the UK and has continued in that role throughout the Every Child a Reader pilot and rollout. He was interviewed in October 2011.

[17] Jean was involved in the planning and pilot stages of Every Child a Reader and became a director of Every Child a Chance Trust in 2009. She was interviewed in February 2012.

[18] In Nottinghamshire, Marion is the local authority manager and Jose is the teacher leader. They were interviewed in February 2012.

[19] Gill is the national lead for the Better Reading Partnership, interviewed in January 2012.

[20] Jayne is a headteacher at a Manchester school, interviewed during 2010–11. Permission has been given to use selected material about her experiences.
[21] Joy is an Every Child a Reader teacher leader, interviewed in October 2011.

References

Allen, G. (2011) 'Early Intervention: The next steps'. An independent Report to HM Government. Online. www.dwp:gov.uk/docs/early-intervention-next-steps.pdf (accessed 8 January 2012).

Barber, M. (2004) 'Courage and the lost art of bicycle maintenance'. Paper presented at the Primary National Strategy Consultant Leaders' Conference. London, February.

Brooks, G. (2007) *What Works for Pupils with Literacy Difficulties?* London: DCSF.

– (2013, 4th ed.). *What Works for Children and Young People with Literacy Difficulties? The Effectiveness of Intervention Schemes*. Bracknell: Dyslexia-SpLD Trust.

Blatchford, P., Bassett, P., Brown, P., and Webster, R. (2009) 'The effect of support staff on pupil engagement and individual attention'. *British Educational Research Journal*, 35 (5), 661–86.

Coburn, C.E. (2003) 'Rethinking scale: Moving beyond numbers to deep and lasting change'. *Educational Researcher,* 32(6), 3–12.

Coburn, C.E. and Stein, M.K. (eds) (2010) *Research and Practice in Education: Building alliances, bridging the divide*. Plymouth, NJ: Rowman and Littlefield.

Datnow, A., Hubbard, L., and Mehan, H. (2002) *Extending Educational Reform*. New York: RoutledgeFalmer.

DCSF (1997) *The National Literacy Strategy*. London: DCSF.

– (1998) *The National Numeracy Strategy*. London: DCSF.

– (2008) *Every Child a Reader Toolkit*. Online. www.everychildachancetrust.org/ (accessed 9 January 2012; no longer available May 2013).

DfE (2011) *Evaluation of Every Child a Reader (ECaR)*. London: DfE.

DfES (1989) *The National Curriculum*. London: DfES.

– (2003) *Managing Wave 3 Literacy Interventions: Good practice guidance for local education authorities*. London: Primary National Strategies.

Douëtil, J. (2005) 'Reading Recovery™ Annual Report for UK and Ireland 2004–05'. London: European Centre for Reading Recovery. Online. www. readingrecovery.ioe.ac.uk/reports/ (accessed 13 January 2012).

Douëtil, J. (2011) 'Reading Recovery™ Annual Report for UK and Ireland 2010–11'. London: European Centre for Reading Recovery. Online. www. readingrecovery.ioe.ac.uk/reports/ (accessed 13 January 2012).

Drucker, P.F. (1994) 'The age of social transformation'. *The Atlantic Monthly*, 274 (5), 53–80.

Earl, L., Watson, N., and Katz, S. (2003) 'Large-scale Education Reform: Life cycles and implications for sustainability'. Reading: CfBT. Online. www.cfbt.com/ evidenceforeducation/pdf/Lifecycles.pdf (accessed 12 January 2012).

Elias, M.J., Zins, J.E., Graczyk, P.A., and Weissberg, R.P (2003) 'Implementation, sustainability, and scaling-up of social-emotional and academic innovations in public schools'. *School Psychology Review*, 32 (3), 303–19.

Ellis, V. (2011) 'What happened to teachers when they played "The Literacy Game?"'. In A. Goodwin and C. Fuller (eds), *The Great Literacy Debate: A critical response to the literacy strategy and the framework for English*. London: Routledge.

Elmore, R.F. (2000) 'Building a New Structure for School Leadership'. Online. www. politicalscience.uncc.edu/godwink/PPOL8687/Wk10%20March%2022%20 Accountability/Elmore%20Building%20a%20New%20Structure%20for%20 Leadership:pdf (accessed 8 January 2012).

European Centre for Reading Recovery (2012) *Standards and Guidelines*. Online. http://readingrecovery.ioe.ac.uk/about/documents/Standards_and_Guidelines.pdf

Every Child a Chance Trust (2nd ed., 2009) 'The Long Term Costs of Literacy Difficulties'. Online. www.readingrecovery.ioe.ac.uk/reports/documents/ The_long_term_costs_of_literacy_difficulties_2nd_edition.pdf (accessed 22 February 2012).

Every Child a Reader, *Every Child a Reader Annual Reports*. Online. http:// readingrecovery.ioe.ac.uk/reports/37.html (accessed 24 July 2012).

Every Child a Reader, *Every Child a Reader Case Studies*. Online. http:// readingrecovery.ioe.ac.uk/about/56.html (accessed 18 October 2012)

Every Child a Reader, *Every Child a Reader Studies*. Online. http://readingrecovery. ioe.ac.uk/reports/37.html (accessed 24 July 2012).

Fischer Family Trust (2004) *FFT Wave 3*. A report of findings from a 10 week pilot in the ambit of the local education authorities of Redcar and Cleveland, Manchester, Brent, and Bradford.

– (2009) *FFT Wave 3*. A report based on data and reports submitted by the local education authorities of Birmingham, Bradford, Devon, Leeds, Liverpool, Redcar and Cleveland, Sandwell, Sheffield, and Tameside.

Fullan, M. (2005) 'The tri-level solution: School, district, state synergy'. *Education Analyst* (Society for the Advancement of Excellence in Education), winter.

Fullan, M. (2010) 'The BIG ideas behind whole system reform'. *Education Canada*, summer, Canadian Education Association.

Fullan, M. (2011) 'Choosing the wrong drivers for whole school system reform'. *Centre for Strategic Education Seminar Series Paper No. 204* (April).

Fullan, M., Hill, P., and Crévola, C. (eds) (2006) *Breakthrough*. London: Sage.

Fullan, M., Rolheiser, C., Mascall, B., and Edge, K. (2001a) 'Accomplishing large scale reform: A tri-level proposition'. Article prepared for the *Journal of Educational Change*, November 2001. Online. www.michaelfullan.com

Hall, G.E., and Loucks, S.F. (1978) 'Innovation Configurations: Analyzing the adaptation of innovations'. Paper presented at the annual meeting of the American Educational Research Association, Toronto, Canada. Online. https:// eric.ed.gov (accessed 1 November 2011).

Hargreaves, A. (2005) *Extending Educational Change: International handbook of educational change*. Dordrecht: Springer.

Hargreaves, D.H. and Hopkins, D. (1991) *The Empowered School: The management and practice of development planning*. London: Continuum.

Hatch, T. (2000) 'What does it take to break the mould? Rhetoric and reality in new American schools'. *Teachers College Record*, 102, 561–89.

Hattie, J. (2009) *Visible Learning: A synthesis of over 800 meta-analyses relating to achievement*. London: Routledge.

Hopkins, D. (2001) *School Improvement for Real*. London: RoutledgeFalmer.

Hurry, J. and Holliman, A. (2009) *The Impact of Reading Recovery Three Years after the Intervention*. London: Institute of Education, University of London.

Hurry, J. (2012) *The Impact of Reading Recovery Five Years after Intervention*. London: Institute of Education, University of London. Online. www.ioe.ac.uk/about/documents/Hurry_London_follow_up_2012_Report_december_12.pdf (accessed 2 May 2013).

Kemmis, S. and Smith, T.J. (eds) (2008) *Enabling Praxis: Challenges for Education*. Rotterdam: Sense Publishers.

KPMG Foundation (2006) *'The Long Term Costs of Literacy Difficulties'*. Online. www.kpmg.co.uk/pubs/ECR2006.pdf (accessed 2 May 2013).

Moss, G. (2004) 'Changing practice: The National Literacy Strategy and the politics of literacy policy'. *Literacy*, 38 (3), 126–33, November.

Moss, G. (2009) 'The politics of literacy in the context of large-scale education reform'. *Research Papers in Education*, 24 (2), 155–74.

Mullis, Ina V.S., Martin, Michael O., Gonzalez, Eugenio J., and Kennedy, Ann M. (2003) *PIRLS 2001 International Report: IEA's study of reading literacy achievement in primary school in 35 countries*. Boston: Boston College. Online. http://timss.bc.edu/pirls2001i/pirls2001_pubs_ir.html (accessed 9 January 2012).

Ofsted (2004) *Reading for Purpose and Pleasure: An evaluation of the teaching of reading in primary schools*. London: HMI

Stringfield, S., and Datnow, A. (1998) 'Scaling up school restructuring designs in urban schools'. *Education and Urban Society*, 30 (3), 269–76.

UNESCO (2010) 'The Vision of Education Reform in the United States' (transcript of a speech by Arne Duncan, given in Paris). Online. www.ed.gov/news/speeches/vision-education-reform-united-states-secretary-arne-duncans-remarks-united-nations-ed (accessed 18 October 2011).

Chapter 6

From innovation to normalization

Sue Burroughs-Lange

In order for innovation in education to fulfil its aims in terms of children's lives and achievements, it must progress from being something optional or extra to becoming an essential part of school provision. In this chapter, the major themes and topics of the preceding chapters are summarized and drawn together to demonstrate how this can be achieved through Reading Recovery and Every Child a Reader. The steps towards the 'normalization' of innovation, keeping the balance between integrity and evolution, are enumerated; the challenge of adjustment to different value systems is considered; and the central role that the transfer of knowledge plays in effecting change is described. While highlighting factors that may challenge the future of that change, this chapter ends by exploring current threats to the literacy learning needs of young children and to their ability to thrive in English schools.

Introduction: What's in a name?

The government report *Every Child Matters* (Department for Education and Science, 2002) was familiar to everyone working with young children, and the words 'every child' came to preface a number of initiatives; following Every Child a Reader came Every Child Counts, supported by the organization Every Child a Chance, and others such as Every Child a Writer. Despite over-use of its banner, the goals, activities, and outcomes of Every Child a Reader strengthened during the six years of its expansion. With Every Child a Reader now widely appearing in its abbreviated form 'ECaR', understanding precisely what it offers as an effective early response to literacy difficulties risks being obscured by an acronym.

Metaphors that are used in education are illuminating, offering a lens through which to gain understanding of a conceptual base or to look closely at unexamined premises. For example, the term 'cascade' is often used in the rollout of an innovation. 'Cascade' conveys an image of knowledge, practice, resource, and the tools of change flowing down in an ever-widening stream but with diminishing force. By contrast, the schools and teachers who participated in Reading Recovery with Every Child a Reader were empowered through greater understanding of literacy processes derived from the *central* role afforded to extending and continuing professional development: that is, quality was not diluted by distance from the ideas' origins.

Even the name 'Reading Recovery' does not encompass the breadth of the teaching and learning to which it refers, since the intervention includes writing and oral language development as well as reading, with each aspect providing mutual support to ensure literacy success (Clay, 2001). Every Child a Reader practitioners ceased to refer to Reading Recovery as a 'programme'. 'Programme' is often understood as a prescribed pedagogy, with predetermined content and progression, through which the child is expected to learn. Reading Recovery, by contrast, is characterized by the teacher's moment-by-moment decision-making, informed by current records, observation, and formative assessment, and it is this that makes the content of each child's lesson and the pattern of each learner's growth unique. When Reading Recovery became the foundation of expertise for the Every Child a Reader initiative, it was helping to achieve a broader approach to early literacy learning and literacy difficulties: Clay (1987: 40) had realized that 'an innovation cannot move into an educational system merely on the merits of what it can do for children', and Rinehart and Short (1991: 89–109) characterized 'Reading Recovery as a re-structuring phenomenon'.

The tension between preserving integrity and meeting the challenges of change

Successful innovation in education must address an unknown futurescape. All educational change is based on the belief that the intended activity will result in better teaching and learning outcomes, and research plays a significant role in showing the direction that change should take. Reading Recovery is arguably one of the most evaluated educational activities, including extensive longitudinal research into its effectiveness. Research provided a strong foundation on which to base the innovations required to bring effective literacy intervention to a greater proportion of six-year-olds than had previously been reached. Reading Recovery had safeguarded its integrity, remaining faithful to its original design through layers of quality assurance, monitoring, and ongoing evaluation, while incorporating new knowledge derived from educational research (see Chapter 3 and Chapter 4).

Rapid expansion poses risks to the maintenance of integrity. Without sufficient attention to evidence drawn from theory and practice, effectiveness is compromised and the goals of the innovation risk being undermined. For example, there was pressure to reduce the intensity of initial and ongoing professional development because it was expensive and time-consuming; this was resisted because the importance of the professional development processes was continually demonstrated through pupil outcomes. The management of innovation to achieve expansion without loss of integrity or threat to pupil outcomes is always critical to success, as it was in the case of Every Child a Reader. However, a blanket resistance to change will certainly hamper an innovation's potential to deliver its full impact.

Three aspects of change are considered:

- changes resulting from challenges to fundamental assumptions about learning to read
- changes in practical and proactive forms of engagement by stakeholders
- changes brought about by rapid growth and the challenge to participants' roles.

Change: Challenges to fundamental assumptions about learning to read

The efficacy of Reading Recovery was established in the early stages of its implementation. But challenges to the reasons for this efficacy appeared from a variety of contexts, including from experts such as Chapman and his colleagues (Chapman *et al.*, 2001) who held different views about the causes of reading difficulty.

The Primary National Strategy did not expose teachers to theory. Instead, it emphasized the changing of practice: this was an example of Coburn's (2003) linear model, in which practitioners are distanced from theory (see Chapter 3). In contrast, professional development in Reading Recovery requires detailed examination of literacy acquisition theory, leading to a new understanding.

To abandon the developmental or genetic view of literacy acquisition requires a willingness to review the relationship between learner potential, and teaching and learning. Reading makes significant mental demands (on experience and visual perception, and as cognitive activity) but only low-level physical demands (such as looking at and manipulating the text source). Brain-imaging research has attempted to show where brain activity or neural connections may be faulty or underused in some children who have literacy difficulties and who are sometimes described as dyslexic. However, it is still unclear whether the area of the brain that relates to reading spontaneously becomes active through the process of reading itself, or conversely that it remains underdeveloped until it is 'taught to read'. This aspect of the nature-versus-nurture debate (explored in such writings as those of Dehaene *et al.*, 2010) is discussed in Chapter 3. What policymakers and change agents believe about the malleability of the young brain affects the approach that might be adopted as an early intervention.

Change: Challenge to forms of engagement by stakeholders

Stakeholders, whether the long-term committed or those newly recruited in support of the goals of Reading Recovery and Every Child a Reader, found themselves called upon to respond somewhat untypically in playing a part in changing outcomes for early readers.

Behavioural change, whether minor or more substantial, plays a part in moving innovation along its path. For example, in Every Child a Reader:

- the director of a charitable trust realized that her role had changed from that of grant-giver to that of broker so as to allow her to bring funding partners together;
- the head of the School of Early Childhood and Primary Education at the Institute of Education became directly involved in attracting funding, which was unusual for that time and for a programme directed at children rather than research;
- the director of a multinational finance company left his City desk to engage directly with teachers, school governors, head teachers, literacy consultants, and local school groups to encourage them to become part of the new initiative.

These examples of unusual hands-on involvement helped to generate momentum for the re-emergence of Reading Recovery and the launch of Every Child a Reader as a concept and as a way of effecting change. These small changes in ways that people can act and react are often overlooked in change theory, but collectively they can contribute to the momentum necessary for driving change.

Change: Rapid growth and the challenge to perceptions of interlocking roles

In the early stages, change brings an inevitable challenge of having to do more with less in order not to lose forward thrust while capacity is built. The greatest challenge is to ensure that early decisions, driven by expediency, are sufficiently sound and far-sighted to underpin the working of the systems required by the expanding implementation. These systems need to support the organization centrally and regionally with equal success.

(i)   TENSIONS OF HIGHER DEMAND VERSUS LEADERSHIP INTEGRITY

The central leadership team evolved new ways of working to extend their reach and capacity. Following the efforts of those involved during the two-year lead-in to the start of Every Child a Reader in 2006, support structures were put in place to achieve the goal of expansion. It was evident to the central leadership team that, in order to work effectively on a larger scale, significant change would be required. Not only was expansion at every level required: diversification was also needed (see Chapter 2 and Chapter 5).

Some of these changes involved streamlining ways of communicating with external organizations; for example, protocols were developed to communicate with both the Primary National Strategy and the Every Child a Chance Trust. These protocols improved communication between leadership teams, and additional benefits were derived from the trust's promotional activities, and from links with government and opinion-makers. However, while these protocols were largely successful, the fact that the National Literacy Strategy and Reading Recovery teams were not in close physical proximity meant that the potential benefits were not always identified and shared in ways that could also have built complementary skills across the teams.

Other changes were internal: scaling up the programme meant the need to consider individual team members' strengths, as the demands on the enlarged team necessitated the diversification of roles. This move away from a team in which everyone could do everything was accompanied by some concerns about personal professional identities and a sense of self-efficacy (see Chapter 4). While the leadership team acknowledged that changes were necessary, its highly prized democratic ethos was challenged by the pragmatic need to adopt a more differentiated approach. For example, new leadership team members had been recruited over these years. They undertook intensive professional development in their new responsibilities. Members of the senior team leading the new members' development programme were anxious that they should have the opportunity to engage with the broad spectrum of the theory and practice underpinning the leadership and implementation role, and not be moved too soon into specialisms that risked a premature narrowing of their professional preparation.

While changes to decision-making requirements stemming from working with external partners might have seemed superficial, they symbolized differences in deeply held views about how to work with professional networks (see Chapter 5). One example of this was the need to adopt different forms of record-keeping and reporting as an accountability procedure expected by the Primary National Strategy. The latter's format was not predicated on a conceptual model of professional activity in which formative feedback loops and the valuing of reflection were foremost. Therefore, the quality assurance processes of the PNS were elaborated by the Every Child a Reader team so that they now included the dialectic and mentoring interactions that had been shown to be effective in bringing about change in professional knowledge and embedding practice (see Chapter 4). Thus the needs of both the PNS and Every Child a Reader were served.

(ii) REGIONAL AND LOCAL LEADERSHIP WAYS OF WORKING

The working patterns and responsibilities of the localized leadership of Reading Recovery and Every Child a Reader, including teacher leaders and local authority line managers, were forced to change due to the demands of rapid expansion. Before the expansion of Every Child a Reader, local leaders of Reading Recovery regularly met in clusters across the year to focus on problem-solving and to share practice. In addition, they shared information regarding the regional enterprise's fitness to feed into local and national planning.

With Every Child a Reader, the need to demonstrate the impact of maximum investment led to some local authorities being grouped into larger consortia, with a shared teacher leader. In the early stages, these consortia created frustrations for teacher leaders, particularly when they had no clear chain of command or communication with senior management in all the participating authorities. It became clear that the existing infrastructure was not equipped to support the effectiveness of Every Child a Reader in consortia (for examples of this, see Chapter 5). To resolve the problem, the leadership team at the Institute of Education and Primary National Strategy regional managers worked together to find ways to improve the implementation. Significantly, this joint problem-solving was also beneficial in increasing leaders' mutual understanding of each others' decision-making systems.

As the outcomes for children became more evident (e.g. in Every Child a Reader Annual Reports for the first three years and accompanying media profile), there was a relaxation in many of these tensions and an emerging sense of mutual professional development derived from working together on a national scale.

Reading Recovery teachers leading Every Child a Reader particularly benefited from being part of the expanding implementation. There was a wider range of opportunities for learning from one another and engaging in professional development interactions, both in consortia and at national-level events. Less obviously, perhaps, the awareness of belonging to a larger innovation gave teacher leaders more confidence in their work in schools.

Shared problem-solving generated a number of positive changes that were built into successive rounds of expansion (see Chapter 5).

Those who rose to the challenge of change did so because they were sufficiently engaged to participate in Every Child a Reader. Their engagement stemmed from professional obligations, the opportunity to be associated with a success story, altruism, and curiosity. They also had to acknowledge the evidence that previous ways of working had not been effective, or (even grudgingly) from their own evidence of impact on the child. Significantly, for those whose roles were distanced from school learning, the trigger often took the form of the cathartic experience of coming face to face with the very real agonies of a child struggling to read.

Policy-based evidence making

All governments want children to learn to read. Government-set learning targets have long acted as a tool for demonstrating the success of their policy. Ministers embark on policy to show what their government can achieve (Coles, 2012). The use of performance indicators in the political arena has become a prominent tool of government accountability: for instance, the National Literacy Strategy set itself a target of 80 per cent, later revised to 85 per cent, for the proportion of children having reached Level 4 on their entry to secondary school.

'High-stakes testing' contributes to accountability and to determining whether policy is being deployed effectively. National testing existed as a part of the English school landscape throughout the lifetime of Every Child a Reader. At first the lack of diagnostic sensitivity of national testing tools was viewed negatively by many educators, including those engaged in Reading Recovery. However, the national publication of standardized results at Key Stage 1 (children aged 7) in a widely understood format was helpful in demonstrating effectiveness where Reading Recovery and Every Child a Reader were operating, while also highlighting the numbers of children not progressing in literacy learning. In practice, standardized testing does not control how children are taught, but it merely specifies what will be tested.

We have long known that teachers' expectations play a role in learners' actual achievements (Rutter *et al.*, 1976) and curriculum policy can affect these expectations. The achievement levels of children involved in Every Child a Reader challenge and reform the expected 'bell curve' of the normal distribution of early reading acquisition (see figure 6.1), and these children's post-intervention progress continues along a revised trajectory (KS2 results, 2012).[1]

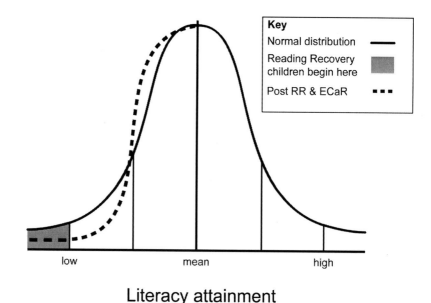

Key	
Normal distribution	——
Reading Recovery children begin here	▨
Post RR & ECaR	▪▪▪

low   mean   high

Literacy attainment

Figure 6.1: The reconfiguring of the curve of normal distribution in literacy achievement after Every Child a Reader and Reading Recovery implementations

However, the reduction or near-disappearance of the low end of the achievement curve does not fit with existing assumptions about normal distribution. Politicians may be more comfortable with trying to raise the peak of the bell curve (the average) rather than considering the impact of contraction of the low-end tail on normative assumptions.

So what challenge does an effective educational intervention, such as Every Child a Reader, bring to politicians when it achieves results with a population that they regard as falling outside the 85 per cent level required for a stated political policy success?

To gain a position within a policy cycle, Every Child a Reader had to be shown to be essential for government accountability. As discussed in Chapter 1 and Chapter 2, this accountability came in the form of international pressure. In 2006, the Progress in International Reading Literacy Study (PIRLS) showed that in England 8.8 per cent of children were at or below the '400' level (that is, they 'did not display even minimal reading skills'), whereas the average across the other countries involved was 4.7 per cent (Hilton, 2006). The 'what works' evidence of Reading Recovery and Every Child a Reader became more attractive to literacy curriculum policymakers. But its attractiveness was, and still is, constrained by the slow pace of attainable growth rates in reaching sufficient numbers of children who form that 8.8 per cent. Expansion is built on each year-cohort of school-based highly skilled teachers, and on area-based highly skilled literacy teacher-educators, who take time to acquire their expertise (see Chapter 4). Governments, like their policy cycles, need quick results (Moss, 2009). For example, if children's outcomes that were raised at 6 years of age, were included in the PISA (OECD, 2009) study of 15-year-olds, their impact on assessment results would be around nine years after tuition in Reading Recovery – well beyond a government's term of office.

The implementation of Every Child a Reader remains vulnerable because of several factors:

- the need to change teachers' beliefs about and attitudes towards the potential of some children
- the time required to build capacity at teacher and school level so that the full extent of the changes and benefits of Reading Recovery/Every Child a Reader can become apparent by the second and third year of intervention
- in terms of influence on national policy, the slow impact of the benefits of Every Child a Reader on national and international assessment measures.

Knowledge transfer

With a rational linear model of change such as in the National Literacy Strategy (see Chapter 2), there is an assumption that transferring the right knowledge to the right place will change what people do and thereby produce different and, by inference, better outcomes (Taylor, 1997).

Repeated rounds of educational reform imply two possibilities: either that the present pedagogical system is effective, as some schools and areas produce high outcomes, which suggests that more efficient management systems are all that is required to replicate this success on a wider scale; or that a systematic approach to knowledge transfer is required to raise standards on a uniform basis. Which assumption about reform does implementing Reading Recovery and Every Child a Reader imply? We first consider the role of knowledge transfer in effecting change.

(i) Evaluating features of Every Child a Reader as knowledge transfer in effecting change

As more Reading Recovery teachers completed their professional development, Every Child a Reader acquired a school-based source of knowledge able to set in motion identified waves of intervention, reaching beyond those children with the greatest literacy support needs. These waves were graphically portrayed as a ripple effect. Developed in Every Child a Reader's first year, this model essentially provided the context for knowledge transfer around the processes of change, as well as its literacy learning content and pedagogical strengths, which were shared with class teachers. In adopting this model, local ownership was assumed from the start. Supported by their professional community, experienced Reading Recovery teachers devised ways of drawing on their theories about child and adult learning and used their existing pedagogical strengths to undertake cycles of reform based on locally identified needs. They aimed to engage key school and area personnel in these change processes.

This process of achieving change through the transfer of knowledge and ongoing pedagogical development (see Chapter 3) increased the scope of the knowledge base within Reading Recovery. Every Child a Reader often provided a vehicle for changing a school's perceptions of its Reading Recovery teacher, thus empowering them to play a greater part in reforming literacy teaching across the school (see Chapter 5). Chapter 2 and Chapter 4 include a description and evaluation of the concept of layers of intervention, of the processes of intervention mapping, and of comprehensive assessment, matched to the extent of children's need for specialized help. This approach provided the scope to extend beyond Reading Recovery and so to address many more children's needs in planned, monitored, and more cost-effective ways.

Table 6.1: How transfer of knowledge pedagogy and process interact in implementing Every Child a Reader

Knowledge transfer	Investment	Activity
MAIN Direct, high-level expertise (regional hub)	High investment, high unit cost, and therefore argument for longer-term savings	Reading Recovery teaching for individual 6-year-old children, the lowest achievers in literacy, whose reading and writing are raised to appropriate age levels.

INDIRECT Medium-level, locally owned	Lower investment, lower unit costs; a school-based asset, which reaches more children	Low-cost professional development and monitoring structure provided by the Reading Recovery teacher, who shares content and pedagogy with other school personnel (teachers, teaching assistants, and volunteers), who then deliver interventions to children with lower-support literacy needs (Every Child a Reader 'layers').
RESOURCE Device for organizational and pedagogical knowledge transfer (*Book Bands for Guided Reading*)	Very low investment, access to regular updates, highlights schools' strategic investment in reading resources	Reading Recovery teacher refers to *Book Bands* as the source of information regarding children's published texts and how to match these to the learner's cutting edge in literacy development. *Book Bands*, adopted by the National Literacy Strategy and the Primary National Strategy as a device for capacity-building in teachers (for instance, pedagogical and practical teaching models), also functions as an organizing plan for the class/school library, and is based on the understanding of the need to enthuse and entice children into reading, while also ensuring a successful reading experience every time.

(ii) Pedagogical environments, knowledge transfer, and Every Child a Reader

Every Child a Reader did not operate within a policy vacuum and was subject to changes in the broader policy context, particularly policy change in relation to curriculum content and pedagogy. To survive, Every Child a Reader needed to be sufficiently robust and flexible to operate within differing policy cycles.

Reading Recovery and Every Child a Reader have both achieved success before and during the Primary National Strategy (see the various European

Centre for Reading Recovery *Annual Reports*) and have adapted to additions to the Primary National Strategy including *Progression in Phonics* (DfES, 2005) and *Letters and Sounds* (DfES, 2006), and the more recent focus on discrete early phonics instruction (e.g. Primary phonics check, DfE, 2012). An explanation for this lies in Reading Recovery's and Every Child a Reader's constant diagnostic focus on the learner, which enables the teacher to select from a full range of appropriate teaching approaches. The focus of the pedagogy is adjusted during tuition and on reflection, to capitalize on each child's strengths and to focus on weaknesses, and aspects of literacy that a child may be finding confusing or has not yet tackled (see Chapter 3 and Chapter 4).

Brooks (2007, 2013), Clay (2001), and Slavin *et al.* (2009) demonstrate that effective classroom programmes will always require additional tools to ensure success in literacy acquisition for individual students. A school's success might be measured by the diminished size of the group for whom something extra has to be provided, and for how long. With a structured yet flexible pedagogical approach, including a systematic approach to knowledge transfer and the implementation of layers of tailored support, classroom environments, whatever the current policy emphasis for instruction, can be developed to respond to all learners' particular needs. Pupils who have become self-monitoring and self-generating learners will also become inured to the vagaries of policy and practice (see Chapter 3 and Chapter 4).

Value systems: Challenge, resistance, adjustment, and change

Confronting new knowledge – for example, about teaching or managing learning, as in Every Child a Reader – necessitates a review and revision of assumptions. Some uncomfortable facts and feelings may only be resolved by an adjustment of system and individual values (Fullan, 2004). Taking account of this is crucial to the successful introduction and embedding of innovation.

(i)   *Demonstrating that Every Child a Reader innovation is cost-effective challenges value systems relating to budgetary management*

The experience of initiating and expanding the implementation of Every Child a Reader included the need to link claims of its cost-effectiveness to evidence about its success both in the long and the short term (see Chapter 1 and Chapter 5).

Primary schools bear the most direct and immediate costs of helping children who find it difficult to learn to read but there are little or no additional costs to primary schools in implementing Every Child a Reader (KPMG

Foundation, 2006; 2009). Their Reading Recovery teacher works directly with those 6-year-olds who have the most severe difficulties and, indirectly in Every Child a Reader, through empowering and resourcing other school personnel to work with a larger number of children experiencing a lesser degree of difficulty in their acquisition of early reading. Cost–benefit analysis has shown that the amount that primary schools already spend on their failing readers is equivalent to what they would spend if they implemented Reading Recovery. The main differences are:

- with Reading Recovery the expenditure is made at one point in time for a struggling learner (aged six), who then requires little, if any, extra expenditure to succeed in literacy;
- for schools without Reading Recovery, expenditure is spread across the child's primary years, with his/her difficulties persisting throughout this time and undermining his/her engagement with all other primary learning opportunities.

(KPMG Foundation, 2006; 2009)

There are also savings on special educational needs provision. The outcomes of Reading Recovery and Every Child a Reader result in a high proportion of children regaining the mainstream rather than going on to be assessed for mild or moderate learning difficulties or dyslexia. With successful intervention at the age of 6, especially pertinent in financially stringent times, available funding can be directed towards those with longer-term, more complex needs.

There are concomitant savings in secondary schools. Close to 30,000 children in England who begin their secondary schooling at the age of 11 are only reading at or below the literacy level of a 7-year-old (DfE, 2012). Poor literacy attainment impedes their access to opportunities in the secondary curriculum and they generate additional costs as they require further literacy support. Wider socio-economic benefits in the long term accrue through the reduction in poor self-esteem and other attendant difficulties that result from not learning to read at an early age (KPMG Foundation, 2006, 2009). The argument for early intervention made in Chapter 1 includes examples of research showing the link between poor literacy and many other socially destructive, medically depressing and intergenerational effects, including loss of productivity in the UK's workforce and lower tax revenues.

(ii) *Working with government and education providers to meet a declared 'moral imperative'*

Reducing inequality is a declared goal for governments. Currently in England, pupil premium funding for additional educational provision is linked to free school meals status. But it can be hard to discern the strategic impact of various policies across the gamut of government actions and anticipated life of one parliament. For example, will the increasing devolution of funding to schools subsequently allow a government to say of Every Child a Reader: 'The same amount of funding continued to be made available. If the results show little or no improvement in lifting children's literacy achievement, then schools are not doing a good enough job?' That is to say that the onus of blame has moved from government (and its policies) to schools and local authorities.

Greater financial autonomy is only emancipating when those empowered have the required knowledge base and experiential evidence to make optimum decisions. The experience of Every Child a Reader showed that, especially in those schools with a concentration of underperforming children, convincing them that all their 6-year-olds would be able to read is very hard until they had seen the results of effective intervention on their own pupils. One has sympathy with the schools' dilemma. Unless headteachers have experienced at first hand the transformation of these 6-year-olds when they become engaged in literacy, then they are easily drawn away to the many other areas of schooling that demand attention, particularly in schools serving poorer areas.

The sustainability of innovation is generally accepted as being vulnerable from a number of directions, particularly in the first few years while it moves from being novel to becoming typical, and then gradually becomes locally owned and understood within the culture of each school. Ring-fencing of some funding streams is needed to sustain targeted, evidence-based, effective initiatives, especially through the early period of implementing change before the benefits reach full impact levels. Only when funding is targeted to enable the high-performing initiative to become embedded can the moral imperative to teach *all* children to read be seen to be sustained.

(iii) Demonstrating success for a nation that cares about literacy

The problem of how to demonstrate the longer-term effectiveness of educational reform is especially great when intervening with children at the age of 6. Yet '[S]eeking quick fix wins with "low hanging fruit" reform typifies governments early in their tenure' (Bangs *et al.*, 2011: 187). A new government may be attracted to investing in its own 'new' answer rather than supporting pre-existing initiatives, even when these have already demonstrated their effectiveness.

Since the coalition government came into power in 2010, there has been a reduction in the scale of implementations of Reading Recovery with

Every Child a Reader in England. However, the impact of this on national standardized assessment results may be hidden. If, as proposed, some primary-school assessment points are abolished and only early phonic knowledge is tested between the ages of 5 and 11, then the real extent of the fall in literacy standards at Key Stage 1 may not become publicly visible for many years hence, or well beyond the term of this government.

While comparison studies are useful in demonstrating the difference an intervention can make, governments can argue that changes in classroom practice invalidate such findings. Follow-up studies pointing to gains maintained in the long term (Hurry and Holliman, 2009; Hurry, 2012) attract similar comment.

Evaluating features of Every Child a Reader and policies for whole-school improvement.

Fullan (2004) points to the value of investing in local communities of practice as a significant way of taking teaching improvements forward. However, too much adaptation risks lack of coherence and loss of the 'reform identity'. It has been important to show that rapid expansion resulted in Every Child a Reader being no less effective than when it started. The route to continuing embedding Every Child a Reader in schools lies in looking further into aspects that may be amenable to local adaptation. If these can be fostered without threatening the strong efficacy base of teaching and learning, then outcomes already achieved with this population of children experiencing literacy difficulties will continue.

Fullan (ibid.) suggests that feedback loops for central monitoring and decision-making allow 'safe' space for local innovation. Reading Recovery and Every Child a Reader have invested in the development of web-based data to provide detailed information on the progress of children, teachers, schools, and regional teacher leaders. Information-gathering begins with the child's initial assessment and first lesson, and is updated regularly. This permits more frequent searching of diagnostic data to constantly monitor the integrity of practice while enabling local responses and ownership.

In England, governments have made school improvement a political goal. Improved literacy achievement is seen as an indicator of this. To this end the current government has taken responsibility for deciding on the content of literacy teaching based on its own research and curriculum reviews. Levers of several kinds have been used to guide, enforce, motivate, reward, and restrict teachers' choices; for example, a school's purchase of 'approved' phonics teaching resources supported by up to £3,000 in matched funding (Department for Education, 2012). Governments condemn any activity outside their policy-directed teaching content and practice as liable to dilute the improvements in outcomes that that new policy is set to achieve. However, it is at the policy development level, rather than the pedagogical one, that a government's role is likely to be more effective in bringing about improvement for learners (Bangs *et al.*, 2011).

At the outset, government policy did not provide the impetus for Every Child a Reader. However, once the scale of funding support from business was demonstrated, the government matched this funding for Every Child a Reader's first three years. In its second three-year round of implementation, funding and control were taken over by government. As administration was contracted to a third-party organization, this government change in involvement resulted in additional management costs, which unfortunately could be represented as increased per-child in programme costs. In a review of eight school-improvement initiatives from across the world, Earl *et al.* (2003: 11) highlight this: 'It's quite clear from the trajectory of these reforms that nothing is stable and that any reform will evolve and adapt as a result of the context in conditions that surround it. Within a few years reforms may be unrecognizable; with school-based management for instance the outside administrative structures that were eliminated were often reinvented'. The authors suggest that building internal capacity is needed for sustainability. Every Child a Reader was, and is, well placed to draw on its internal capacities in terms of people and systems. These capacities come from the pre-existing infrastructure of Reading Recovery; its goals of whole-school and system change (Rinehart and Short, 1991) that continue to build capacity in the development and transfer of knowledge; and maintaining an expanding infrastructure underpinned by the development of quality assurance and related data-collection systems.

Vulnerability to change

Fullan (2001) outlines the impact and problems encountered in trying to effect change through an 'islands of innovation' model.

(i)   *'Islands of innovation' and sustained change*

In a school, a district, and even a university setting, 'islands of innovation' are found in the history of Reading Recovery and Every Child a Reader. Reading Recovery began in *'islands'* and its early history matches the features identified by Mioduser *et al.* (2006):

- Surrey teacher leader trained – *local initiatives*
- small-scale trial prompted by HMI interest – *taken up by enthusiasts*

- and accessing an already available funding stream (GEST) – *implemented through top-down management decisions*
- raising achievement of lowest literacy learners early – *focused on a particular content area or a particular task* (see Chapter 1).

Fullan (2001) and Mioduser *et al.* (2006) agree that top-down *or* localized initiation of innovation affect the motivation and willingness of the system to absorb greater change. This was evident in the advent of the National Literacy Strategy (Ofsted, 2000), where the 'Literacy Hour' used the theory and practice of Reading Recovery adapted for class and small-group teaching, but had no motivation to support the intervention from which it was drawn (see Chapter 1). The impression was given that the focus should be on getting the classroom instruction right first, without recognizing the role that Reading Recovery expertise in schools might play in achieving that goal (Earl *et al.*, 2000). A policy's implication that phonics programmes will fix all the problems of early literacy teaching in the classroom is currently met by a feeling of 'déjà vu'.

Innovation in the 'island' model is implemented with an expectation, at least on the part of the originators and enthusiasts, that when its effectiveness has been demonstrated, it will naturally permeate the whole organization (Fullan, 2001). This model is attractive to management as the innovation will either be seen to fail (not the case for Reading Recovery or Every Child a Reader) without involving too much effort or expense; or, if it seems to be having some success, be considered unlikely to shake the organizational culture too much or too soon. This was the case for Reading Recovery: while its demonstrable impact on children was applauded, far more work and more complex modelling would be needed for it to be turned into a system for reaching all children who needed it (Fullan, 2001). However, although it may not have been generally known, throughout the National Literacy Strategy years and still today, governments and the Institute of Education provided some funding to enable Reading Recovery's central leadership team to continue its support and monitoring role for the early intervention. Without a central team, even a small one, still in place, a model calling for rapid expansion would not have been possible. Every Child a Reader was the strategy developed to tackle this complexity of modelling, which could make links and move beyond 'islands of innovation'.

(ii)   A 'loose coupled organization' and sustained change

In a 'loose coupled' organization (Weick, 1976; Fullan, 2001; Hagel *et al.*, 2010), which might be said to typify the organizational structures at national and local level in Every Child a Reader, there may be space for 'islands of innovation' beginning to effect change in more subtle or less confrontational ways.

Fullan (2001) suggests that there may be problems in gaining acceptance or achieving expansion when an innovation is seen as being hierarchical or compartmentalized in nature. The perception has sometimes been that the 'gatekeeping' of teacher quality and professional development integrity that operates in Reading Recovery and Every Child a Reader appears to be a closed and hierarchical system (Woods and Henderson, 2002). This is a challenge for the communication strategy that is vital to any complex model of innovation. While evidence of pupil outcomes and favourable evaluations of Reading Recovery and Every Child a Reader were widely disseminated (e.g. Brooks, 2007, 2013; Tanner *et al.*, 2011), perhaps less attention was given to promoting the evidence on the quality of capacity-building generated by this interconnected professional development structure. If learner outcomes are the measure of success, then capacity-building of expertise in teaching and pedagogy must precede them and continue throughout the expansion of Reading Recovery and Every Child a Reader (European Centre for Reading Recovery *Annual Reports*, 2006–11).

If Reading Recovery and Every Child a Reader are no longer to be regarded as innovations but rather as 'best practice' in teaching, certain features must be demonstrated to be at work. Earl *et al.* (2003: 17) identify the six features that they see as being necessary in order to embed changes in policy for teaching. These respectively must:

- *Impart understanding at the cognitive, social, and cultural level.* Chapter 3 describes the cognitive changes brought about in children and Chapter 4 shows the impact of this on teacher cognitions and assumptions about learning in early literacy.
- *Provide new or revised content that is deep and detailed.* Through the use of continuous diagnostic assessment across Every Child a Reader, teachers discover for themselves the level of complexity involved in turning a non-reader into a proficient one, and the contingent teaching that can support this. This content had been somewhat simplified for teachers in the National Literacy Strategy (Chapter 2 and Chapter 4), but Every Child a Reader teachers were able to build on that background and put their new ways of working to the 'acid test' of succeeding with those who find it hardest to learn.
- *Promulgate pedagogy that is adaptable for diversity in learners and their strengths.* As the Every Child a Reader annual reports show (ECRR, 2006–11), teachers learn to work flexibly and successfully with

a wide range of children (e.g. boys and girls; those living in poverty; those learning English as an additional language; those from many social and ethnic groups, such as travellers' children, learning in mono- and multicultural inner-city schools; those with speech and language difficulties; and those with other recognized special needs, including children with dyslexia).

Unlike many support teaching strategies, the Reading Recovery principles in place throughout Every Child a Reader succeed with this wide range of needs because they are not deficit-based but focus on extending the learner's strengths to experience success as they gradually acquire the full repertoire of cognitive and practical skills to become self-generating learners (see Chapter 1 and Chapter 4).

- *Include development of emotional understanding: how emotions affect the approach to teaching and impact on children's learning.* Teachers are brought face to face with the potential of children, including some of whose progress they may previously have had low expectations. It is emotionally challenging to acknowledge that it may be their teaching that had let down children they had had in their classes. Seeing the transformation in children who now succeed is both rewarding and a source of self-blame (see the case studies in Chapter 4). In resolving this emotional response with support, teachers develop greater insight to work with the emotions of children who feel they are failures.

- *Help with understanding the change process in teachers and in learners.* The focus in Reading Recovery is on reflective practice and double-loop learning (Argyris, 1991). The pattern of professional development as a community of learners helps to make these overt in the change processes, such as in the critique of lessons through a one-way screen (see Chapter 4). Sharing the evidence for the rate of change in learners calls for articulation of this in sensitive ways for both those in support roles and class teachers.

- *Develop a new professionalism around an ethos of collective responsibility for all pupils.* This has probably been the 'newest' aspect in moving from solely Reading Recovery to Every Child a Reader with Reading Recovery. In the first instance the success of children who had previously not been achieving in the school context raises awkward questions about existing ways of working. Having wider access to detailed assessment, the ability to match children with the most appropriate support and accessing further professional development for improved provision where necessary, results in widening the responsibility and ethos that all children in our school learn to read at the right time. The change in ethos arises from including middle and top school management in committing funding to Every Child a Reader with Reading Recovery as part of a national initiative, which involved very public reporting, incentives of government funds, and publicity such as the Every Child a Reader national awards.

The preceding chapters of this book give many examples of how these features occur, and of what the experience of them looks like and feels like for participants in Reading Recovery and Every Child a Reader. The ethos of change resembled the features of an 'island of innovation' wherever it first occurred but, as it developed, the potential for lasting and greater change grew. Its loose-coupled organization allowed it to adapt but protected it from loss of integrity or efficacy. Engaging in popular and political appeal, especially across a changing and volatile political scene, may be the missing feature in the requirements identified by Earl and his co-authors for an innovation to produce sustained changes in teaching and pedagogical policy.

Conclusion

The term 'Every Child a Reader' encapsulates the idea that we should not be complacent in settling for the status quo where a proportion of children go through our school system, year on year, unable to read and write.

While the label 'Every Child a Reader' may have lost its uniqueness, its meaning became a reality. There is irrefutable evidence that between 2006 and 2011 more schools, children, parents, teachers and teaching assistants, and regional management, experienced what was possible for raising levels of achievements in literacy (ECaR annual report, ECRR, 2011). The London comparison study (Burroughs-Lange and Douëtil, 2007), consistent with other research findings (e.g. Brooks, 2007; Bynner and Parsons, 1997) demonstrated that children who are not making progress in acquiring literacy at around the age of 6 and who are left without appropriate intervention do not catch up on their own (Burroughs-Lange, 2008; Hurry and Holliman, 2009; Hurry, 2012). As their peers progress, they drop increasingly further behind (Brooks, 2007).

Complex cognitive learning cannot be left to a developmental trajectory if that is already delayed. As discussion in Chapter 1 demonstrates, early intervention is now accepted as an effective way to prevent ongoing academic difficulties and their consequences in terms of emotional, social, and financial costs (e.g. Hurry, 2000; KPMG Foundation, 2009). However, professional acceptance of the need for early intervention must be matched by political commitment so that sufficient funding for deployment of proven initiatives is provided. Partial implementation of early intervention is not effective beyond the ambit of the individual child as it does not bring about a universal rise in educational outcomes and does not support system-level school improvement (e.g. Allen, 2011; see also Chapters 2 and 5). Both efficacy and scale together hold the key to reducing the 'tail of underachievement' in literacy. But the support for teacher expertise in schools and positive outcomes for pupils that have been and can continue to be made with Every Child a Reader are at risk where there is insufficient attention to strategic funding at local and national levels (see Foreword).

This book has explored how an effective early response to improving literacy attainment fared in honouring the moral commitment that all children should learn to read at an appropriate age. However, the experiences, expertise developed, and insights gained can be understood in a wider context. Once an innovation responds effectively to an established need and demonstrates sustained or enhanced outcomes through years of implementation and expansion, its availability should be secured for future cohorts of learners. In order to achieve this it needs to continue to move away from the 'island of innovation' model, to become 'normalized' as accepted practice.

Turning a moral purpose into a reality is beset by obstacles. For example, in 2012, greater autonomy over funding offered to schools in England did not guarantee equality of opportunity, nor is equality achieved by undifferentiated teaching. Whatever the curriculum context, each new cohort of 6-year-olds includes a proportion already experiencing difficulty in learning to read and write, and these children will need support for literacy learning. The scale, intensity, and nature of the appropriate response will vary from school to school, according to children's development and stage of learning, the ongoing context of their learning development, the quality of the school's leadership, and the knowledge and experience of the teaching team. All this implies that focused funding needs to be closely tailored to these individual profiles if the right intensity of support is to be provided where and when it is needed.

As this book goes to press, Reading Recovery and Every Child a Reader are at a crossroads. Two or three years were sufficient to convince schools that first took part in the intervention that they should continue to find ways to fund their teacher and teaching assistant salaries as they started to see the impact of whole classes moving up through school without a tail of non-readers, in addition to wider school improvement.

The story of Reading Recovery and Every Child a Reader is not only about the life-changing experiences that they offered to struggling readers, and the success in raising of children's achievements that each successive government might claim for itself. It is about the obstacles that undermine the best efforts to gain support for an innovation, and the need to demonstrate success in an intelligible way to those who have decision-making powers. Showing alignment with moral and educational goals comes more readily than trying to divine what will be perceived as worthwhile in its potential for enabling the achievement of political goals.

Notes
[1] In reading, seven in nine (78 per cent) of the lowest-achieving children who had completed the Reading Recovery programme (either having attained accelerated progress or having been referred for further support at the age of 6) achieved Level 4 or above in their Key Stage 2 national assessments (aged 11), and 95 per cent achieved Level 3 or above. In writing, two-thirds of these children (69 per cent) reached Level 4 or above, and nearly all (98 per cent) attained Level 3 or above (ECRR, 2012).

References

Allen, G. (2011) Early Intervention: The Next Steps. Independent report to H.M. Government. Online. www.dwp.gov.uk/docs/early-intervention-next-steps.pdf (accessed 8 January 2012).

Argyris, C. (1991) 'Teaching smart people how to learn'. *Harvard Business Review,* May–June.

Bangs, J., Macbeath, J., and Galton, M. (2011) *Reinventing Schools, Reforming Teaching: From political visions to classroom reality.* Abingdon: Routledge.

Brooks, G. (2007) *What Works for Children with Literacy Difficulties: The effectiveness of intervention schemes*, Research report 380. London: DfES.

– (2013, 4th ed.) *What Works for Children and Young People with Literacy Difficulties? The Effectiveness of Intervention Schemes.* Bracknell: Dyslexia-SpLD Trust.

Burroughs-Lange, S.G. (2008) *Comparison of Literacy Progress of Young Children in London Schools: A follow-up study.* London: Institute of Education, University of London.

Burroughs-Lange, S.G. and Douëtil, J.D. (2007) 'Literacy progress of young children from poor urban settings: A Reading Recovery comparison study'. *Literacy Teaching and Learning*, 12 (1), 19–46.

Bynner, J., and Parsons, P. (1997) *It Doesn't Get Any Better*. London: Basic Skills Agency.

Clay, M.M. (1987) 'Implementing Reading Recovery: Systemic adaptations to an educational innovation'. *New Zealand Journal of Educational Studies*, 22, 35–58.

– (2001) *Change Over Time in Children's Literacy Development.* Auckland: Heinemann.

Chapman, J.W., Tunmer, W.E., and Prochnow, J.E. (2001) 'Does success in the Reading Recovery program depend on developing proficiency in phonological-processing skills? A longitudinal study in a whole language instruction context'. *Scientific Studies of Reading*, 5 (2), 141–76.

Coburn, C.E. (2003) 'Rethinking scale: Moving beyond numbers to deep and lasting change'. *Educational Researcher*, 32 (6), 3–12.

Coles, J., (2012) *Research and Policy*. Keynote address delivered at the British Educational Research Association Conference, University of Manchester, 4–6 September.

Department for Education (2012) 'National Curriculum Assessments at Key Stage 2 in England: Academic year 2011 to 2012'. Online. https://www.gov.uk/government/publications/national-curriculum-assessments-at-key-stage-2-in-england-academic-year-2011-to-2012

Department for Education and Science (2002) *Every Child Matters*. London: DfES. Online. http://webarchive.nationalarchives.gov.uk/20130401151715/https://www.education.gov.uk/publications/eOrderingDownload/CM5860.pdf (accessed 2 May 2013).

Department for Education and Science (2005) 'Communication, Language, Literacy Development (CLLD): Letters and Sounds'. Online. http://webarchive.nationalarchives.gov.uk/20110809091832/www.teachingandlearningresources.org.uk/early-years/communication-language-and-literacy-development-clld

– (2005) 'Communication, Language, Literacy Development (CCLD): Progression in Phonics (PiPs)'. Online. http://webarchive.nationalarchives.gov.uk/20110809091832/http://www.teachingandlearningresources.org.uk/early-years/communication-language-and-literacy-development-clld

Dehaene, S., Pegado, F., Braga, L.W., Ventura, P., Nunes Filho, G., Jobert, A., Dehaene-Lambertz, G., Kolinsky, R., Morais, J., and Cohen, L. (2010) 'How learning to read changes the cortical networks for vision and language'. *Science*, 330 (6009): 1359–64.

Earl, L., Fullan, M., Leithwood, K., and Watson, N., with Jantzi, D., Levin, B., and Torrance, N. (2000) *Watching and Learning 1. First Annual Report*. London: Department for Education and Employment.

Earl, M.J., Watson N., and Katz, S. (2003) *Large Scale Educational Reform: Life cycles and implications for sustainability*. Reading: CfBT.

European Centre for Reading Recovery (2012a) *Every Child a Reader (ECaR) Annual Report 2010–11*. London: Institute of Education, University of London (and previous annual reports, under various titles, since 2006).

– (2012b) *Reading Recovery™ Annual Report for UK and Ireland 2011–12*. Online. http://readingrecovery.ioe.ac.uk/reports/documents/Reading_Recovery_annual_report_for_the_United_Kingdom_and_Ireland_2011-12.pdf (and previous annual reports since 2005, online at http://readingrecovery.ioe.ac.uk/reports/37.html).

Fullan, M. (3rd ed., 2001). *The New Meaning of Educational Change*. New York: Teachers College, Columbia University.

Fullan, M. (2004) *Systems Thinkers in Action: Moving beyond the standards plateau: Teachers transforming teaching*. London: Department for Education and Skills.

Hagel, J. III, Brown, J.S., and Davison, L. (2010) *The Power of Pull: How small moves, smartly made, can set big things in motion*. New York: Basic Books.

Hilton, M. (2006) 'Measuring standards in primary English: Issues of validity and accountability with respect to PIRLS and National Curriculum test scores'. *British Educational Research Journal*, 32 (6), 817–37.

Hurry, J. (2000) *Review of Intervention Strategies to Support Pupils with Difficulties in Literacy during Key Stage 1*. London: QCA.

Hurry, J. (2012) *The Impact of Reading Recovery Five Years After Intervention.* London: Every Child a Reader Trust.

Hurry, J. and Holliman, A. (2009) *The Impact of Reading Recovery Three Years after Intervention.* London: Institute of Education, University of London.

KPMG Foundation (2006) *The Long Term Costs of Literacy Difficulties.* London: KPMG Foundation.

– (2nd ed., 2009) *The Long Term Costs of Literacy Difficulties.* London: Every Child a Chance Trust.

Mioduser, D., Nachmias, R., Tubin, D., and Forkosh, A. (2006) *Pedagogical Innovation Involving Information Technologies and Communications.* Tel Aviv: Center for Science and Technology Education, School of Education, Tel Aviv University.

Moss, G. (2009) 'The politics of literacy in the context of large-scale education reform'. *Research Papers in Education*, 24 (2),155–74.

OECD (2009) 'PISA 2009 Results: What students know and can do'. Online. www.oecd.org/edu/pisa/2009

Ofsted (2000), *National Literacy Strategy in special schools 1998-2000.* Online. http://www.ofsted.gov.uk/resources/national-literacy-strategy-special-schools-1998-2000 (accessed 2 May 2013).

Rinehart, J.S., and Short, P.M (1991) 'Viewing Reading Recovery as a restructuring phenomenon'. Reprinted in *Journal of School Leadership*, 20, January 2010, 89–109.

Rutter, M., Tizard, J., Yule, J., Graham, P., and Whitmore, K. (1976).'Isle of Wight Studies, 1964–1974'. *Psychological Medicine*, 6, 313–32.

Slavin, R.E., Lake, C., Chambers, B., Cheung, A., and Davis, S. (2009) 'Effective reading programs for the elementary grades: A best-evidence synthesis'. *Review of Educational Research*, 79 (4), 1391–466.

Tanner, E., Brown, A., Day, N., Kotecha, M., Low, N., Morrell, G., Turczuk, O., Brown, V., Collingwood A., Chowdry, H., Greaves, E., Harrison, C., Johnson, G., and Purdon, S. (2011) *Evaluation of Every Child a Reader.* London: DfE-RR114.

Taylor, S. (1997) *Educational Policy and the Politics of Change.* Abingdon: Routledge.

Weick, K.E. (1976) 'Educational organizations as loosely coupled systems'. *Administrative Science Quarterly*, 21, 1–19.

Wood, C., and Caulier-Grice, J. (2006) *Fade or Flourish: How primary schools can build on children's early progress.* London: Social Market Foundation.

Woods, B. and Henderson, R. (2002) 'Early intervention: Narratives of learning, discipline and enculturation', *Journal of Early Childhood Education*, 2 (3), 243–68.

Appendix 1: Annotated timeline showing publications and political context alongside Reading Recovery and Every Child a Reader milestones

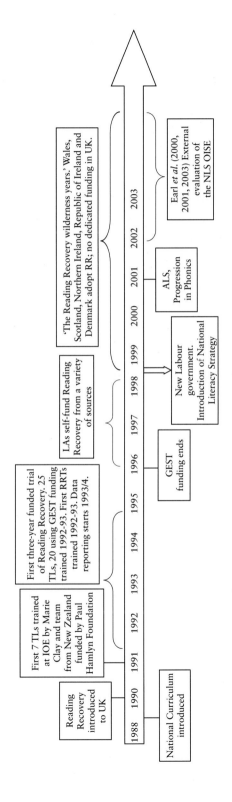

1988 1989 1990 1991 1992 1993 1994 1995 1996 1997 1998 1999 2000 2001 2002 **2003**

Reading Recovery introduced to UK

National Curriculum introduced

First 7 TLs trained at IOE by Marie Clay and team from New Zealand funded by Paul Hamlyn Foundation

First three-year funded trial of Reading Recovery. 25 TLs, 20 using GEST funding trained 1992-93. First RRTs trained 1992-93. Data reporting starts 1993/4.

GEST funding ends

LAs self-fund Reading Recovery from a variety of sources

New Labour government. Introduction of National Literacy Strategy

ALS, Progression in Phonics

'The Reading Recovery wilderness years.' Wales, Scotland, Northern Ireland, Republic of Ireland and Denmark adopt RR; no dedicated funding in UK.

Earl *et al.* (2000, 2001, 2003) External evaluation of the NLS OISE

177

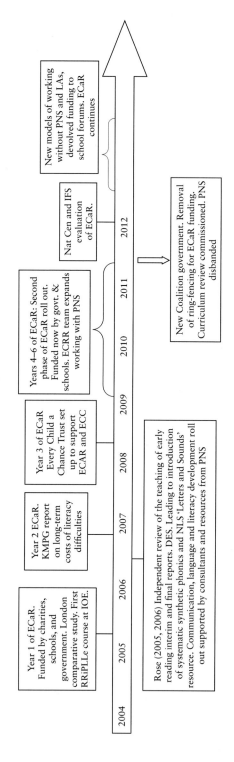

Appendix 2: Overview of the professional master's (MA) degree programme

Aims	Rationale	Learning outcomes	Programme structure
To train teacher leaders for Reading Recovery in the UK and abroad. To equip participants with relevant knowledge and understanding about current research in early literacy, the theories of Marie Clay underpinning Reading Recovery, the skills required to manage an	Reading Recovery teacher leaders (teacher-educators) need to be highly skilled practitioners of Reading Recovery techniques, adept facilitators of teachers' professional development, and proficient administrators of a complex and detailed intervention in an education system.	To train teacher leaders (teacher-educators) to organize, implement, and evaluate an early literacy programme. Participants will: • Develop or enhance their understandings about how the lowest-achieving children can be assisted to overcome their literacy difficulties	The programme is organic, and interplay between practice and theory is an essential element. Work for one module overlaps with that for others. The programme requires full-time attendance for a year and there are three modules: 1. **The Theory and Practice of Reading Recovery** (MMALLD_01) This module earns credits equivalent to half an MA-level requirement. At the start of the year, the programme focuses on children with literacy difficulties and how to teach them effectively using Reading Recovery procedures. While teaching of children continues throughout the year, the emphasis within the module gradually moves to the professional development of teachers. Towards the end of the module, issues concerning the management of literacy intervention implementations are included.

Aims	Rationale	Learning outcomes	Programme structure
implementation in a local authority, school cluster (or equivalent), and the ability to lead high-quality professional development for practising teachers.		• Explore and develop their understandings of Clay's theory of literacy acquisition, which underpins Reading Recovery • Have a thorough knowledge of a range of other theoretical approaches to literacy development, difficulties, and intervention • Have a good knowledge of recent research on early literacy	*Teaching children* Daily teaching of children, using Reading Recovery procedures, supports students to refine their understandings. Seminars at the Institute of Education, University of London (IOE), enable participants to reflect on their practice and deepen their understanding of Clay's theory of early literacy acquisition. Two case studies (one of an older struggling reader and one of a child selected for Reading Recovery) are undertaken to provide contrasting and critical experiences of children with literacy problems. Participants observe teaching sessions and teach for their colleagues behind a one-way viewing screen. *Learning to lead teachers* Opportunities are provided for participants to observe teachers' professional development sessions, led by an experienced teacher leader (teacher-educator) at a Reading Recovery centre. Participants keep a diary of their observations and discuss the progress of the training group in seminars at the IOE, using these, together with reflections on their experiences, to build a portfolio of work.

Aims	Rationale	Learning outcomes	Programme structure
		• Understand the principles of effective professional development for adults • Be able to plan and deliver an effective programme of professional development for experienced teachers • Have sufficient understanding of Reading Recovery to be a competent teacher/ practitioner • Be able to reflect on the experience of a change process that challenges many assumptions	As the year progresses, participants begin to play a more active role as a teacher leader (teacher-educator), and eventually participate in the planning and delivery of the initial professional development programme for teachers. They make visits to teachers to observe their teaching in school and provide feedback, first accompanying an experienced teacher leader for this purpose before making an independent visit. Participants learn to manage an implementation in their own local authority (or cluster of authorities or cluster of schools), including communicating with different audiences about Reading Recovery, advocacy, organization, and administration. **2. Research Methods in Literacy (MMALLD_05)** This module enables participants to gain a firm grounding in research methods in literacy. A 4,000-word critique and comparison of two pertinent research studies is written for assessment.

Aims	Rationale	Learning outcomes	Programme structure
		• Be able to present information about Reading Recovery to different audiences • Be able to organize resources to deliver and monitor a Reading Recovery implementation within a local authority or school cluster and maintain the quality of this implementation	**3. Literacy Development (MMALLD_02)** This module covers the current theory and associated practice around children's learning of literacy. It is assessed through presentation of a 4,000-word assignment on some aspect of literacy acquisition.

Appendix 3: Structure of the fortnightly in-service professional development session in the year-long programme for teachers

Section	Duration	Aim/Purpose	Content
Introduction	10 minutes	To provide a lead into the session, including sharing the emphasis of the session. Moving quickly into introducing the children (in flexible ways), particularly concentrating on what the teachers teaching that day have been working on. Seeking help from the group is a major intention. Encouraging teachers, both those teaching that day and the rest of the group, to be self-reflective enhances the success of this portion of the in-service session.	The emphasis, prepared for in advance, builds around information from a number of sources about where the teachers have reached in their development and where they need to go next in relation to the time in the programme, in relation to literacy acquisition and development for struggling readers and writers. Links may be made to previous sessions, building on these. Crucial information of time in the series of lessons, entry level in book reading and writing, and most importantly, where the child is now in terms of responding to the teaching of literacy and phonics phases, is communicated orally and in a succinct way.

Section	Duration	Aim/Purpose	Content
Teaching	65 minutes	Each of two teachers teaches a child in Reading Recovery behind the one-way viewing screen. The remainder of the group engage in active observation of and hypothesizing about the teaching and learning in the two half-hour lessons.	
Acknowledgement	2–3 minutes	The group acknowledge the teachers for the opportunity provided by the lessons and take the initiative to begin interacting.	The group and teacher leader provide informal supportive comments about the style of the teachers' teaching, such as teacher-child interactions, and appropriateness of choice of materials and of decisions made. The teachers who taught are invited to share briefly their views of the lessons.
Specific discussion of the lessons	20 minutes	The group dialogue constructively, with the teachers who taught, about the lesson and what was talked about behind the screen. Everyone in the group, including the teacher leader, shares in making comments, questioning, providing rationales, tussling with issues, and challenging	To provide effective feedback and support next steps for each of the children, teachers are encouraged to use core theoretical texts to justify their comments, attending to both reading and writing.

Section	Duration	Aim/Purpose	Content
		each other. The teacher who taught talks *with* the group (and the teacher leader) about the lesson, seeking their assistance.	
General discussion	20–25 minutes	In-depth analysis and discussion of both reading and writing using core texts to link theory and practice and to provide a deepened understanding of literacy acquisition for children struggling to read and write.	Usually this is worked on with the whole group, although here, as elsewhere, pairs or small groups may be useful for short periods only. Issues would come from different sources, for example: a) arising from each lesson b) relating to both lessons c) relating to children the group is teaching d) raised by the teacher leader e) raised by the group Earlier in the year this part of the session will involve introducing new materials and teaching procedures and may need a little more time.

Section	Duration	Aim/Purpose	Content
Implementation issues	10 minutes	A short discussion by the group related to learning more about operating Reading Recovery and other literacy interventions.	Topics could include the team approach, parents, liaison in schools, discontinuing children from series of lessons, ongoing monitoring, reporting to the school, etc.
Evaluation	5 minutes	To be effective, evaluation must be genuine and thorough, open and relevant.	Evaluation will have been planned for and built into every in-service session. It may occur spontaneously, it can come into different parts of the session, and may be achieved in different ways throughout the year, but it is a permanent part of every session.

Appendix 4: Outline of the Action Research Module: Reading Recovery in Primary Literacy Leadership (RRiPLLe)

This is a year-long programme of additional professional development for experienced Reading Recovery teachers. At the core of the 'Reading Recovery in Primary Literacy Leadership' programme is action research. It includes planning and conducting a needs analysis in the teachers' schools. The programme supports participants, with community involvement, to identify an issue in literacy learning in their context, and to plan, carry out, and evaluate a collaborative change process to address this issue.

Professional development year

The professional development year involves pre-tasks where teachers are asked to:

- examine data on children from about a year in school onwards
- look at the overall literacy achievements of children of 5 to 7 years of age in their school and undertake some analysis of their strengths and problems.

Professional development knowledge-building workshops

These workshops consist of ten two-and-a-half hour tuition sessions spread across one year, usually more concentrated in the first term. Although some of the sessions may be engaged in as distance learning, forming a local community of learners is valuable in action research. An end-of-year event/ conference in which participants share the learning from the in-school action research activity that they have undertaken is also encouraged.

Locally designed *knowledge-building workshops* focus on the following topics:

- Mentoring and supporting colleagues in school
- Implementing and managing interventions
- Understanding and using data
- Quality-first teaching of writing in Foundation stage and early grades

- Literacy curriculum frameworks and current policy
- Early language development, speaking, and listening
- Involving parents and the wider community
- Selecting, organizing, and using resources for literacy
- Every Child Counts and Every Child a Reader intervention in primary schools
- Assessment for learning

In addition, teachers may elect to follow relevant personal professional interests independently.

Accreditation is available at master's degree level through the Institute of Education, University of London.

Index